THE GLITTER AND THE GOLD

THE GLITTER
AND THE GOLD

Consuelo Vanderbilt Balsan

GEORGE MANN   MAIDSTONE

Consuelo Vanderbilt Balsan
THE GLITTER AND THE GOLD
© Consuelo Vanderbilt Balsan 1953

First published by George Mann 1973

ISBN 0 7041 0002 9

Printed and bound in Great Britain by
Woolnough Bookbinding Ltd of Irthlingborough
For George Mann Books, PO Box 22, Maidstone
In the English County of Kent

"Hit is not al gold that glareth"
Chaucer, "The House of Fame", I, 272
(Tyrwhitt says this is taken from the
Parabolae of Alanus de Insulis, who died
in 1294. *Non teneas aurum totum quod
splendet ut aurum*—Do not hold everything as gold which shines like gold).

"All that glisters is not gold"
Shakespeare, *Merchant of Venice*, Act II,
Scene 7, 1. 65

"All, as they say, that glitters is not gold"
Dryden, "The Hind and the Panther"

CONTENTS

Foreword

FRIENDS HAVE often told me that I should write my story and describe the world of my youth, which was so different from that of today. There are no journals to help me—there are but the meagre notes of engagements made; the press cuttings of recorded events. But the portraits of my friends are etched in memory and stand like figures in a Paul Veronese, brilliant and festive against backgrounds of space and colour where architectural pleasances and an ordered courtesy add beauty to the zest for life.

Looking back to 1895, when I married the ninth Duke of Marlborough and went to live in England, I recall a society whose conventions were closer to the eighteenth than to the twentieth century. Queen Victoria's reign was nearing its end, but those who, like myself, witnessed the splendid pageant of her Diamond Jubilee could not have foreseen that her death would close an era. There are few of us left who can recall that world with its complete acceptance of aristocratic privileges. There are still fewer to whom such anachronisms remain justified. Even then, whispered doubts of their rightfulness could be heard. So is it surprising that an American girl who held democratic views found it difficult to accept the assumption that birth alone confers superiority? Is it not natural when my marriage foundered and I was able to lead my life in the comparative freedom a legal separation ensures that, influenced by the more liberal doctrines of the twentieth century, I should, in the English tradition, have sought a greater usefulness in social service?

Years later, when divorce brought complete freedom, I found happiness in marriage with Jacques Balsan. In writing of those years I recall the homes we made together, the kindly people we lived among, the country I loved. And now, back in my native land, having regained a citizenship I would never have resigned had the law of my day permitted me to retain it, I look back on a long life under three flags. The scenes pictured I have wit-

nessed; the impressions recorded were true of their day. I can
tell no story but my own. I hope it may interest my readers.

Without the constant encouragement of friends I should have
found it difficult to carry this work to a conclusion. Among
them I should like particularly to thank Mr. Henry May for
helping me sketch out the original plan of the book. I am grateful to the present Duke of Wellington for refreshing my
memories of a ball at Apsley House; and I am greatly indebted
to Mr. Stuart Preston for his careful scrutiny of my proofs. My
final thanks go to Miss Mae Lovey, who has performed the
onerous task of typing the book and of keeping track of the
numerous successive corrections in my manuscript.

THE GLITTER AND THE GOLD

CHAPTER ONE

The World of My Youth

IN TRYING to recount events that have influenced my life, it is humiliating to find that I remember very little of my childhood. Watching my great-grandchild Serena Russell at play, so sure of herself, even at the age of three, I wonder if, when she reaches my age, she also will have forgotten events that now appear important to her. That we are both in America—she the child of my granddaughter Sarah Spencer-Churchill, who married an American, and I the wife of a Frenchman—is due to World War II, and to events little anticipated at the turn of the century when I left my native land.

Memories of myself at Serena's age recall a picture painted by Carolus Duran of a little girl against a tall red curtain. She is wearing a red velvet dress with a square *décolleté* outlined with Venetian lace. A cloud of dark hair surrounds a small oval face, out of which enormous dark eyes (much bigger than they were) look out from under arched brows. A pert little nose and dimples accentuate the mischievous smile. There is something vital and disturbing in that small figure tightly grasping a bunch of roses in each fist. "You were *un vrai petit diable,* and only kept still when I played the organ in my studio!" Carolus Duran exclaimed, when again he painted me, this time at seventeen. The second portrait was a very different affair from the first, for the red curtain which had become his traditional background was at my mother's request replaced by a classic landscape in the English eighteenth-century style, and I am seen a tall figure in white descending a flight of steps. For my mother, having decided, in the fashion not uncommon at the time, to marry me either to the man who did become my husband or to his cousin —generously allowing me the choice of alternatives—wished my portrait to bear comparison with those of preceding duchesses

I

who had been painted by Gainsborough, Reynolds, Romney and Lawrence. In that proud and lovely line I still stand over the mantelpiece of one of the state-rooms at Blenheim Palace, with a slightly disdainful and remote look as if very far away in thought.

It is well that my Aunt Florence Twombly, now ninety-eight, could remember not only the street but also the number of the house where I was born, for my birth had never been officially recorded. This information was required when I took back my American citizenship after the French armistice in World War II. It was in one of those ugly brownstone houses somewhere in the forties, which was then the fashionable district of New York, that I first saw the light of day.

My father's family was Dutch and had its origin in the Bilt— that northern point of Holland whence comes our name. It was about the year 1650 that the first member of the family came to the New Netherlands, and succeeding generations lived in the vicinity of New Amsterdam, as New York City was then called. In the first part of the nineteenth century my great-grandfather Cornelius Vanderbilt founded the family fortune, moved from New Dorp, Staten Island, to New York and changed the spelling of our name from van der Bilt to its American version. In later years I met a Professor van der Bilt who taught at a Dutch University. He told me that there was only one family bearing our name in Holland, and in looking through his family archives he had become convinced that the Dutch and American branches had descended from a common ancestor. In the *Patriciat,* a book that is the Dutch equivalent of the *British Landed Gentry,* the Professor pointed out our coat of arms, the three acorns, and the names Gertrude, Cornelius and William, which repeatedly figure in our family Bible.

My grandfather, William H. Vanderbilt, had, considering his numerous philanthropic gifts, an unmerited reputation for indifference to the welfare of others. It was, as is often the case, founded on a remark shorn of its context. This is the version of the "public be damned" story that was given me by a friend of the family. Mr. Vanderbilt was on a business trip and, after a long and arduous day, had gone to his private car for a rest. A swarm of reporters arrived asking to come on board for an interview. Mr. Vanderbilt sent word he was tired and did not wish to give an interview, but would receive one representative of the Press for a few minutes. A young man arrived saying, "Mr.

Vanderbilt, *your* public *demands* an interview!" This made Mr. Vanderbilt laugh, and he answered, "Oh, *my* public be damned." In due course the young man left and next morning his article appeared in the paper with a large headline reading, "Vanderbilt says, 'The Public be damned.' " That he was not so black as painted I have from a cousin to whom my grandmother after her husband's death said, "Your grandfather never said an unkind word to me during all the years we were married."

In "The House of Vanderbilt"* by Frank Crowninshield, I find a reference to my grandmother in which he says, "She was an amazing woman who brought up her children to become people of the greatest cultivation and taste. She had been born Maria Louisa Kissam, the daughter of a clergyman of the Dutch Reformed Church. The Kissams were an old and distinguished family, Mrs. Vanderbilt's father having descended from the Benjamin Kissam who, in 1786, married Cornelia Roosevelt, the daughter of the patriarchal Isaac, and the President's great-great-grandfather." Of my grandmother's eight children my father, W. K., as he was known to his friends, was the second son. I remember my grandmother very well, and our visits to her in the big house on Fifth Avenue directly opposite St. Patrick's Cathedral where she lived. She was a lovely old lady, gracious and sweet as old ladies should be. All her grandchildren—we were, I think, twenty-six—loved her. After my grandfather's death in 1885 she lived alone with her youngest son, George. Uncle George was quite different from my other uncles and aunts. With his dark hair and eyes, he might have been a Spaniard. He had a narrow sensitive face, and artistic and literary tastes. After my grandmother's death in 1896 he created Biltmore, a great estate in North Carolina where he built model houses and fostered village industries.

My father's eldest brother Uncle Corneil, as we called him, was a stern and serious person, or so we thought. He was not gay like my father and Uncle Fred. Of my four aunts I loved my Aunt Emily Sloane best, for, like my father, she was of a joyous nature and had the look of happy expectancy one sees on the faces of those who love life. She and my Aunt Florence were always perfectly dressed, and, with their slight figures and quiet distinction, reminded me of Jane Austen's charmingly prim

* *Vogue* Magazine, November 15, 1941.

ladies. Some time before her death I went to see Aunt Emily. She was sitting at a window overlooking Central Park. It struck me that her days must have been very long, now that she was widowed and that the bridge game she loved was no longer possible because of her failing memory. But when I sympathised with her, she folded her hands and softly smiling answered—"I have such lovely thoughts to keep me company," and when I crept away, fearing to disturb them, I heard her murmuring, as if conversing with ghosts of the past. She lived to be over ninety. At her memorial service the Rector of St. Bartholomew's in New York paid a well-deserved tribute to her lovely character and generous charity.

My maternal grandfather, Murray Forbes Smith, was descended from the Stirlings, and both my mother's given names— Alva Erskine—are Stirling names. The Scotch tradition of large families is borne out in two volumes on the Stirlings in America. This prolific family overflowed from Virginia into the more southern states and produced several governors and people of importance. All this accentuated in my mother a pride in her Southern birth and a certain disdain for the mercenary spirit of the North. Her father, who owned plantations near Mobile, was ruined by the liberation of the slaves and, after the Civil War, moved to Paris. There my mother's eldest sister made her début at one of the last balls given at the Tuileries by Napoleon III. My mother and I used to attribute our love for France to a Huguenot ancestor who escaped to America after the revocation of the Edict of Nantes. Indeed we were happier in France than in any other country, and, following the example of an aunt and a great-aunt, we both returned to live there.

Why my parents ever married remains a mystery to me. They were both delightful, charming and intelligent people, but wholly unsuited to each other. My father, although deep in his business interests, found life a happy adventure. His gentle nature hated strife. I still feel pain at the thought of the unkind messages I was made the bearer of when, in the months that preceded their parting, my mother no longer spoke to him. The purport of those messages I no longer remember—they were, I believe, concerned with the divorce she desired and with her wishes and decrees regarding custody of the children and arrangements for the future. My father had a generous and unselfish nature; his pleasure was to see people happy and he enjoyed the company of his children and friends, but my mother —for reasons I can but ascribe to a towering ambition—opposed these carefree views with all the force of her strong personality. Her combative nature rejoiced in conquests. She loved a fight. A born dictator, she dominated events about her as thoroughly as she eventually dominated her husband and her children. If she admitted another point of view she never conceded it; we were pawns in her game to be moved as her wishes decreed. I remember once objecting to her taste in the clothes she selected for me. With a harshness hardly warranted by so innocent an observation, she informed me that I had no taste and that my opinions were not worth listening to. She brooked no contradiction, and when once I replied, "I thought I was doing right," she stated, "I don't ask *you* to think, *I* do the thinking, you do as you are told," which reduced me to imbecility. Her dynamic energy and her quick mind, together with her varied interests, made her a delightful companion. But the bane of her life and of those who shared it was a violent temper that, like a tempest, at times engulfed us all.

One of her earliest ambitions was to become a leader of New York society. To this end she gave a fancy dress ball for the opening of her new house, 660 Fifth Avenue, on March 26, 1883. In contemporary newspapers I have read how eagerly invitations to this party were sought after. It proved to be, they said, the most magnificent entertainment yet given in a private house in America. My parents, gorgeous in medieval costumes, received the *élite* of what then was New York society. My godmother, who as Consuelo Yznaga had been my mother's bridesmaid, was our house guest and the ball was given in her honour. She was then Viscountess Mandeville and soon after, when her husband succeeded to the dukedom, became Duchess of Manchester. Beautiful, witty, gay and gifted, with the ability to play by ear any melody she had heard, she delighted us with her charm. Her lovely twin daughters who died so tragically young and her son Kimbolton spent that winter with us. Kim had early acquired the sense of importance a title is apt to confer, and one day when the postman left a letter for Viscount Mandeville with the comment, "How I would like to see a real live lord," he was astonished to see a diminutive figure in a sailor suit approach him exclaiming, "Then look at me."

Now firmly established as a social leader, my mother, wishing still further to dominate her world, assumed the prerogatives of an *arbiter elegantiarum*, instructing her contemporaries both in the fine arts and the art of living. Ransacking the antique shops of Europe, she returned with pictures and furniture to adorn the mansions it became her passion to build. She thus set a fashion for period houses, which at that date were little known in the United States. Once she was successfully installed in the three homes she had built, her restless energy must, I imagine, have turned to other projects. It was perhaps then that plans for my future were born.

Courage was one of her prominent characteristics—a courage that was physical as well as spiritual. I shall never forget an incident when I had occasion to realise how intrepid and quick were her reactions. It took place at Idlehour, our home on Long Island. One day when I, aged nine, was out driving, my pony started to run away with me, making straight for a water hydrant. My cart would undoubtedly have been overturned; but without the slightest hesitation my mother, who was standing near-by, threw herself between the hydrant and the racing pony and seized his bridle, thus preventing a serious accident.

Reminiscences relating to one's childhood are apt to be tinged with a self-conscious pity, which in my generation might be considered justified, for we were the last to be subjected to a harsh parental discipline. In my youth, children were to be seen but not heard; implicit obedience was an obligation from which one could not conscientiously escape. Indeed, we suffered a severe and rigorous upbringing. Corporal punishment for minor delinquencies was frequently administered with a riding-whip. I have a vivid memory of the last such lashing my legs received as I stood while my mother wielded her crop. Being the elder, I had the privilege of the first taste of the whip—Willie followed. We had, my brother and I, been sailing in our boat on a pond. Our governess, Fraulein Wedekind, wished to bring us home, but, lost in the pleasure of the sport, we paid no attention to her calls. At length, as we neared the bank, she caught us and, imprudently straddling the water with one leg on shore, she tried to stop us. Alas, how could one prevent the wicked impulse to give a sudden shove with an oar, setting the boat free and seating Fraulein in the water? It seemed very funny at the time, but as we neared home, our governess trailing her wet skirts straight up to our mother, the incident lost its charm.

I bore these punishments stoically, but such repressive measures bred inhibitions and even now I can trace their effects. It
is a melancholy fact that childhood, so short when compared
with the average span of life, should exert such a strong and
permanent influence on character that no amount of self-training
afterwards can ever completely counter it. How different is the
child's education today! Prejudiced as I am by my own experience, I still think that, although my mother's standard was too
severe, it was preferable to the complete lack of discipline I see
in many homes today.

Punishments, which were private affairs, were more easily
borne than ridicule suffered in public. I remember an occasion
when, dressed in a period costume designed by my mother—for
it was her wish that I should stand out from others, hallmarked
like precious silver—I suffered the agonies of shame that the
ridicule of adults can cause children. Then again I was particularly sensitive about my nose, for it had an upward curve
which my mother and her friends discussed with complete dis-
regard for my feelings. Since nothing could be done to guide
its misguided progress, there seemed to be no point in stressing
my misfortune. I developed an inferiority complex and became
conscious not only of physical defects but also of faults that with
gentler treatment might have been less painfully corrected.
Introspection and heart-searching caused hypersensitiveness and
a quick temper to cloud an otherwise amiable disposition.

My brother Willie was my junior by eighteen months. He had
inherited my father's charm and sweet temper. The wistful look
of his big green eyes was appealing, but he was mischievous
and recklessly daring. He used to ride one of those old-fashioned
high-wheeled bicycles at such speed that he took many tosses.
One day my mother threatened to confiscate the bicycle at the
next fall, and Willie went through a lesson before his tutor discovered that in falling he had broken his arm. I had for him the
love little girls expend on their juniors and we shared a keen
sense of fun.

My brother Harold was born seven years later. Returning
from a walk on a Sunday in July, 1884, we found him in my
mother's arms. Nor were we further enlightened until Boya, my
sainted nurse, informed me that God had sent him to us. What
could be more pleasing than so poetic a version of birth and
creation? Though we experienced a certain curiosity as the years

went by, modesty was not sacrificed to the precocious knowledge sex education now confers. Harold, being so much younger than we, took little part in our games. In our eyes he was encircled by the halo his adoring nurse Bridget placed round his lovely head. She was an ardent Catholic—a faith that inspired her with sufficient courage one day to tax my mother with the number of houses she was building: "You have so many houses on earth, Mrs. Vanderbilt, don't you think it is time to build one in heaven?" To which my mother replied: "Oh no, Bridget—you live in my houses on earth, but I look forward to living in yours in heaven"—an answer of classic realism.

We did not live for long in the little nondescript house in which I was born. Choosing Richard Morris Hunt as her architect, my mother built a large ornate white stone house in the French Renaissance style at the north-west corner of Fifth Avenue and Fifty-second Street. It was demolished after my father's death to make room for office buildings. This house stood back from the avenue and was approached by wide steps leading to an iron-grilled entrance. Inside, one saw on the right a great stairway running up three flights. I still remember how long and terrifying was that dark and endless upward sweep as, with acute sensations of fear, I climbed to my room every night, leaving below the light and its comforting rays. For in that penumbra there were spirits lurking to destroy me, hands stretched out to touch me and sighs that breathed against my cheek. Sometimes I stumbled, and then all went black, and, tensely kneeling on those steps, I prayed for courage to reach the safety of my room.

In comparison with this recurrent nightmare, how gay were the gala evenings when the house was ablaze with lights and Willie and I, crouching on hands and knees behind the balustrade of the musicians' gallery, looked down on a festive scene below—the long dinner-table covered with a damask cloth, a gold service and red roses, the lovely crystal and china, the grown-ups in their fine clothes. The dining-room was enormous and had at one end twin Renaissance mantelpieces and on one side a huge stained-glass window, depicting the Field of the Cloth of Gold on which the Kings of England and France were surrounded with their knights, all not more magnificently arrayed than the ladies a-glitter with jewels seated on high-backed tapestry chairs behind which stood footmen in knee-breeches. Next to this big dining-room was a small breakfast-room adorned with Flemish tapestries and Rembrandt's portrait of the Turkish Chief. Then came a white drawing-room hung with a fine set of Boucher tapestries; here were the beautiful lacquer *secrétaire* and commode, with bronzes chiselled by Gouthière, made for Marie Antoinette. Next-door our living-room, a panelled Renaissance salon, looked out on Fifth Avenue.

My father's small dreary room saddened me—it seemed a dull place for so gay and dashing a cavalier who should, I thought, have the best of everything life could give. He was so invariably kind, so gentle and sweet to me, with a fund of humorous tales and jokes that as a child were my joy. But, alas, he played only a small part in our lives; it seemed to us he was always shunted or side-tracked from our occupations. It was invariably our mother who dominated our upbringing, our education, our recreation and our thoughts. With children's clairvoyance we knew that she would prove adamant to any appeal our father made on our behalf and we never asked him to interfere. The hour we spent in our parents' company after the supper we took with our governess at six can in no sense be described as the Children's Hour. No books or games were provided; we sat and listened to the conversation of the grown-ups and longed for the release that their departure to dress for dinner would bring.

Occasionally Willie and I were permitted to join my mother in her handsome bedroom and watch her evening toilet. There was one memorable evening when the safe in which her jewels were kept could not be opened. My mother was going to a big dinner at which it would almost have been considered an offence to wear no jewels. Something of the prevailing feeling of panic must have reached me, for I ran to my room and prayed fervently that a miracle would open the safe. And when I returned the safe was opened—my mother decked in her beautiful pearls. Small wonder that I believe in the efficacy of prayer.

When I was old enough for a room of my own I was moved from the nurseries next to my mother to a room above hers, to which she had access by a spiral staircase in one of the towers that adorned the house. On this floor there was a colossal playroom where we used to bicycle and roller-skate with our cousins and friends. But the chief memory it holds is of a Christmas tree that towered to the roof and was laden with gifts and toys for us and for every one of our cousins.

After heavy snowfalls there were joyous sleigh drives to which we looked forward—the horses with their bells, the fat coachman wrapped in furs, and Willie and myself in the back seat with our small sleigh on which we were allowed to toboggan down slopes in the Park.

After the holidays there were matinées at the Metropolitan Opera House to look forward to, when in my best dress I sat in my father's box near the stage. My earliest operatic recollection is of hearing the great Adelina Patti sing Martha. Her birdlike trills evoked scenes of wild enthusiasm, and mountains of bouquets were heaped round her diminutive form. Gounod's *Faust* was one of my favourites, but Mephistopheles terrified me and folly became associated with love after seeing Marguerite and later Lucia de Lammermoor in their affecting mad scenes.

Every Saturday my mother made me recite endless poems in French, German and English, and in my tenth year there was a memorable occasion when our *solfège* class gave a concert in honour of our parents. Whether from stage fright or emotion, I gave a rendering of 'Les Adieux de Marie Stuart' with so much feeling that I burst into tears. Somebody tossed me a bouquet and I am sure no prima donna ever felt a greater thrill.

Willie and I also went to a weekly dancing class conducted by Mr. Dodsworth, an elderly and elegant instructor who had taught succeeding generations of New Yorkers how to dance and how to behave when in company. Willie disliked being dressed in his best sailor suit and having to dance with elderly girls who steered him around, but I liked wearing my prettiest dress, and the competition of boys who wished to dance with me gave me a sense of superiority I did not often enjoy at home.

Sundays were special days. We went to morning service at St. Marks-in-the-Bouwerie, a long drive in the landau with Willie and myself in our best clothes facing my mother in an elegant costume and my father in a frock-coat, top hat and an overcoat with a fine fur collar. Those long drives were always frightfully tiring, for I was made to sit up very straight and was not allowed to relax for a moment. When my legs began to fidget in uncontrollable twitches, I was strictly admonished against what for some unknown reason my mother dubbed "Vanderbilt fidgets", as if no other children had ever been afflicted thus. Sitting up straight was one of the crucial tests of ladylike behaviour. A horrible instrument was devised which I had to wear when doing my lessons. It was a steel rod which ran down my spine and was strapped at my waist and over my shoulders—another strap went around my forehead to the rod. I had to hold my book high when reading, and it was almost impossible to write in so uncomfortable a position. However, I probably owe my straight back to those many hours of discomfort.

Upon our return from church, we children lunched with our parents in the company of two boys of our age, and after a Scripture lesson spent delirious hours marching armies of tin soldiers across the carpet that represented land, or sailing them over the seas of parqueted floors to fight furious battles for the possession of the forts we built out of blocks.

In contrast to this city life there was the welcome liberty we enjoyed at Idlehour, my father's place at Oakdale, Long Island, where we spent the early summer and autumn months. It was a rambling frame house close to a river; green lawns swept away to the gardens, stables, woods and farms. Here we crabbed and fished in the river and learned to sail a boat. We had ponies, which I rode side-saddle, and a garden to plant, but we were bad gardeners, for my brother Willie, who was of an impatient nature, would pull up the potatoes long before they were ripe. Our earliest bets were made on the number we would find on each root.

Good behaviour found its reward in the pleasure of cooking our supper in the playhouse. Our German governess presided and indulged her taste for sauerkraut, which we did not appreciate, but as compensation I was allowed the chocolate caramels I loved to make. This playhouse was an old bowling alley, and when my mother handed it over to us she insisted as a matter of training that we should do all the housework ourselves. Utterly happy, we would cook our meal, wash the dishes and then stroll home by the river in the cool of the evening.

Boya, my nurse, as near a saint as it is possible for a human being to be, shared these outings with us. High-minded, simple and kind, she had none of the mawkish sentimentality that caused my governess to take affront at the slightest provocation.

There were times when, possibly influenced by Boya, I reflected with some discomfort on the affluence that surrounded me, wondering whether I was entitled to so many of the good things of life. This feeling was sharply accentuated by a visit I paid to the sick child of one of our Bohemian workmen, whose duty it was to cut the grass lawns that surrounded the house. One morning when wishing him good day I noticed how sadly he answered. "Is anything the matter?" I inquired. Then he told me of his little girl, aged ten—"just my age," I commented—a cripple condemned for life to her bed. The sudden shock of so terrible a lot overwhelmed me, and when the next day I drove with my governess to see her, the pony-cart filled with gifts, and found her in a miserable little room on a small unlovely cot, I realised the inequalities of human destinies with a vividness that never left me. How much I owe to Boya! It was from her I learned the happiness helping others brings. For she gave her all in alms and kindness, and later, when she left us, spent her last years directing a Home for Swiss Girls in New York.

When my grandfather died in 1885 leaving the bulk of his fortune equally divided between his two elder sons—Cornelius and my father—my mother was able to give full vent to her ambitions, and the yacht *Alva*, of 1,400 tons, was one of the first results of our new affluence. She was a beautiful and luxurious ship with appointments in simple good taste, but she was a bad sea boat, as we soon found to our discomfort, and was eventually sunk in a collision in a fog. On our first trips we visited the West Indies. In following years we crossed the Atlantic and cruised in the Mediterranean. On one occasion as we left Madeira and headed for Gibraltar a frightful storm overtook us. The waves broke over the high wooden bulwarks in such rapid succession that there was not enough time for the water to drain out through the freeing ports before the next wave hit us. I was lying in the forward deck cabin with my brother Willie and his tutor, who was both frightened and sick. "If we have seven such waves in succession," he informed us, "we must sink." Willie and I spent the rest of the day counting the waves in terrorised apprehension as the green water deepened on our deck. There were several casualties among the crew and the doctor who always accompanied us on our voyages was kept busy.

These yachting expeditions were excessively boring to us children. The doctor, my brother's tutor, my governess and three men friends of my parents made up our party. Heavy seas provided our only escape from the curriculum of work, for even sightseeing on our visits ashore became part of our education, and we were expected to write an account of all we had seen.

Harold, still being in the nursery, was free to amuse himself within the limits a yacht made possible.

On one of our cruises we visited Algiers, Tunis and Egypt. I recall being deeply impressed by the magnificent proportions of the temples of Egypt, but the tombs of the kings gave me the worst kind of claustrophobia and I was terrified by the hundreds of bats that clung to the low ceilings. There was something pathetic about the richly caparisoned mummies surrounded by the worldly possessions they deemed necessary to their future lives, and it seemed positively indecent to disturb the dignified seclusion they had taken such infinite precaution to insure.

On leaving Egypt we went to Constantinople. At the entrance to the Dardanelles our yacht was rudely halted by two shots across the bow, for warships were then not admitted into the Bosphorus and we had been mistaken for a small cruiser. After a twenty-four-hour delay during which the authorities were placated, we were allowed to proceed and soon anchored in that beautiful bay, with Constantinople and its lovely palaces and mosques spread before us. My parents had gone on shore when an anxious captain brought me the news that a pasha had arrived and wished to see my father. As the captain could not speak a word of French nor the pasha a word of English, it was arranged that I should entertain him, since he refused to leave without tendering the Sultan's apologies to my parents for the incivility of our reception. It must have been a new experience for the haughty and sophisticated Turk to talk to a little girl for an hour or more, and it was a proud moment when later a beautiful box of sweets arrived as a tribute to my exertions. At that time Turkish women were strictly secluded, their emancipation from the purdah only being accomplished by Mustapha Kemal in his policy of Westernisation during the first quarter of the next century. My father had an audience with the Sultan, who showed us every courtesy, even having us visit palaces not usually opened to the public.

Our cruise that year ended at Nice, where we arrived in time for the carnival and all its grotesque and riotous gaiety. We took part in the Battle of Flowers and greatly enjoyed throwing what in time became rather dusty nosegays at passers-by. Suddenly a well-meant but clumsily aimed package hit me in the eye. Neither the chocolates it contained nor the compliment attached to it, 'Pour la jolie petite fille,' were allowed to console me, for my mother, fearing that compliments might lead to conceit, said, "It must have been meant for Harold." Harold, aged three, was, I admit, a beautiful child; still I hoped he had not been mistaken for a girl, and had doubts of my mother's veracity.

From Nice we went to Paris, where in recurrent years we spent the months of May and June at either the Hotel Bristol or the Continental. When I think of spring it is of Paris, with its sweet scents of budding chestnut trees and flowering lilac, and of the lilies the hawkers vend in the streets, those sprigs of *muguet* one wears on the first of May. The lovely city has for me a beauty that makes my heart ache. The gracious harmony of its ancient buildings, the shimmering lights, the soft green of the trees, and the fast-flowing Seine glowing red in the evening sun, all nurture a sad and tender reverence. For the beauty of spring is evanescent and loveliness is a fragile thing.

When I was a child, Paris in springtime was a happy place. At the Carrousel we rode wooden horses to gay waltzes. We loved the Punch and Judy shows in the Champs Élysées, and in the little booths we bought pails and shovels to play with on the sand piles, or boats to sail on the round basins in the gardens of the Tuileries. There was a small band of us who met there for several years running when our parents went abroad to race at Longchamps, to shop, or simply to have a good time in the easy carefree way of the nineteenth century. I remember Waldorf Astor, now Viscount Astor, and married to Nancy Langhorne, first woman Member of Parliament. He was a serious little boy, very good-looking, with the remarkable sense of fairness that inspired all his actions to the end. There was also May Goelet, who was bright, amusing and quick, the three natural attributes of an American girl. She was to be my bridesmaid and later to marry Marlborough's cousin, the Duke of Roxburghe, himself a fine man and a great gentleman. She became a Scottish chatelaine and lived at Floors Castle in the lovely Border country where England and Scotland meet. Her chief interests were needlework, salmon-fishing and bridge, which she played well enough to rank with Lady Granard, another compatriot. To these diversions she devoted a good brain which might perhaps have been used to better purpose.

And there was Katherine Duer, who married, first, Clarence Mackay, and then, after divorcing him, Dr. Joseph Blake, the great brain surgeon who rendered such service to France at his

THE WORLD OF MY YOUTH

hospital in World War I. Katherine was very handsome, with a straight nose, and a shock of dark hair that swept back from a low, well-shaped forehead. Her dark eyes flashed with ardour and the love of life. She wanted to dominate us all; she was one of those who assumed it to be her right. She was always the queen in the games we played, and if anyone was bold enough to suggest it was my turn she would parry, "Consuelo does not want to be Queen," and she was right. These days of early spring were the precursors of others that during the summer months we spent at Newport. Here our little band would meet again. My happiest memory is of a farm in the surrounding country where we went for picnics and played at Indians and white men, those wild games inspired by the tales of Fenimore Cooper. Wriggling through thorns, scrambling over rocks, wading through streams, we were completely happy—though what sights we looked in torn clothes with scratched faces and knees as we drove home to the marbled halls and Renaissance castles our parents had built!

In the autumn my family would return to Idlehour and then to New York, where the winter routine would resume. As I grew into my teens, I began to study at what was known as the Rosa classes. My class consisted of six girls and was held at Mrs. Frederick Bronson's house. Mr. Rosa managed to cram such various subjects as English, Latin, mathematics and science into two hours; but if our knowledge was elementary, at least our interest was sharply awakened. Mr. Rosa was especially successful with history and literature, or perhaps it was because they were my favourite subjects that I thought so. We were given essays to write, and pages and pages on the Punic Wars are still treasured among my earliest literary efforts.

Mrs. Bronson lived on Madison Avenue near Thirty-eighth Street, which was then a fashionable residential part of the city. Every morning I walked there with my governess. Fifth Avenue had but very few shops in those days. The big Hotel Windsor at 571 Fifth Avenue, later destroyed by fire, was, with the churches, one of the few large edifices to interrupt the even flow of private mansions. The buses were still drawn by horses and there were many elegant carriages with a coachman and groom on the box seat. I liked these walks better than the return home in my father's brougham, which called for me at one o'clock.

In addition to the Rosa curriculum I had French, German and

music lessons with various governesses, and an hour or so of exercise in Central Park.

In the eighties the foundations of education were laid young. We were not encouraged to consider self-expression more important than the acquisition of knowledge, and if, like children the world over, we painted crude and grotesque pictures, they were not considered to possess artistic merit. At the age of eight I could read and write in French, German and English. I learned them in that order, for we spoke French with our parents, my father having been partly educated at a school in Geneva. We had then a German governess at home; the French governess came in for an hour a day, and I prepared my lessons for her under the supervision of Boya.

There was, because of our travels, a long procession of governesses in my life, and when I grew older there were two so-called finishing governesses in residence, one English and one French. How difficult it was to please them both. What tact and patience it required! It may have taught me to see both sides of a question, for whatever opinion was held by one was invariably contradicted by the other. The English governess remained with me to the day of my wedding. She was one of the best friends I ever had.

Reading early became my favourite recreation. What untold hours of happiness were spent in the company of *Les Petites Filles Modèles, Le Bon Petit Diable* and other creations of Madame de Sègur, whose sympathies with errant childhood I found more to my taste than the sentimental yearnings expressed in a series of German books that also came my way about that time. I remember one entitled *Zwei und Fünfzig Sonntage* from which I gathered that German children, rather like me, regarded Sunday as a day of liberation from a too-encompassing discipline. The books I read in those early days were chiefly French and German. There were fairy tales, Hans Andersen's and *Les Contes de Perrault,* and La Fontaine's *Fables,* which I had to commit to memory. In a German book there was a grotesque creature called Struwwel Peter whose escapades Willie and I thoroughly enjoyed. Later *Robinson Crusoe, Swiss Family Robinson* and Fenimore Cooper's 'Leatherstocking' tales inspired the games we played. There were in those days fewer books written for children. I am bewildered by the choice with which I am now confronted. It was perhaps for this reason that we read what might be described as the Classics. It was only later when Willie went to a day school and I was left alone that my books became sentimental, and Queechy with *The Wide, Wide World* brought tearful hours. And there was Miss Alcott, whose Jo and Meg and Beth and Amy must be household names in every American family. At the age of thirteen I became acquainted with the loves of gods in a lovely book on Greek mythology, and with Charles Lamb's *Adventures of Ulysses,* Henty, Marryat and Jules Verne went on voyages of discovery. *The Scottish Chiefs* I knew practically by heart and Robin Hood was also a favourite hero. It was about then that Plutarch's *Lives* inspired a Spartan austerity which in contrast to the cushioned comfort of my life I found appealing. Unbeknown to my governess—for by then I had been moved to a room near my mother's—I determined to sleep on the floor without a blanket; but a heavy cold soon put an end to that short-lived experiment. The next step in my literary experiences was the discovery of *Ivanhoe, Kenilworth* and *Woodstock,* and Dickens's novels, which held me spellbound. Later came Thackeray's *Henry Esmond* and *The Virginians. Vanity Fair* I was not allowed to read. For water nymphs I developed a special tenderness in Ondine and Kingsley's *Water Babies* and I recited "Die Lorelei" with genuine emotion. Our games of croquet became hilarious when *Alice in Wonderland* and its sequel came our way, and frequent references to "Off with her head" would annoy our adversaries when we croqued their balls out of bounds. But the real emotional crisis was reached when in the yacht's library I found *The Mill on the Floss* and my dreams became interwoven with the romance of Stephen and Maggie Tulliver. In addition to these, my personal books, I read with my governess biographies of the great English and German poets together with their works; from Chaucer's *Canterbury Tales* and Spenser's *Faerie Queene* I turned to the *Nibelungenlied* and *Wallenstein,* from Milton's Puritan idealism to Klopstock's German lyricism —from Shakespeare to Schiller and Goethe. I knew far more of Goethe's loves than my mother surmised, but love was a legendary word and meant to me only what in his lovely poem he describes as *"Himmel hoch jauchzend zum Tode betrübt— glücklich allein ist die Seele die liebt."* I read voraciously of the German Classics with a governess who so inspired a love of German poetry and philosophy that after my marriage I read

the books hitherto forbidden—*Faust* in its entirety, Heine, with
Schopenhauer and Nietzsche. For the heavier philosophies of
Kant and Hegel I had no liking and wasted no time in cudgelling
the little understanding I had of them. But Nietzsche had the
inevitable appeal of poetic vision combined with madness. In
Vienna, years later, on one of those sad pilgrimages to restore
my hearing, I had dreams of translating *Also Sprach Zara-
thustra*—a dream which ended when on inquiry at a bookshop
I discovered there were already some twenty-seven such transla-
tions.

The deepest emotion of my young life was born in my Con-
firmation. Bishop Littlejohn, then the Bishop of Long Island,
was our house guest, and the service took place in the church
at Islip which my father had helped to build. As I knelt at the
altar rails I felt as if I were dedicating my life to God's service
and, had anyone suggested my becoming a nun, I might indeed
have considered changing the white muslin and veil I was
wearing for the more sober garb of the convent. Preparing for
this sacrament at a time when the widening rift between
my parents was causing me sorrow rendered me peculiarly
susceptible to the emotional appeal of Christianity.

In my sixteenth year my family acquired a new 2,000-ton
yacht, the *Valiant*. It brought my father from Birkenhead,
where she was built, to Newport in seven and a half days. His
journey was short and uneventful compared to my great-grandfather's on the S.S. *North Star*, which sailed on the twenty-second
of May, 1853, from Sandy Hook and took ten days, eight hours
and forty minutes to reach Southampton. In a contemporary
magazine I found the following description, which may amuse
my readers:

Commodore Cornelius Vanderbilt built the S.S. "North
Star" for his pleasure. Her size was: 200 feet length of keel
and 270 feet overall, with 38 feet breadth of beam. It was the
largest yacht that had ever been constructed for a pleasure
voyage, and when she had been finished and sumptuously
furnished he started on his holiday trip to the Old World with
all his numerous family of 18 on board—his sons and
daughters and wives and husbands and children, and a great
retinue of servants.

The Commodore and his companions were received with distinguished marks of consideration wherever they went and in Southampton a public dinner was given them by the civic authorities, the day on which it took place being kept a holiday by the citizens.

After a fortnight's sojourn in England, the "North Star" took her departure for Cronstadt, where she arrived safely and the Commodore with his family and followers were hospitably entertained by the Czar and his Court. It was the year before the Crimean War and Russia had not experienced any of the mortifying disasters which broke the heart of the Emperor and caused his premature death.

After enjoying a succession of brilliant feasts and receptions in St. Petersburg the "North Star" left for the South visiting Havre; the principal ports of the Mediterranean, in Spain, France, Italy, Constantinople, Malta, Gibraltar, Madeira and returned to New York in September. And wherever they went, the Commodore and his companions were treated like princes.

The cruise of the "North Star" still remains unparalleled. No similar excursion has ever been since undertaken either in this country or in Great Britain; and the Commodore's holiday excursion remains like his whole career, by itself and not likely to be repeated.

My father's journey, if less eventful, at least had a brilliant ending, for when he arrived at Newport, our new and magnificent home awaited him—Marble House on Bellevue Avenue. This, my mother's second architectural achievement in co-operation with her architect friend Richard Hunt, was inspired by the Grand Trianon in the park of Versailles. Unlike Louis XIV's creation, it stood in restricted grounds, and, like a prison, was surrounded by high walls. Even the gates were lined with sheet iron. But it cannot be gainsaid that Marble House both within and without impressed one with its splendour and grandeur. The hall and staircase were built of yellow marble, and there were fine tapestries flanking the entrance, depicting the Death of Coligny and the Massacre of St. Bartholomew's Eve, which always gave me a momentary chill. The beautiful dining-room, built of red marble, gleamed like fire.

Upstairs my own room was austere. It was panelled in a dark Renaissance *boiserie*. There were six windows, but at best one could only glimpse the sky through their high and narrow case-

ments. An unadorned stone mantel opposite my bed greeted my
waking eyes. To the right on an antique table were aligned a
mirror and various silver brushes and combs. On another table
writing utensils were disposed in such perfect order that I never
ventured to use them. For my mother had chosen every piece of
furniture and had placed every ornament according to her taste,
and had forbidden the intrusion of my personal possessions.
Often as I lay on the bed, that like St. Ursula's in the lovely
painting by Carpaccio stood on a dais and was covered with a
baldaquin, I reflected that there was in her love of me something
of the creative spirit of an artist—that it was her wish to produce
me as a finished specimen framed in a perfect setting, and that
my person was dedicated to whatever final disposal she had in
mind.

On the ground floor just under mine a Gothic room held a
collection of majolica, cameos, and bronzes which a French
connoisseur, Garvais by name, had brought together. It was our
living-room, but stained-glass windows from some famous church
kept out the light, creating a melancholy atmosphere in which a
della Robbia Madonna suggested the renunciation of a worldly
life. It was here that Marlborough later proposed to me, and that
I accepted a sacrifice that, in obeisance to the dictates of my upbringing, I felt was fore-ordained.

It was not strange that, intuitive and sensitive, I should have
been introspective. My life was a solitary one in which my
brothers, both younger, one markedly so, because of their school-
ing took little part. We never shared our lessons, and during the
holidays as they grew older they partook of sports and games in
which I was seldom allowed to indulge.

The restrictions of my girlhood may appear strange to modern
young women accustomed to the freedom that is theirs. But in
my youth there were no telephones—no cinemas—no motor-cars.
Even our clothes prevented the relaxed comfort we now take for
granted. When I was seventeen my skirts almost touched the
ground; it was considered immodest to wear them shorter. My
dresses had high, tight, whalebone collars. A corset laced my
waist to the eighteen inches fashion decreed. An enormous hat
adorned with flowers, feathers and ribbons was fastened to my
hair with long steel pins, and a veil covered my face. Tight
gloves pinched my hands and I carried a parasol. Thus attired
I went to Bailey's Beach for a morning bathe. There, clad in a

dark blue alpaca outfit consisting of a dress under which were drawers, and black silk stockings, with a large hat to protect me from the sun, I bobbed up and down over incoming waves. Needless to add that I was never taught to swim. Tennis and golf played no part in my education, but lessons in deportment cultivated a measured and stately walk. How full of tedious restraint was this artificial life! It was not surprising that I disliked our sojourn at Newport and longed for the greater freedom Idlehour brought me. As I grew older, discipline increased. I then saw little of my contemporaries, and spent my days at my studies. My mother disapproved of what she termed silly boy and girl flirtations, so the picnics at the farm ceased and my governess had strict injunctions to report any flighty disturbance of my thoughts. Luncheon, which was served in the red marble dining-room where the heavy bronze chairs required a footman's help to get them near the table, was my only social distraction.

My mother always lunched at home to be with her children; it was the only meal we had with her. One of my most vivid memories of her is at the head of the massive oak table in our New York house, at which places were invariably laid for six or eight guests who would drop in informally. It was then the fashion for women to drink tea or chocolate with their midday meal. In front of my mother's place there was a sumptuous silver tray on which stood a tea service and a chocolate pot. They were large and heavy and were embossed with scenes from Flemish life recalling those in the tapestries on the walls. They seemed to me much too heavy for my mother's delicate hands to lift.

Men were only occasionally present at these luncheons, my father being kept at his business, and as I grew in years and listened to the arid gossip women talk when in each other's company, I developed a decided preference for the society of men whose conversation, it seemed to me, held much more of interest. My studies at the Rosa classes had made me very much alive to events other than those discussed among my mother's women friends. I sometimes longed to express my views in the general conversations that took place, but a look from my mother repressed me. Art was a favoured topic, and I listened to the appreciations of certain self-termed connoisseurs whose appraisals were dictated by the cost rather than the beauty of an object. I was not surprised when later in Mrs. Oelrich's pseudo-marble palace or Mrs. Goelet's Renaissance château I saw objects that with their heavy gilding and rich velvets looked expensive but had neither the fine proportions nor the restraint art imposes. Period houses were then rising like mushrooms in the competitive atmosphere of Newport's plutocracy. Mrs. Stuyvesant Fish, who lived in a frame house of some distinction but no pretensions and claimed to be a social leader, is reported to have been annoyed by such ostentation. On one occasion when her hostess, whose knowledge of history was as limited as her appreciation of art, announced, "And this is my Louis Quinze salon!" Mrs. Fish with a polite but studied insolence exclaimed, "And what makes you think so?" Such distinctions gave pleasure to the little set of elegants who still occupied the simple houses of their fathers and gazed with affronted eyes at the vulgar extravagances of newcomers.

As a child I would note these new mansions rising when in the afternoons I drove my pony Dumpling up and down Bellevue Avenue. My governess, Miss Harper, shared the seat beside me in the low dog-cart specially built for me; behind sat a small groom. One day, shopping in the town of Newport, I learned how the rich are exploited, for when Marble House was mentioned as our address the shopkeeper informed me he had mistaken the price he had given me, and added a good fifty per cent. Even Miss Harper seemed taken aback, and I was aghast at what I conceived to be dishonesty.

As I grew older, I was increasingly happy to leave the artificial life of Newport and to return to Idlehour in the autumn. Here, when I was sixteen, a last peaceful interlude awaited me before our departure on a long cruise to India.

I saw little of the Rosa classes from then on. It was perhaps as well that the competitive ardour examinations evoked should be over, for I worked myself into such a state of apprehension that I still wonder how I managed to secure the *cum laude* with which our teacher rewarded our best efforts. Encouraged by my English governess, I had had hopes of going to Oxford after my graduation, with an honours degree in modern languages in view, but all this came to naught when at the age of eighteen I became engaged to be married.

CHAPTER TWO

A Debutante of the '90s

I HAD reached an age when the continual disagreements between my parents had become a matter of deep concern to me. I was tensely susceptible to their differences, and each new quarrel awoke responding echoes that tore at my loyalties. Profoundly unhappy in my home life, I awaited the rupture which I felt could not be long delayed. Divorce in those days was considered shocking, and because of its novelty would create a dire scandal. But of this I knew nothing and cared still less. The immediate cause of my unhappiness was to be found in the constant scenes that so deeply wounded my father and harried my mother beyond control—scenes that embittered the sensitive years of my girlhood and made of marriage a horrible mockery. It was in such an atmosphere of dread and uncertainty that our last and longest yachting expedition was undertaken in my seventeenth year.

We left New York on November 23, 1893, with India as our destination. The party included my parents, my brother Harold, a doctor, a governess and the three men friends who were our constant companions. Willie, being at school, remained at home. My mother, claiming that my governess gave sufficient trouble, refused to have another woman on board.

Our way to Bombay lay through the Atlantic, the Mediterranean, the Suez Canal, the Red Sea and the Indian Ocean, calling only at Tunis and Egypt. We spent two days in Cairo while the yacht passed through the Suez Canal and coaled at Suez. The harbour of Bombay was a welcome sight after so long a voyage, but when we started to cross India in a private sleeping-car attached to a regular train we realised what discomfort in a train could amount to. At every station angry natives seeking transportation tried noisily to force their way into our bedrooms, which opened directly on to the station platforms. Luckily the doors were locked, but the din was formidable, and in the night those angry mobs seemed threatening. No one slept, and the next day we continued our journey in the comparative luxury and seclusion of a private train.

Thus we crossed India—stopping at Ahmedabad, Jaipur, Delhi, Benares, Lucknow and Agra. Accompanying my parents, I did all the sights in tourist fashion, and spent a night of lurid memories in Lucknow. I had read a vivid description of the gallant defence of its English garrison during the Indian Mutiny and of how they were finally overcome and massacred by Indian troops. In my hotel bedroom, which was accessible to any marauder, the horrors of that massacre assumed nightmare proportions. Hotels at that time were small hostels one storey high, built to accommodate commercial travellers; the front of the rooms gave on to a court, while the back looked out on an open drain. Fortunately, most of our nights were spent on the train, which was backed on to a siding. Even then we knew little comfort, for it was difficult to secure bath water and the food was incredibly nasty. We lived on tea, toast and marmalade.

It was wonderful to find all the luxuries of home on the *Valiant*, which had come round India from Bombay and lay anchored in the Hooghly. My parents spent a week as guests of the Viceroy and Lady Lansdowne at Government House, Calcutta. My mother, whose habit it was to impose her views rather than to invite discussion, had already, on occasion, revealed the hopes she nourished for my brilliant future, and her admiration for the British way of life was as apparent as was her desire to place me in an aristocratic setting. These intentions, I am sure, crystallised during her visit at Government House. In the Viceroy and Lady Lansdowne she found exemplified the qualities she admired, which the prerogatives of a privileged life had but enhanced; and in conversations with her hostess, who was Marlborough's aunt, the possibility of my marriage to him may have been discussed. It is certain that it was then her ambitions took definite shape; for she confessed to me years later that she had decided to marry me either to Marlborough or to Lord Lansdowne's heir.

While we were in Calcutta, I went to spend a day with Lady Lansdowne's younger daughter at a place the Viceroy had on the river. She was just my age and later on was to become my cousin by marriage, since both Lady Lansdowne and Lady Blandford, my future mother-in-law, were daughters of the Duke of Abercorn—'Old Magnificent,' as he was dubbed while Lord Lieutenant of Ireland. She and I compared the books we were reading and I was surprised to find how scanty was her knowledge. Little time or trouble was spent on the education of English girls. It was still customary for them to have, sometimes inherited from a previous generation, what Lady Mary Wortley Montagu has humorously described as a "good homespun" governess. They read Miss Young's *History of Greece*, but Virgil, Gibbon, Hallam and Green were all equally unknown to them. I pitied the limited outlook given by so restricted an education, and wondered what chance a girl so brought up had against a boy with a public school and college background. Later on I was to find that English girls suffered many handicaps, and I came to realise that it was considered fitting that their interests should be sacrificed to the more important prospects of the heir.

It was with no regrets that I left India. It seemed to me a cruel country. Women had so little part either in its history, its life or its religion. Their lives were spent in purdah, in petty squabbles and intrigues which sometimes culminated in ugly tragedies. How glorious in comparison was Greece, where women as goddesses or hetæræ had inspired the arts. How transcendent the Acropolis with its amphitheatre of mountains in the distance, the sea near-by and the little theatre where the tragedies of Sophocles and Euripides were first heard. Even without the statues of Praxiteles and the friezes of Phidias, now scattered in museums, one realised the splendour that must have been the Athens of Pericles. Nostalgic memories lay in the shade of those Greek olives and myrtle; whether evoked by the loves of pagan gods, or by heroes of an illustrious past, or yet again by the fine concepts of the Stoics, I did not know, but I felt that on this hill greatness had dwelt.

We spent the spring in Paris. I can still see the view over the Tuileries Gardens from our windows, still enjoy our walks under the flowering chestnuts of the Champs Élysées and our drives in the Bois de Boulogne in our carriage and pair. Every day there were visits to museums and churches and lectures at the Sorbonne, but the classical matinées at the Théâtre Français were my greatest pleasure. The impression made by Mounet-Sully in *Œdipe Roi* is unforgettable—his moving voice, his noble gestures and bearing, his handsome appearance and the dramatic quality of his acting stirred me deeply. In Legouvé's play, *Adrienne Lecouvreur*, the beautiful actress murdered by the Duchesse de Bouillon, jealous of the former's love for Maurice de Saxe, was impersonated by Mademoiselle Bartet, with Albert Lambert as the hero. The tragic intensity of their love scenes established a standard I have rarely seen attained. How elegant is the French language when spoken as it was at the Comédie Française with its great tradition of perfect diction. At times I have wondered whether it was anticipation of my future that caused my mother to arrange for me to have lessons in elocution with an actress from so classic a school, or whether she already realised that any daughter of hers would find causes to champion. Whatever her motive, the lessons produced a voice that carried.

On Sundays my governess and I would go to Saint-Sulpice and sit with Widor, the celebrated organist. Years later, when Rheims Cathedral was reopened after World War I, I was to hear his lovely Mass for two organs. How deeply moving was that Mass in its spiritual ascendancy of an inviolate Faith. There was in that beautiful church, in that vast assembly, a dedication, such as had animated the crusades, that sanctified the participant.

In the Paris of my youth there were no motor-cars. One used to stroll along the boulevards or sit and watch the passing crowd. The little open victoria in which it so delighted the Princess of Wales to drive incognito was, with the boats that plied the Seine, the pleasantest conveyance. The Rue de la Paix was the fashionable shopping centre and names of the great dressmakers —Worth, Doucet, Rouff—were printed on small doors admitting one to modest shops. Inside, the array of lovely dresses, expensive furs and diaphanous lingerie fairly took one's breath away. I longed to be allowed to choose my dresses, but my mother had her own views, which unfortunately did not coincide with mine.

For my first ball, at the Duc de Gramont's in the Avenue des Champs Élysées, where I made my début at a party given for the Duchess's eldest daughter, I wore a white tulle dress made by Worth. It touched the ground with a full skirt, as was the fashion in those days, and it had a tightly laced bodice. My hair was piled high in curls and a narrow ribbon was tied round my long and slender neck. I had no jewels and wore gloves that came almost to my shoulders. The French dubbed me *La belle Mlle. Vanderbilt au long cou.* It is difficult for a girl of the present day to visualise a white ball, as those dances given for débutantes were then called. A *bal blanc* had to live up to its name of purity and innocence; it could not inspire the mild flirtations of a pink ball where young married women were included. The men who attended them, no doubt with the intention of selecting a future spouse, were expected to behave with circumspection. There was no opportunity for conversation. A débutante was invited to dance, and once the dance was over she was escorted back to her mama. Rows of chaperones lined the walls, discussing the merits of their charges. The young girls stood diffidently beside them. The terror of not being asked to dance, the humiliation of being a 'wallflower', ruined the pleasures of a ball for those who were ill-favoured. With the politeness inherent in the French, a galaxy of partners presented their respects to me and I was soon at ease and happy. Curiously enough, my second husband, Jacques Balsan, who was present, told his mother the following day, "I met at the ball last night the girl I would like to marry." It was twenty-seven years later that his wish came true.

We spent the whole of May and June in Paris, and I had five proposals of marriage. When I say I had, I mean that my mother informed me that five men had asked her for my hand, as the French saying goes, but Jacques was not among them. She had, as a matter of course, refused them, since she considered none of them sufficiently exalted. There was only one, a German prince, whose cause I was allowed to consider. Prince Francis Joseph was the youngest of the four handsome Battenberg Princes. The eldest, Prince Alexander, had in 1879 been freely elected Prince of Bulgaria by the people, but in 1886, falling into disfavour with Russia, had been kidnapped and carried into that country by Russian partisans, and eventually had to abdicate. Of the other two, Prince Henry had married Queen Victoria's youngest daughter; Prince Louis had already begun his brilliant career in the British Navy which was cut short by the war.

I met Prince Francis Joseph at an evening party given by Madame de Pourtalès in her house close to the Madeleine. That the Comtesse Mélanie de Pourtalès had been a famous beauty could still be seen. She was a typical *grande dame* and in her salons were to be found the *beau monde* of Paris. I felt lost as I entered that brilliant throng of statesmen, diplomats and elegant women, but my hostess with inimitable charm called me to her side and put me at ease. I sensed by the way she drew me out that her interest was not inspired purely by kindness to a little débutante and I wondered what lay behind it. Later in the course of the evening while I was with the Prince I saw my mother engrossed in conversation with our hostess; they were observing us with interest. Instinct suggested and made me fearful of some deep-laid plot. I was grateful for the distraction offered by the Comte Louis de Turenne's witty comments on those present. He was a diplomat of the old school and seemed to know the history of everyone worth knowing. It was, he told me, then the fashion for great ladies to aspire to political power through protégés whose ambitions they fostered. It was also common knowledge that intrigues were on foot to displace Prince Ferdinand of Saxe-Coburg, who, though elected ruler of Bulgaria a few years before by the Great Powers against the wishes of Russia, had not yet been accorded general recognition. Pointing to Prince Francis Joseph, the Count said it was rumoured that at least one of the Powers would be willing to elect him King in Ferdinand's stead, and that he appeared to be assured of success if provided with the necessary financial backing. The stage seemed set for a political intrigue and my hostess's ambition to place her protégé on a throne showed signs of succeeding. I think that for a moment my mother's intentions to marry me to an English duke faltered! A royal crown glittered more brightly than a coronet! So the Prince continued his courtship unhindered, unfolding his ambitions to my apprehensive ears. It seemed I was but to exchange one bondage for another. Such a marriage could mean only unhappiness. Separated from my family and my friends, living in a provincial capital, ironbound in a strict etiquette with a man whose views were those of a prejudiced German princeling —how could I reconcile myself to such a life? Only a great love could make such a marriage possible, and I felt aversion rather than attraction for the dapper man of the world for whom I realised I was only a means to an end. My mother on second thoughts decided to adhere to her former intentions and raised no objections when I confessed my feelings to her. So nothing more was heard of the project—Prince Ferdinand of Bulgaria, backed by the Great Powers, assumed the title of Czar, and Prince Francis Joseph of Battenberg's royal aspirations later

became reconciled to a minor role in his marriage to a
Montenegran princess, sister to Queen Hélène of Italy.

Soon after this we left Paris to spend the summer in England
at a rented house near Marlow on the Thames. Having begun a
divorce suit against my father, my mother wished to await its
conclusion abroad and had invited Mrs. William Jay with her
daughters, who were my friends, to visit us. My parents definitely
parted that spring in Paris. I felt relief that the sinister gloom
of their relationship would no longer encompass me. But I did
not realise how irrevocably I would be cut off from a father I
loved nor how completely my mother would dominate me from
then on.

We first went to London and settled in a fashionable London
hotel, a dingy structure in a narrow street. The rooms were
frowsty in the true English sense and contained a bewildering
medley of the rubbish of centuries. Rigid armchairs had lace
antimacassars; comfortless couches stood stiffly against the wall;
footstools and whatnots impeded one's progress, and a black
grate held black coal at an impossible angle. A chandelier with
gas flares hung over a large round table on which were spread
The Times, The Morning Post, a copy of *Punch,* and the fashionable weekly, *The World,* in which Belle's 'Letters' castigated
the *beau monde* like a genteel precursor of Cholly Knicker-
bocker. Over the windows hung heavy plush curtains, and the
meagre light was still further dimmed by the heavy lace window-
curtains. I thought with longing of our gay and handsome suite
at the Hotel Continental and of the lovely view over the Tuileries
Gardens to the Seine.

Our carriages and horses, the imposing French coachman and
the no less distinguished English footman had preceded us, and
our first outing was a visit to Lady Paget, one of my mother's
oldest friends. She was born Minnie Stevens of New York and
with my godmother, Consuelo Duchess of Manchester, Lady
Randolph Churchill and Mrs. Cavendish-Bentinck, represented
the American element of the smart coterie known as "the Prince
of Wales's set". Lady Paget was considered handsome; to me,
with her quick wit and worldly standards, she was Becky Sharp
incarnate. She was married to a tall handsome officer who in
time became a general. She lived at 35 Belgrave Square, a fine
house with lofty rooms in which there was an immense amount
of nondescript furniture and numerous tables that were littered

with signed photographs in silver frames. She received us with a mixture of the affection due to an old friend and the condescension that seemed to infect the habitués of the inner circles of London society. Once greetings had been exchanged I realised with a sense of acute discomfort that I was being critically appraised by a pair of hard green eyes. The simple dress I was wearing, my shyness and diffidence, which in France were regarded as natural in a débutante, appeared to awaken her ridicule. My lack of beauty, for I was still in the ugly duckling stage, made me painfully sensitive to criticism. I felt like a gawky graceless child under her scrutiny.

"If I am to bring her out," she told my mother, "she must be able to compete at least as far as clothes are concerned with far better-looking girls."

It was useless to demur that I was only seventeen. Tulle must give way to satin, the baby *décolletage* to a more generous display of neck and arms, naïveté to sophistication. Lady Paget was adamant.

It was at a dinner-party at her house, soon after, that I met the Duke of Marlborough. My hostess had placed the Duke on her right and had put me next to him—a rather unnecessary public avowal of her intentions. He seemed to me very young, although six years my senior, and I thought him good-looking and intelligent. He had a small aristocratic face with a large nose and rather prominent blue eyes. His hands, which he used in a fastidious manner, were well shaped and he seemed inordinately proud of them.

By that time the London season was well over, and the festivities and balls of June and July had petered out in the dust and heat of August. Society had gone its different ways to Cowes, to Scotland, to do a cure, or simply to country houses. We went to our house on the Thames, accompanied by Mrs. Jay and her daughters, who were younger than I. My brother Willie joined us. His tutor, blessed with the appropriate name of Noble, had brought him from St. Mark's School to spend the holiday with us. With Miss Harper and my brother Harold we were a pleasant little party. Being the eldest and hard put to finish my studies, I worked a considerable part of the day while Willie and Mr. Noble ran a motor-launch on the Thames. There were occasional breaks in our routine, such as the day my mother, posing as an English chatelaine, gave a party for the village children. To our discomfiture, they complained that American ice-cream gave them tummy-ache and clamoured for hot tea, which we had not provided. Occasionally we had guests; among them I remember particularly Paul Deschanel, a good-looking and cultured Frenchman. He used to read French poetry to my mother, but one day, breaking off a couplet, he asked her permission to pay me his court. He told her of his ambitions, and in no uncertain tones announced that one day he would be President of the French Republic. He was at this time a member of the Chamber of Deputies, of which he soon became President. There were no more readings of French poetry after so indiscreet a disclosure of his ambitions, and the next day Monsieur Deschanel departed, taking a tearful farewell of *"le petit philosophe rose"*, as he named me. Years later, as President of the French Republic, Deschanel paid an official visit to England and, as fate strangely decreed, I was selected as his partner in the state quadrille at the Court Ball at Buckingham Palace. The Lord Chamberlain informed me that he relied upon me to steer my partner through the intricate figures. We were dancing opposite King George, who expected his aristocracy to avoid false steps in the quadrille as well as in other matters. I could not help smiling at the President's bewilderment when, confronted by a tall lady glittering in jewels, he recognised the *petit philosophe rose* he had once wished to marry. During the dance he managed to whisper, "Did your mother tell you that I had made up my mind one day to be President of the French Republic?" and I answered truthfully, "Yes, but only after your departure." His end was sad, for after several undignified exhibitions of folly he threw himself out of a railway train in a tunnel and soon after died from his injuries.

That summer I received two or three other proposals from uninteresting Englishmen, which I found slightly disillusioning. They were so evidently dictated by a desire for my dowry, a reflection that was inclined to dispel whatever thoughts of romance might come my way.

In the early autumn of the year 1894 we returned to America. I looked forward to being in my own country and to coming out in New York society with feelings of pleasure. The few balls of Paris and London had awakened a zest for more and I was anxious to see something of my friends from whom I had been separated for many months. It was with relief that I realised that

the dangers of a foreign alliance were at least for the time being
in abeyance and that my mother's ambitions appeared to have
waned, since that one dinner with the Duke of Marlborough
remained our only meeting.

We settled at 660 Fifth Avenue, from which my father had
temporarily been banished. Society, not yet hardened to divorce,
was inclined to take sides. During the following months I was
to suffer a perpetual denial of friendships and pleasures, since
my mother resented seeing anyone whose loyalties were not
completely hers. I had moreover to render a strict account of the
few parties I was allowed to attend without her, and if I danced
too often with a partner he immediately became the butt of her
displeasure. She knew how to make people look ridiculous and
did not spare her sarcasm about those to whom I was attracted,
reserving special darts for an older man who by his outstanding
looks, his distinction and his charm had gained a marked
ascendancy in my affections.

The following March, on my eighteenth birthday, a succession
of floral offerings arrived in staggering profusion. It was then
the custom to send American Beauty roses to the object of one's
affections, and when I opened a small box and found a perfect
rose alone on its green foliage I instinctively knew who had
sent it, though no name was attached. Later that day I received
the only proposal of marriage I wished to accept. We had gone
to Riverside Drive to bicycle, which was at that time a fashionable amusement, and my Rosenkavalier and I managed to out-
distance the rest. It was a most hurried proposal, for my mother
and the others were not far behind; as they strained to reach us
he pressed me to agree to a secret engagement, for I was leaving
for Europe the next day. He added that he would follow me,
but that I must not tell my mother since she would most certainly
withhold her consent to our engagement. On my return to
America we might plan an elopement. Alas for those hurried
promises! I have never succeeded in hiding my feelings and my
mother must have guessed the cause of my new radiance. She
laid her plans with forethought and skill, and during the five
months of our stay in Europe I never laid eyes on Mr. X, nor
did I hear from him. Later I learned that he had followed us to
Paris but had been refused admittance when he called. His
letters had been confiscated; my own, though they were few, no
doubt suffered the same fate. When one is young and unhappy

the sun shines in vain, and one feels as if cheated of one's birth-right. I knew that my mother resented my evident misery, and her complaints about what she satirically termed my "martyrdom" did not improve our relations. Like an automaton I tried on the clothes she ordered for me. Visits to museums and churches were varied by concerts and lectures. I went to a few of those deadly débutante balls which I no longer cared for and danced with men who had no interest for me. Then we moved to London, where events began to move rapidly, and I felt I was being steered into a vortex that was to engulf me.

One ball stands out clearly because of the beauty of the hostess and of her surroundings. It was given by the Duke and Duchess of Sutherland at Stafford House. The young Duchess was a glittering apparition in her silver dress and diamonds as she stood at the top of the great staircase receiving her guests. There were endless reception rooms thronged with people. I had few acquaintances and felt lost and ill at ease. It was the custom then to have cards on which your partners wrote their names, and I can still recall the surge of gratitude with which I welcomed the first to do so. Marlborough, whom I had not seen since the dinner at Lady Paget's the previous year, claimed several dances.

We were but a short time in England, and a visit to Blenheim Palace was the outstanding event. At that time Marlborough lived there alone. His two unmarried sisters sometimes stayed with him, but his mother, Lady Blandford, was seldom invited. She had after many years of unhappiness with Marlborough's father finally divorced him, and he had contracted a second marriage with Mrs. Hammersley, an American widow, whose wealth had been freely spent installing central heating and electric light at Blenheim.

Blenheim always impressed one by its immense size and by the beauty of its situation and surroundings. It has a stately grandeur—the word Palace best describes the intentions Sarah, Duchess of Marlborough, and the architect, Sir John Vanbrugh, had in mind when they built it. We entered the park through a stone arch. A porter in livery carrying a long wand surmounted by a silver knob from which hung a red cord and tassel stood at attention and the great house loomed in the distance. At the right of us and below lay an ornamental lake spanned by a monumental bridge. We turned into a fine avenue of elms and passed through another arch leading into a court around which were disposed audit rooms, laundries, a porter's lodge and various offices. On its southern façade it was flanked by hot-houses which formerly had housed a collection of Titian's works. The gallery was kept locked, since the ladies were not allowed to view the pictures, and great was their delight when it was destroyed by a fire.

Passing through still another stone arch we drove into the central court surrounded by the house. To the open north one looked across the bridge to the monument built to the first Duke, a column around which, as legend would have it, trees were planted in the order in which the British regiments stood at the opening of the Battle of Blenheim. It was this legend which gave rise to the question asked by so many tourists with more curiosity than knowledge of either history or geography: "At which exact spot was the battle fought?" From the column the High Park sloped gently down in green glades to the lake. There were great oaks, some accounted over a thousand years old, including one credited to have hidden King Alfred, for the park had been part of the royal forest of Woodstock. There was also Fair Rosamond's well, named after a king's love, and the High Lodge where the wicked Earl of Rochester, High Ranger to Charles the Second, had taken his pleasure. The High Lodge was a small house with a lovely view over the park and surrounding country; in my time it was used only for picnic luncheons when the men shot pheasants and rabbits in the park.

A flight of shallow steps led up to the main entrance of the Palace. The doors opened on to an immense hall with a domed ceiling. It was so high that I had to crane my neck to see the Great Duke dressed in a Roman toga driving a chariot. He was surrounded by clouds and I realised that he was hurrying through celestial spheres, no doubt to join Julius Cæsar and Alexander the Great. Even Napoleon, I thought, could not have imagined a finer apotheosis. The architect Vanbrugh had unfortunately forgotten to provide space for the monumental staircase such a house required and one had to climb a long and narrow flight with an ugly handrail. A family group painted by Hudson was the only ornament to enliven one's endless peregrinations up and down. From the hall, red baize druggets showed the way to which tourists must adhere.

We followed one into the Great Saloon, where again we viewed

the first Duke and his household in wall frescoes painted by the
French artist Laguerre, who must have rued the day he came to
exploit his country's humiliation. Here there were two impressive
mantelpieces and in front of one a tea-table had been set. In due
course Marlborough, accompanied by his sisters, Lady Lilian and
Lady Norah Spencer-Churchill, joined us. Lilian, a pretty blonde
a few years my senior, immediately won my heart by her simple
unaffected kindness. Two or three young men completed a party
which seemed lost in so big a house. As I looked about I saw
drawing-rooms stretching in vistas on either side of the saloon,
on the west towards the Long Library and on the east to the
private apartments. We spent the evening listening to the Duke's
organist, a famous musician from Birmingham, who played for
us on the organ Marlborough's father had installed in the Long
Library.

The following day, Sunday, my host showed me his estate.
We also drove to outlying villages, where old women and children
curtsied and men touched their caps as we passed. The country
round Blenheim is rural, with ploughed fields and stone fences.
The villages are built of grey stone and the lovely old churches
delighted me. Each cottage had its small garden gay with flowers.
I realised that I had come to an old world with ancient traditions
and that the villagers were still proud of their Duke and of their
allegiance to his family. They earned little, but were cared for
when sick. There were as yet no stump orators to inform them
of better conditions; politicians were Liberal or Conservative,
which meant in either case much of a sameness to the tiller of
the soil. That Marlborough was ambitious I gathered from his
talk; that he should be proud of his position and estates seemed
but natural; but did he recognise his obligations? Steeped as I
then was in questions of political economy—in the theories of
the rights of man, in the speeches of Gladstone and John Bright
—it was not strange that such reflections should occur to me.

I don't know what Marlborough thought of me, except that I
was quite different from the sophisticated girls who wished to
become his Duchess. My remarks appeared to amuse him, but
whether he considered them witty or naïve I never knew, except
that much later, after our separation, he said on the occasion of
some trivial catastrophe, "Consuelo must be laughing at this—
she has such a sense of humour!" Luckily for me I have always
been able to laugh, even at my own discomfiture. It was that

afternoon that he must have made up his mind to marry me and to give up the girl he loved, as he told me so tragically soon after our marriage. For to live at Blenheim in the pomp and circumstance he considered essential needed money, and a sense of duty to his family and to his traditions indicated the sacrifice of personal desires.

When I left Blenheim after that week-end I firmly decided that I would not marry Marlborough. And, homeward bound, I dreamed of life in my own country with my Rosenkavalier. It would, I knew, entail a struggle, but I meant to force the issue with my mother. I did not relish the thought, but my happiness was at stake.

My mother had invited Marlborough to visit us in Newport some time in September. I barely had six weeks to make my plans and I was nervous and worried, not knowing when or where I could get into touch with the man to whom I considered myself engaged.

On reaching Newport my life became that of a prisoner, with my mother and my governess as wardens. I was never out of their sight. Friends called but were told I was not at home. Locked behind those high walls—the porter had orders not to let me out unaccompanied—I had no chance of getting any word to my fiancé. Brought up to obey, I was helpless under my mother's total domination. Despairing of ever seeing him, I had succumbed to despondency, when at a ball we met. We had one short dance before my mother dragged me away, but it was enough to reassure me that his feelings towards me had not changed.

Driving home my mother observed an ominous silence, but when we reached the house she told me to follow her to her room. Thinking it best no longer to dissemble, I told her that I meant to marry X, adding that I considered I had a right to choose my own husband. These words, the bravest I had ever uttered, brought down a frightful storm of protest. I suffered every searing reproach, heard every possible invective hurled at the man I loved. I was informed of his numerous flirtations, of his well-known love for a married woman, of his desire to marry an heiress. My mother even declared that he would have no children and that there was madness in his family. I had no answer to these accusations, but in my silence she must have read how obstinately I clung to my choice. In a final appeal to

my feelings she argued that her decision to select a husband for
me was founded on considerations I was too young and inexperi-
enced to appreciate. Though rent by so emotional a plea, I still
maintained my right to lead the life I wished. It was perhaps my
unexpected resistance or the mere fact that no one had ever
stood up to her that made her say she would not hesitate to shoot
a man whom she considered would ruin my life.

We reached a stage where arguments were futile, and I left
her then in the cold dawn of morning feeling as if all my youth
had been drained away. No one came near me and the morning
dragged on its interminable course. I could not seek counsel
with X, for there was no telephone. I could not write, for the
servants had orders to bring my letters to my mother, neither
could I get past the porter at the gate. The house was full of
ominous rumours. I heard that my mother was ill and in her
bed, that a doctor had been sent for; even my governess, usually
so calm, was harassed. The suspense was becoming unbearable.
There was no one I could consult; to appeal to my father, who
was away at sea and who knew nothing of my mother's schemes,
would, I knew, only involve him in a hopeless struggle against
impossible odds and further stimulate my mother's rancour.

Later that day Mrs. Jay, who was my mother's intimate friend
and was staying with us at the time, came to talk to me. Con-
demning my behaviour, she informed me that my mother had
had a heart attack brought about by my callous indifference to
her feelings. She confirmed my mother's intentions of never con-
senting to my plans for marriage, and her resolve to shoot X
should I decide to run away with him. I asked her if I could see
my mother and whether in her opinion she would ever relent. I
still remember the terrible answer, "Your mother will never
relent and I warn you there will be a catastrophe if you persist.
The doctor has said that another scene may easily bring on a
heart attack and he will not be responsible for the result. You
can ask the doctor yourself if you do not believe me!"

Still under the strain of the painful scene with my mother,
still seeing her frightening rage, it seemed to me that she might
indeed easily suffer a stroke or a heart attack if further provoked.
In utter misery I asked Mrs. Jay to let X know that I could not
marry him.

How sad were those summer days of disgrace and unhappiness,
my mother turned away from me, my father out of reach, my

brothers engrossed in their personal pleasures—Willie cruising in his small boat, and Harold too young to mix himself in my problems. My friends who had wearied of being rebuffed no longer called, and with an ingrained reticence I kept my worries to myself.

How gratefully then I looked to Miss Harper for consolation and advice, how wisely she spoke of the future awaiting me in her country, of the opportunities for usefulness and social service I would find there, of the happiness a life lived for others can bring. And in such gentle appeals to my better nature she slowly swung me from contemplations of a purely personal nature to a higher idealism. Brought up to obey, I surrendered more easily to my mother's dictates than others nurtured in a gentler discipline might have done. It seemed to me impossible further to risk her displeasure, implying as it did persecution of the man I loved and the danger to herself the doctor had indicated.

History records many marriages of convenience. Even in my day they were still in vogue in Europe, where the interests of the two contracting parties were considered to outweigh the wishes of the bride. So that what to many of my compatriots may appear an unwarranted prerogative was to my mother but a reasonable decision concerning my future.

Thus disciplined and prepared, I found with Marlborough's arrival a sudden change of scene. Determined to outdo all previous entertainments, my mother gave a ball described in contemporary newspapers as "the most beautiful fête ever seen in Newport". The favours for the cotillion, which she had selected herself in Paris, consisted of old French etchings, fans, mirrors, watch-cases and sashes of ribbons, all of the Louis XIV period. Lanterns which were a facsimile of Marble House and bagpipes which really squeaked added an amusing note. Each favour was marked with a medallion representing Marble House. "The young Duke of Marlborough," the papers continued, "stood by Mrs. Jay in the grand salon and viewed the pretty women with interest."

Once again launched into the gaieties of a season from which I had so recently been withdrawn, I went to dinners and balls escorted by Marlborough, chaperoned by my mother. In the harbour, on one of those sumptuous yachts millionaires then owned, John Jacob Astor and his beautiful wife, later Lady Ribblesdale, entertained us; a cruise with the Pembroke Joneses was declined as Marlborough claimed he was too bad a sailor. My father's yacht, the *Valiant*, was away in other waters; we did not meet until later in New York. And the man I longed to see had withdrawn from so gay a scene.

How leisurely were our pleasures! In the mornings, with my mother, we drove to the Casino in a sociable, a carriage so named for the easy comfort it provided for conversation. Face to face on cushioned seats permitting one to lean back without the loss of dignity, we sat under an umbrella-like tent. Dressed in one of the elaborate batistes my mother had bought for me in Paris, with Marlborough opposite in flannels and the traditional sailor hat, we proceeded in state down Bellevue Avenue. And society rolled by in the elegant equipages one saw in those days when to be well turned out on wheels with a handsome pair of horses was as necessary to one's standard of luxury as a fine house. At the Casino we met the *beau monde* and its belles, young Mrs. J. J. Astor, Miss Grace Wilson, later to marry my cousin Cornelius Vanderbilt, and the two lovely Blight girls, who during their seasons in Paris impressed the Faubourg with the charm, distinction and gaiety their generation achieved. But to my mind the most beautiful of all, with a classic perfection of face and form, was Louise Morris, who later, married to Henry Clews, bequeathed that beauty to her daughter the Duchess of Argyll. How charming they all were in their picture hats and organdies, so incompatible with comfort, but so becoming.

Returning to Marble House, perhaps for a luncheon party, we would often see Oliver H. P. Belmont, a noted whip, bowl swiftly by on his coach, skilfully guiding his blue-blooded leaders Rockingham and Hurlingham. Oliver Belmont was a man of taste. He had at that time a unique stable of carriage horses. In order to be closer to them he had built over his stables near Bellevue Avenue an apartment where he lived with his books and a collection of equestrian knights in medieval armour. Below he housed his carriages—a cabriolet, a curricle, a spider phaeton and various types of gigs and buggies and breaks. These carriages were made in France and were copies of the ones we admire in the pictures of Carle Vernet and the drawings of Guys. They were beautifully turned out with the attention to detail Mr. Belmont's knowledge insured. Sometimes he drove us to the Polo Field, where the young Waterbury boys were giving early proof of the dash and skill that later placed them in the team known as the Big Four, when with my cousin Harry Whitney and that great back Devereux Milburn they won back the Westchester Cup from England. The rivalry of international matches had not as yet caused polo ponies to become as valuable as jewels and the pace so furious as to be almost dangerous. We sat round the Field in our carriages and strolled off to tea at the end of a game.

It was in the comparative quiet of an evening at home that Marlborough proposed to me in the Gothic Room, whose atmosphere was so propitious to sacrifice. There was no need for sentiment. I was content with his pious hope that he would make me a good husband and ran up to my mother with word of our engagement. There was no time for thought or for regrets. The next day the news was out, and a few days later Marlborough departed to see something of a country he even then announced he would never revisit. There was in his sarcastic comments on all things American an arrogance that inclined me to view his decision with approval. When I broke the news of our engagement to my brothers, Harold observed, "He is only marrying you for your money," and with this last slap to my pride I burst into tears. It was obvious that they would have preferred me to marry a compatriot, but unable to speak of the emotional turmoil I had so recently experienced I could not enlighten them. Indeed an immense distance now separated me from them, for I had grown years older.

In October we returned to New York to a new house my mother had taken since her divorce had become final. It was on Seventy-second Street and has only recently been demolished.

November 5th was fixed for our wedding, but it was changed to the 6th when Marlborough said that November 5th was Guy Fawkes Day and that it would not be suitable for him to be married on a day that an attempt had been made to blow up the House of Lords. I could not understand why Guy Fawkes's attempt to blow up Parliament almost three centuries before should affect the date of our marriage, but this was only the first of a series of, to me, archaic prejudices inspired by a point of view opposed to my own.

Ordering my trousseau, always an exciting event in a girl's life, proved of slight interest since I had very little to say about it, my mother not troubling to consult the taste she claimed I did not possess.

The marriage settlements gave rise to considerable discussion. An English solicitor who had crossed the seas with the declared intention of "profiting the illustrious family" he had been engaged to serve devoted a natural talent to that end. Finally the settlements were apportioned in equal shares, at my request.

The strain my engagement imposed on my feelings was further intensified by these material considerations. However, with my engagement, vigilance had relaxed and my correspondence was no longer subjected to scrutiny, a circumstance that permitted a host of proposals to reach me. They were penned by would-be knights anxious to prevent the unhappiness so unromantic a marriage seemed to hold in store. Rendered sceptical by recent experiences, I viewed these offers with less enthusiasm than did their begetters.

As the wedding approached there came presents. My mother had forbidden me to receive any gifts from my Vanderbilt relatives and I felt hurt and pained when I was made to return them without excuse or thanks. My grandmother was the only Vanderbilt whom I was allowed to visit, and the only one invited to my wedding, but she naturally refused to come to a ceremony from which her entire family was to be excluded. My eight bridesmaids had been selected by my mother from among her friends for her own reasons, and some of them were several years older than I. They were Edith Morton, Evelyn Burden, Marie Winthrop, Katherine Duer, Elsa Bronson, May Goelet, Julia Jay and Daisy Post. They wore long dresses of white satin with blue sashes and their big picture hats were most becoming. The arrival of my wedding dress brought the realisation that my mother had ordered it while we were still in Paris, so sure had she been of the success of her plans.

Mine was the first international marriage that had taken place for some time. It created great interest and every incident of my engagement had been publicised. Reporters called incessantly, anxious to secure every particle of news, from the cost of my trousseau to our future plans. Since little news was given out, accounts were fabricated. I read to my stupefaction that my garters had gold clasps studded with diamonds, and wondered how I should live down such vulgarities.

I spent the morning of my wedding day in tears and alone; no one came near me. A footman had been posted at the door of my apartment and not even my governess was admitted. Like an automaton I donned the lovely lingerie with its real lace and the white silk stockings and shoes. My maid helped me into the beautiful dress, its tiers of Brussels lace cascading over white satin. It had a high collar and long tight sleeves. The court train, embroidered with seed pearls and silver, fell from my shoulders in folds of billowing whiteness. My maid fitted the tulle veil to my head with a wreath of orange blossoms; it fell over my face to my knees. A bouquet of orchids that was to come from Blenheim did not arrive in time. I felt cold and numb as I went down to meet my father and the bridesmaids who were waiting for me. My mother had decreed that my father should accompany me to the church to give me away. After that he was to disappear. We were twenty minutes late, for my eyes, swollen with the tears I had wept, required copious sponging before I could face the curious stares that always greet a bride. To my mother, who had preceded us to the church, the wait appeared interminable and she wondered whether at the last moment her plans would miscarry.

There were the usual crowds of curious sightseers on Fifth Avenue. When we reached St. Thomas I saw an endless aisle with clusters of white flowers, and at the altar stood the Bishop of New York and the Bishop of Long Island. So many eyes pried my defences, I was thankful for the veil that covered my face. As I followed my lovely bridesmaids I remembered to press my father's arm gently to slow his step. Marlborough, with the best man, his cousin Ivor Guest, was waiting for us. The usual hymns glorifying perfect love were sung, and when I glanced at my husband shyly I saw that his eyes were fixed in space.

As we came out of the church the crowd surged towards us and women tried to snatch flowers from my bouquet. There were spasmodic cheers and less friendly sallies. At the luncheon which followed at our house the British Ambassador, Lord Pauncefote, made a charming speech, to which Marlborough responded fittingly. The best man toasted the bridesmaids, but the ushers—chosen from the ranks of those who had perhaps from similar notions aspired to be in Marlborough's place—were not called upon to demonstrate their goodwill in speeches.

Driving away from my home I looked back. My mother was at the window. She was hiding behind the curtain, but I saw that she was in tears. 'And yet,' I thought, 'she has attained the goal she set herself, she has experienced the satisfactions wealth can confer, she has ensconced me in the niche she so early assigned me, and she is now free to let ambition give way to a gentler passion.' In seeking a divorce, she had persuaded my father much against his will to give her the grounds a decree in New York State requires—a code in which the subtle charges of mental cruelty cannot be stretched to a complaisant elasticity. I was happy to think that in her marriage to Oliver H. P. Belmont she would find happiness. I did not then know how tragically short their married life would be.

CHAPTER THREE

A Marriage of Convenience

THERE WERE no tunnels to Long Island and no parkways in 1895. Brooklyn Bridge alone spanned the East River. We took a ferry to Long Island City and then a special train to Oakdale.

Settled in an observation car, Marlborough whiled away the journey reading congratulatory telegrams, handing them on to me with the proper gestures of deference or indifference the senders evoked. Thus I could gauge the importance of each person, and received my first lesson in class-consciousness. Unfortunately, there was no silver platter on which to present Her Majesty Queen Victoria's missive, but it was read with due respect, and a sense of her intimidating presence crept even into that distant railway car. It became clear that the royal family and his own families, the Spencer-Churchills and the Hamiltons, were ready to accord me a gracious welcome, though tempered with the reserve marriage with a foreigner evoked. From the Churchills, more immediately concerned, since Blenheim was their home, came a jubilant note; but from the Hamiltons there seemed to emanate a distinct warning that my person rather than my fortune would be my claim to their good graces.

The Hamiltons were a formidable clan headed by the Dowager Duchess of Abercorn, who was proudly conscious of her family and their alliances. Herself the daughter of a Duke of Bedford, she was a typical example of the hereditary aristocrat. A few years later, I was included in a photograph she had made of herself and of her one hundred and thirty descendants in the garden of Montagu House in Whitehall—at that time the residence of her son-in-law, the Duke of Buccleuch, and subsequently the Ministry of Labour. I can remember still my surprise when one member after another of that well-bred company remarked to me that I was the first American she had condescended to receive! Could they imagine they were paying me a compliment?

Of the Duchess's thirteen living children, six daughters had all been ordered to marry into the peerage and no one beneath an earl. My mother-in-law, Lady Blandford as she was known, since she had divorced her husband before he succeeded to the duke-dom, had been forbidden to accept the proposal of a gentleman of lesser degree, who later contracted another ducal alliance. Sensing the similarity of our experiences, we became knit in a close and sympathetic understanding, which caused her to stand by me in any differences that arose.

Added to these royal and family congratulations were cables from political organisations, from county dignitaries, from ten-ants, from employees and from a host of friends, all together bringing me a realisation of the complex and ordered society I was to join. The messages expressed so much deference that they seemed to me ridiculous, for after all we were only two very young people. But in time I learned that snobbishness was an enthroned fetish which spreads its tentacles into every stratum of British national life.

My husband spoke of some two hundred families whose lineage and whose ramifications, whose patronymics and whose titles I should have to learn. Then Blenheim and its tenants, its employees and its household servants would claim my attention. It was only later that I found that my personal reactions towards what to me appeared absurd distinctions must be repressed and that I must not expect even a servant who stood high in the hierarchy to perform a task he considered beneath his dignity. On ringing the bell one day I was answered by the butler, but when I asked him to set a match to an already prepared fire he made me a dignified bow and, leaving the room, observed, "I will send the footman, Your Grace," to which I hastily replied, "Oh, don't trouble, I will do it myself."

Such pomp and ritual were considerations of prime importance in the country that was to be mine. To me, seated beside the man who now ruled my life, absorbed as he was in contemplation of the future at a moment when the present should mean so much, the outlook loomed sombre.

It was a relief to reach the little station of Oakdale, but there was no carriage awaiting us and we found ourselves surrounded by a large crowd. Rather than remain the objects of their curious scrutiny, we sallied forth on foot, accompanied by members of the Press who were overjoyed at the scoop this bit of news would represent in headlines next day: "Duke and Duchess start honeymoon on foot."

It was not long before the carriage found us and the gates of Idlehour closed behind us. Seeing my old home brought a flood of memories of happy days when my father and mother had been united and I had my brothers as companions. How different from the present when alone I faced life with a comparative stranger. The house looked cheerful with its blazing fire in the living-hall, from which wide steps of polished oak led to the landing above. Here my mother's room had been prepared for me and my room next-door for Marlborough. A sudden realisation of my complete innocence assailed me, bringing with it fear. Like a deserted child I longed for my family. The problem created by the marriage of two irreconcilable characters is a psychological one which deserves sympathy as well as understanding. In the hidden reaches where memory probes lie sorrows too deep to fathom.

After the week's seclusion custom has imposed upon reluctant honeymooners, we returned to New York, and spent an evening at the fashionable horse show, where our box was mobbed by crowds which policemen had to move along. It was pleasant to escape from the glare of publicity that was focused upon our every act, and I left the city with few regrets.

Since Blenheim was being renovated we could not go there before March, and since Marlborough, never having travelled, wished to see something of the world before settling down, we embarked for the Mediterranean. Crossing the Atlantic in those days was not the luxurious affair it is now. Ships were much smaller and there were no beautifully decorated suites, no Ritz restaurant, no cinema and no radio. There being no ocean liners to Italy, we travelled on a small cargo boat. The captain's suite, which he had turned over to us, was gloomy and boasted but a minimum of comfort.

As a good sailor, I did not mind the long, extremely rough passage, but I was worried about Marlborough. There was no doctor on board; we were, I think, the only passengers, and the captain's ministrations did not help him. Sea-sickness breeds a horrible pessimism, in which my husband fully indulged, and it took all the optimism I possessed to overcome the depressing gloom of that voyage.

We left the ship at Gibraltar instead of going on to the port in

Italy we had aimed for, since another sea voyage was not considered advisable for him. A visit to Madrid, Seville and Granada was arranged and we then intended to proceed by way of the French Riviera, Rome and Brindisi to our eventual destination, Egypt. Winters in Spain are apt to be cold and bleak. In Madrid icy winds made visits to poorly heated museums unpleasantly chilly. The galleries which contain so many masterpieces—and also so many rows of inferior pictures—were at that time atrociously arranged. My enthusiasm waned and, because I had overgrown my strength, I also felt exhausted.

We spent a pleasant evening with the English Ambassador, Sir Henry Drummond-Wolff, who proved a charming and courteous host. There I met Lord Rosebery, then leader of the Liberal party in the House of Lords. His short Government of little more than a year had fallen in 1895 but had given him time to realise his greatest wish, that of winning the Derby while Prime Minister, which he did in 1894 and again in 1895. An exceedingly brilliant man with a caustic wit, he had, in spite of a bourgeois appearance, an aristocratic arrogance rendered less aggressive by the twinkle of his blue eyes and a kindly humorous smile. Someone told me that his mother, the Duchess of Cleveland, who in England lived at Battle Abbey, always requested her guests to write not only their names but also an appreciation of their stay in her visitors' book; and the following entry by an unappreciative guest: "From *Battle* murder and sudden death good Lord deliver us" was just the sort of sentiment I thought Lord Rosebery himself might have indulged in. Realising that no better pass to the favour of the Dowager Duchess of Marlborough could be found, I deemed myself lucky when he told me that he was sending her a good account of me.

It was less pleasant to envisage a more immediate consequence of our meeting. When Marlborough heard that Lord Rosebery was to be received in audience by the Regent of Spain, Queen Maria Christina, he wished also to be accorded this honour. The stringent etiquette of the Spanish Court intimidated me as much as did the fear of Lord Rosebery's ridicule; nevertheless, when we met at the Palacio Real on the appointed day and were conducted through endless reception rooms, I managed to acquit myself with dignity and, on reaching the royal presence, to drop the three ceremonial curtsies Spanish custom required. The Queen Mother led a cloistered life, and my sympathy went out to the little King, Alfonso XIII, whom we saw in a gloomy palatial distance. No one then could foresee his tragic exile and his death in a foreign land. But for an Epicurean he was a remarkable stoic; later, when I met him in England, he told me that he had always considered death his close companion and that immunity from bombs had been but a lucky chance.

Of my visits to Seville and Granada I remember little. The vastness of the Cathedral of Seville impressed me, but my æsthetic eye was shocked by the statues of the Madonna adorned as if for a carnival, with mantles of velvet and ermine and with garish jewels fashioned as necklaces, bracelets and tiaras. After the Gothic austerity of these sombre churches I came with relief to the Alhambra, whose wide terrace overlooked fertile plains to the rocky heights of the Sierra Nevada. Here evidence of the Moorish love of gardens and of running water, of graceful arches and of slender columns, reminded me of the Taj in India. Had my frame of mind been happier and had our visit occurred during the summer I might have found gaiety in Spanish music and in the fiestas with their colourful crowds; as it was, I have a sombre picture of an austere country whose customs and religion have remained very much as they were in the sixteenth century.

From Spain we went by train to France. It was a complete and startling contrast to arrive at the little principality of Monaco in brilliant sunshine with the blue Mediterranean at our feet. My honeymoon had so far been a serious and depressing introduction to a life I had imagined would at least be gay, but now my spirits rose. They have always depended on blue skies, and I looked forward to pleasant days in cheerful surroundings. We stopped at the fashionable Hôtel de Paris, eating our meals among a lively crowd of beautiful women and elegant men, many of whom were acquaintances of my husband. When I asked him who they all were I was surprised by his evasive answers and still more startled when informed that I must not look at the women whose beauty I admired. It was only after repeated questioning that I learned that these were ladies of easy virtue whose beauty and charm had their price. It became increasingly complicated when I heard that I must not recognise the men who accompanied them, even though some of them had been my suitors a few months before. In those days there were ladies of the *demi-monde* who vied in beauty, in elegance, in wit and charm with the greatest ladies of the Faubourg. These women—perhaps the nearest approach to the Greek hetæræ the Christian world has seen—had beautiful houses where they received the intelligentsia of Paris, smart carriages in which to air their charms, handsome jewels to adorn their persons. At the opera and at the races in their incomparable toilettes they were the cynosure of all eyes. The two outstanding beauties of the *demi-monde* were La Belle Otero, a dark and passionate young woman with a strong blend of Greek and gypsy blood, who was always flamboyantly dressed to set off her magnificent figure; and lovely Liane de Pougy, who looked the *grande dame* she eventually became by her marriage to the Roumanian Prince Ghika.

There was rivalry between them, and they were proud of the precious stones that adorned them as visible signs of the eminence they had reached in their profession. Fortunes were spent and lost for them and bets were exchanged on the relative value of their jewels. It was not surprising therefore that Otero should challenge her rival by appearing at the Casino one night covered from head to foot with priceless jewels. It was a dazzling display, but in seeking to outdo her rival Otero had sacrificed good taste and had lent herself to ridicule. Excited conjectures about Pougy's rejoinder were promptly answered. The next evening, appearing in a simple white gown without a single jewel, she was followed by her maid gorgeously arrayed in jewels that far outshone Otero's.

In such extravagant ways was stressed the immense importance men attached to beauty, and it seemed to me then unfair that *ces dames du demi-monde* should be permitted to enhance their beauty with cosmetics which were forbidden to *la femme du monde*. For the respectable woman, as she was called, had to observe a neutral role; her clothes as well as her "make-up" had to be discreet. To pass unnoticed was the dictum imposed by the good, if hypocritical, society of the day. Any extravagance of fashion was condemned as bad taste, and no well-bred woman could afford to look seductive, at least not in public. Lipstick and powder alone were considered fast, and any further embellishments would immediately have committed one to the world of the *déclassé*, that sad middle state where recognition is withheld both by the upper and the lower worlds. How different was this life from the prim monastic existence my mother had enforced. The goddess Minerva no longer sat enthroned. Beauty rather than wisdom appeared to be everyone's business.

I was further aghast at the importance food had suddenly assumed. "Considering," I was told, "that it is the only pleasure one can count on having three times a day every day of one's life, a well-ordered meal is of prime importance." We seemed to spend hours discussing the merit of a dish or the bouquet of a vintage. The *maître d'hôtel* had become an important person to whom at meals most of my husband's conversation was addressed.

Without a doubt the *demi-monde* was brilliant, seductive and gay, but the *beau monde* glittered no less enticingly. Dandies, roués, spendthrifts and scions of great European families were to be seen recklessly gambling away colossal fortunes. Even the United States of America, that Mrs. Grundy in so profligate a world, had its representative in no less a spectacular figure than the great James Gordon Bennett, millionaire owner of the New York *Herald* and its continental mouthpiece, the Paris *Herald,* he who had sent H. M. Stanley to Central Africa to find Livingstone and had organised a Polar Expedition as well. When I knew him he owned a villa at Beaulieu-sur-Mer and was a great friend of my mother. The trains used to rush through his garden, and Mr. Bennett invariably ran to his windows to watch them pass. I thought it unusual for one who had his yacht, the famous *Lysistrata,* anchored in the quiet bay at his feet to find so much to excite him in passing trains. But James Gordon Bennett was an eccentric and there were curious tales concerning his fancies. Among those he invited to dine on the *Lysistrata* were the American belles Lily, Lady Bagot, and Adele, Countess of Essex, who with another compatriot, the malaprop Mrs. Moore of Paris, had one evening an extraordinary adventure. Suddenly in the midst of dinner Mr. Bennett retired to his cabin and the yacht weighed anchor and moved out to sea. On seeing the coast of France disappear in the distance the guests rushed out to question the captain on so unexpected a departure, clamouring for an immediate return. "I have Mr. Bennett's orders to proceed to Egypt," the captain answered, "and nothing but his word will change that order." But the owner of the luxurious yacht was locked in his cabin, and the guests perforce spent an unpleasant night in various stages of active discomfort, since the sea was rough and they had only their evening clothes.

The next morning fortunately brought the host back to reality and the yacht was ordered to return to Monte Carlo. There the furious and outraged guests were disembarked in broad daylight still wearing their evening dresses. Profuse apologies accompanied by extravagant presents finally restored more friendly relations, but in the future visitors were less easily persuaded to dine on the *Lysistrata*.

In this international world it was perhaps the Russians who were the greatest gamblers, led by the Grand Dukes Alexis and Vladimir. It must have been a family failing, for the Grand Duchess Anastasia was later also to prefer the gaming tables of Monte Carlo to the stern and stuffy atmosphere of her German husband's Court. In the 1920s, when my mother was her neighbour at Eze-sur-Mer, we used to watch the Grand Duchess during our rare visits to the Casino. Invariably she was recklessly throwing her last louis on the table—her semi-Oriental eyes glistening green as she watched them go. When after a particularly disastrous night she was found dead in bed there were ominous rumours of too many sleeping pills. What a typical Russian she looked—lean, dark and sinister, but exquisite in satin and jewels. She wore her black hair tightly coiffed to her narrow head, which she still held proudly, and her lips curled disdainfully. She was completely indifferent to anything but her personal wishes and desires.

From the infrequency with which anyone was presented to me I concluded that my circle would be all too select. It was pleasant, therefore, to meet another young bride. English, blonde and pretty, she was a self-assured young woman with a shrewd appraisal of social standards. Amazed at my unworldliness, she ripped the blinkers from my eyes. In the tarnished mirror of a crude materialism my values appeared absurd and I listened to her vitriolic gossip with mounting concern. Seeing with her eyes those I was to meet, gauging as she meant me to the enmity of certain of my husband's friends, the future loomed complex and difficult. Finally, emphasising the need for fine clothes, for rich jewels and a lavish expenditure, she added, "With our money, our clothes, our jewels we will be the two successes of the coming London season, and all the women will be jealous of us."

Depressed and concerned, I left the sophisticated set we had found in Monte Carlo to proceed to Rome. Settled in the high

c

bare rooms of the hotel for my first Christmas without family and friends, I felt strangely lonely and sad. It was an unfortunate moment to choose to insure my life, but it appeared no time was to be lost. A doctor's certificate was needed to complete the transaction. Medical supervision in the form of check-ups was rare in my youth; a doctor was sent for to cure rather than to prevent. I shall always remember the brutal manner in which the pretentious Roman doctor who came to examine me informed me that I had probably only six months to live. However, a specialist summoned from London assured us that organically I was sound and had but outgrown my strength. He imposed a régime of rest, and in the solitude of those long hours I began to realise what life away from my family in a strange country would mean. At the age of eighteen I was beginning to chafe at the impersonal role I had so far played in my own life—first a pawn in my mother's game and now, as my husband expressed it, "a link in the chain". To one not sufficiently impressed with the importance of ensuring the survival of a particular family, the fact that our happiness as individuals was as nothing in this unbroken chain of succeeding generations was a corroding thought; for although I greatly desired children, I had not reached the stage of total abnegation regarding my personal happiness. Nevertheless, to produce the next link in the chain was, I knew, my most immediate duty and I worried at my ill-health.

My husband spent his time with art dealers, ransacking the antique shops of the city. I was not allowed to accompany him because he claimed that my appearance in furs and furbelows caused prices to rocket. We were lucky in securing a beautiful privately owned Boucher tapestry which a famous English dealer had missed buying by a day. Later it hung in my bedroom at Blenheim until it was sold by my husband to Mr. Edward Tuck; it now hangs in the Petit Palais in the fine collection that he presented to the city of Paris.

From Rome we went to Naples, which I advise honeymooners to omit, since a visit to the buried towns of Pompeii and Herculaneum is bound to awaken discord. I, at least, found it a humiliating experience to be left outside the ruins while my husband went below with a guide to inspect the paintings and statues erected to the worship of Priapus, the god and giver of life.

At Brindisi we boarded a small steamer and after another rough journey reached Alexandria, then proceeded to Cairo and up the Nile. I viewed the *dahabiya* with distrust—it was a sail-boat and depended on a steam launch to haul us up-stream. It was, moreover, small and uncomfortable, and my maid and Marlborough's valet shared my dislike of these cramped quarters. Even the glorious sunsets which redden sands and sky and turn the Nile into a molten stream were less beautiful when seen with a small tug ahead. Progress was incredibly slow. We tied up every night and spent our days in the inevitable excursions by donkey to temples or burial vaults. During my previous trip with my father the donkeys had borne American names; now, however, Yankee Doodle had become John Bull. One night nautch girls were summoned to perform their dances. Not yet hardened to such exhibitions, I retired below and was not altogether sorry to hear that one had fallen into the river, from which she was fished none the worse for her immersion.

We returned finally to Cairo, then at Suez boarded a P. & O. steamer for Marseilles. In Paris we took an apartment in the Hôtel Bristol on the Place Vendôme.

I was happy to be in Paris again and while there completed the purchase of my trousseau. Since I had little experience in shopping, everything having always been bought for me by my mother, Marlborough took it upon himself to display the same hectoring rights she had previously exercised in the selection of my gowns. Unfortunately, his taste appeared to be dictated by a desire for magnificence rather than by any wish to enhance my looks. I remember particularly one evening dress of sea-blue satin with a long train, whose whole length was trimmed with white ostrich feathers. Another creation was a rich pink velvet with sables. Jean Worth himself directed the fittings of these beautiful dresses, which he and my husband considered suitable, but which I would willingly have exchanged for the tulle and organdie that girls of my age were wearing.

My father had generously told me to get whatever I wanted as a gift from him, but I was surprised by the excess of household and personal linens, clothes, furs and hats my husband was ordering. Marlborough's ideas about jewels were equally princely, and since there appeared to be no family heirlooms, jewels became a necessary addition to my trousseau. It was then the fashion to wear dog-collars; mine was of pearls and had nineteen rows, with high diamond clasps which rasped my neck. My mother had given me all the pearls she had received from my father. There were two fine rows which had once belonged to Catherine of Russia and to the Empress Eugénie, and also a *sautoir* which I could clasp round my waist. A diamond tiara capped with pearl-shaped stones was my father's gift to me, and from Marlborough came a diamond belt. They were beautiful indeed, but jewels never gave me pleasure and my heavy tiara invariably produced a violent headache, my dog-collar a chafed neck. Thus bejewelled and bedecked I was deemed worthy to meet English society. With the first days of spring we crossed the Channel.

London looked immense as the train slowly wound through endless dimly-lit suburbs. They seemed drab to me, but the streets were clean and the little houses had gardens. There was a general air of homeliness. In those days there was little dis-content—England was prosperous and only the intelligentsia ventured to discuss socialism. Feeling anxious and diffident at meeting so many strangers—strangers who were to become my family—I gazed anxiously at the station platform where a small group of people were waiting to welcome us. Lady Blandford, my mother-in-law, with her daughters Lilian and Norah, was there; Ivor Guest, the good-looking but supercilious cousin who had come to our wedding; Lady Sarah Wilson, an aunt; Lady Randolph Churchill with her son, young Winston Churchill, yet another cousin; and numerous friends. I felt the scrutiny of many eyes and hoped that my hat was becoming and that my furs were fine enough to win their approval. They all talked at once in soft voices and strange accents which I knew I should have to imitate, and I felt thankful that I had no nasal twang. The sight of these strangers, Marlborough's family, brought the loneliness of my position sharply into focus. I realised that he would from now on be surrounded by friends and distractions that were foreign to me and that the precarious hold I had during our months alone secured in his life and affections might easily become endangered.

The family dinner that night disclosed a feud between the Churchill and the Hamilton clans. Lady Blandford, a Hamilton by birth, was a typical *grande dame* of the late Victorian era—Disraeli had made her the heroine of one of his novels. She had the narrow aristocratic face of the well-bred, a thin slightly arched nose and small blue eyes that were kind and appraising. Her black hair was arranged in a profusion of curls and puffs which took so long to dress that once done they had to last the day. She had the high bust and tightly laced waist that fashion imposed and was proud of her small feet and hands, boasting that no manicurist had ever touched her nails. Her outlook was limited, for she had received an English girl's proverbially poor education, but she possessed shrewd powers of intuition and observation, and that she liked me I immediately realised. Lady Sarah Wilson—a Churchill—was quite different. She told me to call her Sarah since she thought herself too young to be an aunt, and I felt an enmity I could not then account for. She seemed to me as hard as her polished appearance, and her prominent eyes, harsh voice and sarcastic laugh made me shudder. She disliked my mother-in-law, "Bertha", as she called her, and plainly showed that she considered her a fool. To me she was kind in an arrogant manner that made me grit my teeth, for I had no intention of being patronised. I was glad to turn to Winston, a young red-headed boy a few years older than I. He struck me as ardent and vital and seemed to have every intention of getting the most out of life, whether in sport, in love, in adventure or in politics. He was the next heir to the dukedom and I wondered how he and his mother, the American-born Lady Randolph Churchill, would regard me. At any rate, I thought, they will be pleased to notice that there is as yet no sign of an heir. Lady Randolph was a beautiful woman with a vital gaiety that made her the life and soul of any party. She was still, in middle age, the mistress of many hearts, and the Prince of Wales was known to delight in her company. Her grey eyes sparkled with the joy of living, and when, as was often the case, her anecdotes were *risqué* it was in her eyes as well as in her words that one could read the implications. She was an accomplished pianist, an intelligent and well-informed reader and an enthusiastic advocate of any novelty. Her constant friendship and loyalty were to be precious to me in adversity.

During this welcoming dinner the conversation veered to America, and Lady Blandford made a number of startling remarks, revealing that she thought we all lived on plantations with negro slaves and that there were Red Indians ready to scalp us just round the corner. She was greatly aggrieved to think that, having once been in India, she should not have been allowed to visit America, and complained that she had not been able to attend our wedding because her son refused to pay her passage over. Then Sarah tittered and also regretted that she had not been present. "But," she added, "the Press did not spare us one detail," and I felt that the word "vulgar" had been omitted but not its implications.

Ignorance of our history and of our geography appeared to be prevalent. An American cousin who came to spend a week-end at Blenheim told me of her astonishment when her neighbour at dinner, an elderly nobleman, remarked that he had never been able to understand the war between North and South America.

"Considering the distance between you, what could you have fought about?" he asked.

"But we never had a war with South America," she answered, puzzled.

"Oh yes, you did," he said. "It was in 1861."

She had difficulty in making him understand that it was the Southern states of the Union and not South America the North had fought.

The next day, a dull raw morning of early March, was dedicated to family visits. The first of these ordeals was my presentation to the Dowager Duchess of Marlborough, my husband's grandmother, a daughter of the fourth Marquess of Londonderry. She was a formidable old lady of the Queen Anne type. By that I mean that she could be arrogant and familiar in baffling succession, that she had large prominent eyes, an aquiline nose, and a God-and-my-right conception of life. An English duchess to her was the highest position any woman not of royal birth could reach, and like Sarah Jennings, first Duchess of Marlborough, she felt capable of matching her wits against any queen's—though I imagine Queen Victoria would have been less easily gulled than Queen Anne had been by Sarah.

The Duchess was seated in an armchair in the drawing-room of her house at the corner of Grosvenor Square where she had lived since her widowhood. Dressed in mourning with a little lace cap on her head and an ear-trumpet in her hand, she bestowed a welcoming kiss in the manner of a deposed sovereign greeting her successor. After an embarrassing inspection of my person, she informed me that Lord Rosebery had reported favourably on me after our meeting in Madrid. She expressed great interest in our plans and made searching inquiries concerning the manner of life we intended to live, hoping, she said, to see Blenheim restored to its former glories and the prestige of the family upheld. I felt that this little lecture was intended to show me how it behoved me to behave. Then fixing her cold grey eyes upon me she continued, "Your first duty is to have a child and it must be a son, because it would be intolerable to have that little upstart Winston become Duke. Are you in the family way?" Feeling utterly crushed by my negligence in not having insured Winston's eclipse and depressed by the responsibilities she had heaped upon me, I was glad to take my leave. We then went on to Hampden House, the residence of the Duke of Abercorn, who was head of the Hamilton family and my husband's uncle.

This house had all the charm and beauty of Georgian panelling, with spacious rooms that gave on to a little garden enclosed in brick walls. The Duke, a small fragile man, was seated near the fire; he had embroidered slippers on his feet, and a velvet smoking-jacket, for he was convalescing from some minor ailment. When I saw him it struck me that Marlborough was much more like the Hamiltons than the Churchills in appearance, and that he also had their mannerisms. The Duke was restless and fussy, and ran round the room pointing out family portraits by Lawrence, of which there was a lovely collection. He insisted upon removing my coat, which was of green velvet entirely lined with Russian sables.

"What a wonderful coat, what priceless furs!" he exclaimed. "I must send for my sables to compare them."

Whereupon he rang the bell and had his valet bring his coat. To his deep concern, it did not equal mine! There followed a great deal of family tittle-tattle, and finally, as we got up to go, he looked me up and down and, with an amused twinkle in his eyes, said, "I see the future Churchills will be both tall and good-looking."

Both sides of the family were evidently equally concerned with the immediate necessity of an heir to the dukedom, and were infecting me with their anxiety.

Our next visit was to the Marchioness of Lansdowne, an aunt Marlborough greatly preferred to his mother. At that time Lord Lansdowne was Secretary of State for Foreign Affairs in Lord Salisbury's Government. Their London residence was Lans-

downe House in Berkeley Square, whose garden adjoined that of
Devonshire House in Piccadilly. Designed by Robert Adam,
Lansdowne House with high porticoes and classical pillars was a
masterpiece of English eighteenth-century architecture. The
beautiful rooms were filled with Greek and Roman sculpture and
with pictures. Lady Lansdowne was very like my mother-in-law
in appearance except that she was better-looking. They were
both gay and loved to gossip, and giggled at the slightest
provocation. She had not forgotten the pomp and circumstance
that had surrounded her during the years that she had been
Vicereine of India. To Marlborough she showed affection and
the mild flirtatiousness of the Victorian *grande dame*. I sensed
that she was curious to know what lay under the shy and
diffident schoolgirl I still was. For I was different from English
girls and better educated, and she realised that there was
independence of thought in my reactions to her advice.

I gathered from her conversation that an English lady was
hedged round with what seemed to me to be boring restrictions.
It appeared that one should not walk alone in Piccadilly or in
Bond Street, nor sit in Hyde Park unless accompanied; that
one should not be seen in a hansom cab, and that one should
always travel in a reserved compartment; that it was better to
occupy a box than a stall at the theatre, and that to visit a
music-hall was out of the question. One must further be very
careful not to be compromised, and at a ball one should not
dance more than twice with the same man. One must learn to
take one's place in the social hierarchy and if one had the good
fortune to belong to two prominent families one must learn all
their ramifications. One must, in other words, memorise the
Peerage, that book that with the *Almanach de Gotha* in Europe
and the *Social Register* to a lesser degree in America establishes
pedigrees and creates snobs. I found that being a duchess at
nineteen would put me into a much older set and that a measure
of decorum beyond my years would be expected of me. Indeed
my first contact with society in England brought with it a
realisation that it was fundamentally a hierarchical society in
which the differences in rank were outstandingly important.
Society was definitely divided into castes. They were not so
rigid, it is true, as those in the older Hindu civilisation, nor did
they contain untouchables, except those who intentionally
sinned against its standards. Thus a gentleman caught cheating

at cards or a woman publicly branded with adultery were equally ostracised. There were cast-iron laws that governed the conventional code of behaviour, but an aristocratic sensitivity in manners was definitely more important, and it decreed discretion in one's indiscretions. Arrogance was apparent in the relationships between superiors and those of lesser degree and was so firmly inculcated that even servants observed it in their treatment of each other. It is so much a part of English consciousness that a Labour Government has not dared to abolish the House of Lords, nor has it been able to find a better principle on which to establish a second chamber. A title still evokes particular relish and "Your Grace" is at times pronounced with almost reverent unction. I still recall with mirth an occasion when a clergyman before luncheon one day addressed my husband thus: "May I say grace, Your Grace?"

How fortunate that the day we left for Blenheim was cold, since Marlborough had decided that I must wear my sable coat. Blenheim is only sixty-five miles from London and can be easily reached by car in less than two hours; but in those days there were no automobiles and we went by train to Oxford, where a special engine took us the seven short miles to Woodstock. The little station was festive and beflagged; a red carpet had been laid on the platform and the Mayor in his scarlet robes, accompanied by members of the Corporation, greeted us in a welcoming speech. Turning to me he said, "Your Grace will no doubt be interested to know that Woodstock had a Mayor and Corporation before America was discovered."

Feeling properly put in my place, I managed to give the awed smile I felt was expected, although a riposte was seething on the tip of my tongue. A carriage from which the horses had been unhitched was awaiting us and our employees proceeded to drag us up to the house. Somewhat discomfited by this means of progress, at which my democratic principles rebelled, I nevertheless managed to play the role in fitting manner, bowing and smiling in response to the plaudits of the assembled crowds. Triumphal arches had been erected, schoolchildren were waving flags, the whole countryside had turned out to greet us, and I felt deeply touched by the warmth of their welcome. We stopped at the Town Hall, where addresses on parchment written in a lovely illuminated script were given to us, and flowers were brought to me by the children. At last we reached the house,

C*

but here again ceremonies awaited us. Tenant farmers, employees and household servants were ranged in groups, and each had prepared a welcoming speech and a bouquet which had to be presented in the customary manner and fittingly responded to.

As I stood on the steps listening to the various speeches, I realised that my life would be very strenuous if I was to live up to all that was expected of me. My arms were full of bouquets, the fur coat felt heavier and heavier, the big hat was being blown about by the winds, and I suddenly felt distraught, with a wild desire to be alone. My maid was waiting for me, a tea gown of satin and lace laid out, a hot bath ready, and I dressed for the ritual of dinner such as Marlborough, the chef and the butler had decreed it to be.

How I learned to dread and hate these dinners, how ominous and wearisome they loomed at the end of a long day. They were served with all the accustomed ceremony, but once a course had been passed the servants retired to the hall; the door was closed and only a ring of the bell placed before Marlborough summoned them. He had a way of piling food on his plate; the next move was to push the plate away, together with knives, forks, spoons and glasses—all this in considered gestures which took a long time; then he backed his chair away from the table, crossed one leg over the other and endlessly twirled the ring on his little finger. While accomplishing these gestures he was absorbed in thought and quite oblivious of any reactions I might have. After a quarter of an hour he would suddenly return to earth, or perhaps I should say to food, and begin to eat very slowly, usually complaining that the food was cold! And how could it be otherwise? As a rule neither of us spoke a word. I took to knitting in desperation and the butler read detective stories in the hall.

My first duty concerned my household. Taking them in domestic status, first came the butler, or house steward. He was addressed as Mr. So-and-So by the other servants, and his chief concern was to keep everyone, including himself, in his place. His rule in the men's department was absolute—only the two electricians, who at that time were treated with the respect due to men of science, were his equals. The groom of the chambers ranked next. One of his duties was to keep the numerous writing tables supplied with paper, pens and ink, an expensive item, as I was to find when we had guests who preferred to use our writing-paper rather than their own. They must often have departed with reams, for I remember receiving a letter headed Blenheim Palace from a guest who had long left us. He had evidently forgotten to whom he was writing.

Marlborough's valet shared the prestige that tails and striped trousers conferred. Such a costume was considered necessary to uphold the standard of elegance of the steward's room, where the valets and maids had their meals, strictly seated according to the rank given their masters upstairs. I remember Jacques Balsan on one of his visits to us telling me that he had to lend his valet a discarded dinner-jacket to wear, since his blue serge had been looked down upon by the other valets present. The Marchioness of Bath in her little book entitled *Before the Sunset Fades* describes the etiquette of life below stairs at Longleat:

> A strange ritual took place over the midday meal in the servants' hall. The under servants first trooped in and remained standing at their places until the upper servants had filed in in order of domestic status. After the first course the upper servants left in the following manner: When the joint, carved by the house steward, had been eaten and second helpings offered, it was ceremoniously removed by the steward's room footman, who carried it out with great pomp, followed by the upper servants, who then retired to the steward's room for the remainder of their meal; while the housemaids and sewing-maids scurried off with platefuls of pudding to eat in their own sitting-rooms. This seems to have been the recognised custom of most large houses at that time.

The procession of head servants leaving the Hall arm-in-arm is amusingly illustrated by Cecil Beaton. But in my day there was no such ritual at Blenheim, and the upper servants remained entrenched in their own dining-room, to which such newcomers as chauffeurs were refused admittance and sent packing to the servants' hall. Next in the servants' hierarchy came the under butler and three or four footmen. There were also humble individuals who were known by the strange name of odd men— not, I was to observe, because of any personal oddity, but rather because they were expected to carry out the butler's wishes however strange they might be. They were kept busy carrying coal to the fifty or more grates; they also washed the windows, which they boasted they cleaned only once a year, since it took them twelve months to go the round!

On the distaff side, the housekeeper ruled. I felt sorry for her, for she had only six housemaids, which was an inadequate staff to keep so colossal a house in order. The difficulty was further accentuated by Marlborough's fastidiousness. I shall not easily forget the day when our worthy and competent housekeeper came to me in a state of flurry and indignation.

"His Grace," she said, pulling herself erect and speaking slowly and distinctly, "has accused one of my housemaids of stealing."

"Oh come, Mrs. R.," I said, "surely you have misunderstood him."

"Not at all," she said. "His Grace says that on the table in the second window of the Green Drawing Room a small china box is missing—in fact he says it has been missing for several days and that I have not even noticed that it is no longer there."

The housemaid supposedly responsible was sent for and, crying, she said she wished to leave as she had never before been accused of stealing. When at last I managed to soothe them both I went to see Marlborough, who laughingly informed me that he had himself hidden the box to see if they would notice that it was no longer there.

The housemaids lived in the Housemaids' Heights up in a tower where there was no running water, but since housemaids had so lived for nearly two centuries I was not allowed to improve their lot. There were, further, five laundresses, and a still-room maid who cooked the breakfasts and the cakes and scones for our teas. The still-room looking on to the Italian garden and the china-room, which with its enchanting walls festooned with lovely china, were two of my favourite resorts.

A French chef presided over a staff of four. Frequent rows between him and the housekeeper ensued over the intricacies of breakfast trays, since meat dishes were provided by the kitchen, and the kitchen and still-room were separated by yards and yards of damp, unheated passages so that the food was often cold.

Later, when there was a nursery, a fourth estate came into being. This was ruled over by the head nurse. She was perhaps the most typical example of snobbishness, and when my second son was born she refused to hand over the 'Marquess' to the second nurse, as by rights she should have done, claiming that

he was still a baby. It was to her humiliating to push the peram-
bulator which contained the younger son, in spite of the fact
that Ivor, who was a lovely child, was frequently held up by
admiring ladies. Nanny was an autocrat, with the strange
hostility to any youthful pleasures that is sometimes caused by
the lack of personal happiness. She had, as an Englishwoman,
the traditional dislike of the French nursery-maid, who, she complained to me, refused to take a bath; but when I taxed the girl
I found it was only Nanny's personal supervision she objected
to. The dourness Nanny showed to her wards was fortunately
not extended to my sons or to me. On my frequent visits to the
nursery she greeted me with a pleasant smile, and I felt
welcomed to those lovely hours I spent romping with my babies.

Still another important person in the household was my maid.
She was with me twenty years and died in my service. My
mother-in-law had chosen her for me. Jeanne, the French maid
who had accompanied me on my honeymoon, was not considered suitable by my husband, who wrote to his mother to
have one already used to English ways awaiting me. Mindful
of my youth, Lady Blandford selected a staid and elderly person
completely devoid of joy. She was the old maid personified and,
disliking men in general and my husband in particular, she
made me the object of a loyal but somewhat hectoring devotion.
A Swiss with the sterling qualities of her race, she had a strong
sense of duty and an equally acute dislike for the full, eager life
of youth. Her one wish was to remain quietly at home. She
hated the week-end parties which, as time went by and I lived
alone, were the relaxation I most enjoyed after a busy week. It
was with fear and trembling that I would announce that we were
spending Sunday at Esher or Taplow or Hackwood. She hated
them all, for she knew that she would share a room with other
maids. At times I would argue with her and say, "You have
five quiet days in the week; don't grudge me my two gay ones."
With an unanswerable logic she would answer, "You always
have your room to yourself!"

These visits had for her other drawbacks, and the fight for
the bathroom became a painful subject which, though recurrent,
was best ignored. English country houses contained few bathrooms and they were usually installed in some inconvenient
place at the end of a passage. It therefore became a strategic war
of movement among the various maids to secure the bathroom

for their ladies. Sometimes, coming up to dress for dinner, I would see a queue of them standing with sponges, towels and underwear, waiting in sulky enmity for possession of the bathroom. There was one distressing evening when, coming up late after a game of bridge, I was greeted angrily by my maid with, "Twice have I prepared your bath tonight and twice has it been stolen from me." "Never mind," I answered contritely, "I'll do without one," but she refused to be mollified. Poor Rosalie, she died of a dread disease and left what for her was a large sum of money. A year later a letter from her Swiss relatives informed me that she had so tied up her legacies that there would be very little left for them to inherit. Her lawyer told me that, inspired by the will of a millionaire she had seen published in the news, she had insisted upon imposing the same safeguards and restrictions on her pounds, shillings and pence that he had on his millions. Such, alas, can be the unfortunate result of a good example!

Between the various departmental heads there were frequent difficulties which it became my business to adjust. I sometimes wished at first that my nineteen years had provided me with a greater experience.

Our own rooms, which faced east, were being redecorated, so we spent the first three months in a cold and cheerless apartment looking north. They were ugly, depressing rooms, devoid of the beauty and comforts my own home had provided. Just across the hall overlooking a small inner court were rooms known as Dean Jones's—where, incidentally, Winston Churchill was born. The Dean had been private chaplain to the first Duke and his portrait can be seen in the murals painted by Laguerre. He had a stout form and a florid countenance and looked as if he must have enjoyed the good things of life unchecked by his spiritual vocation. It seemed strange to me that he should haunt the ugly apartment that had been his, but there was no doubt that various people who slept there were terrified by his appearance. A young woman, a miniature painter who was doing my portrait, begged me to change her room, hysterically declaring that she had been awakened in the night by a blaze of light and had seen the Dean bending over her. A male guest had had a similar experience, and impressed me by his evident terror. So the rooms remained empty during my reign. They have now become famous as Winston Churchill's birthplace, and to his other achievements may be added the fact that it seems he has exorcised a ghost, since no one now mentions having seen Dean Jones; no doubt disgruntled by his eclipse he no longer haunts the scene. When eventually we moved into the apartment usually occupied by the Duke and Duchess I found it equally uncongenial. It is strange that in so great a house there should not be one really livable room. Planned to impress rather than to please, Blenheim gave rise to Abel Evans's famous epitaph for Vanbrugh:

> Under this stone, reader, survey
> Dear Sir John Vanbrugh's house of clay.
> Lie heavy on him earth, for he
> Laid many a heavy load on thee.

Blenheim was perhaps not designed as a home; its creators may have preferred the characteristics one of Vanbrugh's enemies described in his lines upon the Duke of Marlborough's House at Woodstock:

> See, Sir, see here's the grand Approach,
> This Way is for his Grace's Coach;
> There lies the Bridge, and here's the clock,
> Observe the Lyon and the Cock,
> The spacious Court, the Colonade,
> And mark how wide the Hall is made!
> The Chimneys are so well design'd,
> They never smoke in any Wind.
> This Gallery's contriv'd for walking,
> The Windows to retire and talk in;
> The Council-Chamber for Debate,
> And all the rest are Rooms of State.
>
> Thanks, Sir, cry'd I, 'tis very fine.
> But where d'ye sleep, or where d'ye dine?

We slept in small rooms with high ceilings; we dined in dark rooms with high ceilings; we dressed in closets without ventilation; we sat in long galleries or painted saloons. Had they been finely proportioned or beautifully decorated I would not so greatly have minded sacrificing comfort to elegance. But alas,

Vanbrugh appears to have subscribed more readily to the canons of dramatic art than to those of architecture, for he had been a playwright before becoming an architect. Alexander Pope's criticism of Blenheim: "I never saw so great a thing with so much littleness in it," and again: "In a word the whole is a most expensive absurdity and the Duke of Shrewsbury gave a true character of it when he said it was a great quarry of stones above ground," may have been inspired by the scorn a writer feels for one who transfers his affections to another Muse.

My bedroom had a very high ceiling and a deep frieze on which golden cupids held flowered garlands. The room was comparatively small and just at the foot of my bed on the opposite wall there was a marble mantelpiece that looked to me like a tomb. On its flat surface I read the words: "Dust Ashes Nothing". This bleak inscription in large black letters greeted my waking, and I wondered why Marlborough when re-decorating the rooms should have left this morbid sentiment, a survival of his father's philosophy, in so prominent a place. I began to be intrigued by a personality that could have chosen such a motto with which to face two brides, for, of course, I had not known the preceding Duke. He evidently enjoyed proclaiming his mordant views, for on another mantelpiece he had had printed: "They say. What say they? Let them say", which I gathered he lived up to. In spite of the depressing reflections caused by these rather sinister admonitions, a sense of humour and the companionship of my sisters-in-law helped me to forget them.

My happiest times were daily rides with our estate agent, an accomplished horseman. We used to gallop across country to our outlying farms, where I met Marlborough's tenants. They were fine men, good farmers, and loyal friends, and some had lived on the estate for over fifty years. Their sons enlisted in the County Yeomanry, in which Marlborough was an officer. The Oxfordshire Yeomanry, as this Volunteer Regiment was called, used to train in our High Park and the three weeks they spent there under canvas were a gay time, with dinners and dances and sports. I remember an exciting paper-chase which I won on a bay mare, thundering over the stone bridge up to the house in a dead heat with the adjutant.

Visits to county neighbours were less pleasant than those I

paid to tenant farmers. The informality of horseback was not to be thought of. Instead I had to drive in an old landau—sometimes accompanied by my sisters-in-law, more often alone—the long miles that separated the various estates. Etiquette dictated a visit of at least twenty minutes. This was usually prolonged to an hour or more, as our neighbours invariably wished to show me their houses and give me tea; besides, the coachman had told me that the horses required a rest before the eight miles home and I realised that he wanted to gossip about me as well. There is always a certain jealousy of what is considered the most important family or the finest estate in a county. It was apparent that the older families whose roots were embedded in Oxfordshire regarded the Churchills, who moved there in the eighteenth century, rather as the Pilgrim Fathers looked upon later arrivals in America. Perhaps also to impress me, they stressed their ancient lineage, seeming to imply that lives lived in a long-ago past conferred a greater dignity on those lived in the present.

One of our most charming neighbours was Lady Jersey. She was a witty and cultured lady and a fine public speaker. The Earl of Jersey had been Governor-General of Australia, and on one occasion when addressing a large audience was greatly put out by a rude heckler who shouted, "We have had enough of you, bring out the old girl!"

There was one family in particular which for no other reason than the extraordinary appearance of its members excited our merriment. Had they appeared on any vaudeville stage as they did on their visits to Blenheim I am sure they would have been greeted with hilarious applause. No sooner would the butler announce their visit than my sisters-in-law and I felt a nervous desire to giggle; we had to bite our lips and avoid looking at each other to prevent the roar of laughter invariably provoked by these two old maids of fifty years and more. They were enormously fat and dressed in black bombazine which accentuated the generous curves of their anatomy. On their colossal chests were to be seen a variety of spots and crumbs, vestiges of their last meal. Their feather boas hung straight instead of curled. They had masses of coarse grey hair on which they perched at saucy angles picture hats trimmed with lilacs and roses, which were held to their heads by black dotted veils that exhaled a musty odour. Their large red hands were half hidden in black cotton mittens and they firmly grasped parasols. On their feet were high black shoes with elastic sides. They used to burst in on us bubbling over with jocular good fellow-ship, pressing us to their bosoms with the utmost goodwill. It was hard to escape the kiss that their black moustaches rendered almost painful, but they were so full of gaiety in spite of their drab lives that we were soon all physically exhausted by the merriment they created.

My duties also consisted in visits to the poor, whose courtesy I found congenial. In almshouses founded and endowed by Caroline, Duchess of Marlborough, there were old ladies whose complaints had to be heard and whose infirmities had to be cared for, and there were the blind to be read to. There was one gentle, patient old lady whom I loved. She used to look forward to my visits because she could understand every word I read to her while sometimes with others she could neither hear nor follow and was too polite to tell them so. I grew to know the Gospel of St. John by heart because it was her favourite. Dear Mrs. Prattley—when I looked at her lovely peaceful face, the thin hands folded in her lap, the black shawl crossed neatly on her chest, the bowed head, the closed sightless eyes, the lips repeating the words of St. John after me, I felt the peace of God descending into that humble home and I was happy to go there for the strength it gave me.

It was the custom at Blenheim to place a basket of tins on the side table in the dining-room and here the butler left the remains of our luncheon. It was my duty to cram this food into the tins, which we then carried down to the poorest in the various villages where Marlborough owned property. With a complete lack of fastidiousness, it had been the habit to mix meat and vegetables and sweets in horrible jumble in the same tin. In spite of being considered impertinent for not conforming to precedent, I sorted the various viands into different tins, to the surprise and delight of the recipients.

Our days during those first months were busy but uneventful. Marlborough spent a good deal of time away in London and I was left with his two unmarried sisters to keep me company. The mornings began with prayers in the chapel at nine-thirty, after which breakfast was served. If one overslept, it was a great scramble to be ready, and I often had to run across the house to the chapel fastening the last hook or button, and ramming on a hat. At the toll of the bell housemaids would drop their dusters, footmen their trays, house-men their pails, carpenters their ladders, electricians their tools, kitchenmaids their pans, laundrymaids their linen, and all rush to reach the chapel in time. Heads of departments had already taken their seats in the pews allotted them. The curate in his surplice read the prayers and a lesson, and after the short service, when I accompanied him to the door, he told me of any sick or poor who needed my personal attention. On Sunday afternoons we had evensong and hymns, which I chose, and the school-children came up to sing. On Sunday mornings we attended service at Woodstock. Indeed, I had ample proof of the Sunday feeling which D. H. Lawrence found so blighting in England.

The Palace chapel was small but high and Rysbrack's ambitious monument to John Duke took up a whole wall. Our pews faced this monument with the altar on our left. I often wondered whether the architect had wished to suggest that allegiance to John Duke came before allegiance to the Almighty. Having been confronted with Marlborough's victories in the tapestries that adorned the walls, having viewed his household in the murals painted by Laguerre, his effigy in silver on our dinner-table, his bust in marble in the library, his portrait over mantels, his ascent to celestial spheres on the ceilings, my feelings as I faced the funeral monument were akin to those of the Bishop of Rochester who says in a letter to Alexander Pope, speaking of the first Duke's funeral, at which he was to officiate: "I go tomorrow to the Deanery (of Westminster) and I believe I shall stay there till I have said Dust to Dust and shut up that last scene of pompous vanity."

The first Duke and his Duchess were buried under this chapel. Some years after my arrival we were dismayed by a smell of putrefaction. On investigation it was found that some of the coffins were such light shells that they had burst open. It was fortunate that there was room only for the Dukes and their consorts in the chapel. Smaller fry were buried in the little churchyard of Bladon across the park from the house.

These few months of my first English spring spent quietly at Blenheim proved an introduction to the serious side of life in England. It was then that I sampled the fine tradition of public service which English men and women have willingly subscribed to, a tradition to which they owe their greatness. I came to realise that when Marlborough spoke of a link in the chain he meant that there were certain standards that must be maintained, whatever the cost, for what was a generation but such a link?—and to him it was inconceivable that he, given the greatness of his position, should fail to uphold the tradition of his class. The English countryside was still rural, the farmers and labourers loyal to their landlord, the standard of living possible for those whose needs were elementary. It was not for me, with my more democratic ideals, to upset the precarious balance. I should have to adopt the role expected of me by my marriage and fulfil its obligations as conscientiously as possible. It was with these good resolutions that I left Blenheim early in May to go to London for my first season. I might almost say for my coming out, for there had been little gaiety in my previous life, and that sporadic, without sequence and without results—a few balls in Paris, London and New York, with no time for friendships or even understanding.

CHAPTER FOUR

Mistress of Blenheim Palace

THE MARLBOROUGH family had no London residence, since Marlborough House had reverted to the Crown and was occupied by the Prince and Princess of Wales. We took a tiny house in South Audley Street for the months of May, June and July. Those who knew the London of 1896 and 1897 will recall with something of a heartache the brilliant succession of festivities that marked the season. There were seasons in European capitals —the Paris season, the Vienna season, the St. Petersburg season—but nowhere was there anything to equal the sustained brilliance of the London season. To me it appeared as a pageant in which beautiful women and distinguished men performed a stately ritual. One year I even witnessed a tilting tourney in which Marlborough, encased in medieval armour, charged his horse full tilt against an opposing knight. There was a tremendous impact as their lances crashed, and my husband was declared the victor. It was, I believe, at a performance organised by Lady Randolph Churchill for the benefit of some charity that this romantic episode was staged. It is recorded among the spectacular celebrations of those early years.

I was impressed by the splendour of the receptions I attended. The stately houses in which they were given had a lordly air, though they could not, I thought, compare with the lovely homes the French aristocracy had built *entre cour et jardin* in Paris. Nevertheless, they were ideal for entertaining and in their galleries and drawing-rooms one could admire treasures from Italy and France often acquired on the European tours young noblemen of the eighteenth century considered the fitting climax to their education.

In Devonshire House, which no longer stands behind its gates in Piccadilly, the Duke and Duchess had always ruled the more liberal circles of society, but in my day the Duke's party was

Liberal Unionist and his Duchess was no longer a passionate
Whig—nor would her kiss have won an election, as did
Georgiana Duchess's in the Westminster Election of 1784, when

> Arrayed in matchless beauty Devon's fair
> In Fox's favour takes a zealous part;
> But oh! where'er the pilferer comes, beware!
> She supplicates a vote, but steals a heart.

Just behind stood Lansdowne House. Alas, that so perfect an
example of an Adam house should have been demolished! In
its fine rooms the Marquess of Lansdowne, Queen Victoria's
Secretary of State for Foreign Affairs, entertained everyone of
importance. Montagu House in Whitehall, which in Stuart days
stretched its gardens to the River Thames, still stands, but in
shrunken grounds. At a ball given there by the Duchess of
Buccleuch, the Queen's Mistress of the Robes, a typical
Victorian scandal occurred. An Indian shawl presented to her
by the Queen, which the Duchess had, with several others,
kindly provided for any guests who wished to sit in the garden,
was not returned by its wearer. The affair became, as it were, a
symptom of the downward glide of modes and manners and
shocked great ladies into startled disapproval.

At Apsley House, which overlooks Hyde Park and Rotten
Row, I recall a ball given some years later by the Duke and
Duchess of Wellington at which King Edward VII, Queen
Alexandra, the Duke and Duchess of Sparta and a vast number
of Royalties were present. The Waterloo Gallery, in which it was
held, was hung with red damask and with the pictures belonging
to the Royal Spanish Collections captured from Joseph Bona-
parte at the Battle of Vittoria and subsequently presented to the
Duke by the King of Spain. As always in those days, there was a
royal quadrille in which only those invited took part. A
colourful figure at the ball was the Austrian Monsignor Vay de
Vaya, Apostolic Protonotary. I knew him well, for he often
came to Blenheim, where, in his violet cassock—made, it was
rumoured, by a celebrated Paris *couturier*—his jewelled chain
and pectoral cross, he gave just the right note of eighteenth-
century ecclesiastical elegance. There were also present two
great foreign ladies of considerable beauty—the Princess di
Teano, later the Duchess of Sermoneta, who in her *Memoirs*

describes this evening, and Princess Henry of Pless—the golden-haired Daisy Cornwallis-West. I thought the women had never looked lovelier—perhaps because the rooms were lit by candles. The Duke had prepared a bridge room for the King's use, with cards of the kind he was supposed to prefer brought specially from Vienna. The procession into supper—strictly in order of precedence—consisted of the seventy or eighty most important people at the ball. It was arranged at five tables in the dining-room where dinner had previously been served to seventy-two guests. As was customary then, the dinner had an endless number of courses, which were served on silver platters and plates presented to the first Duke of Wellington. The family owned a series of such services; one presented to the Duke by the Portuguese Government after the Indian campaigns, the service he used when Ambassador in Paris, and still others given to him by foreign sovereigns.

The foreign Embassies were houses of importance. The Ambassadors then were aristocrats and diplomats of the old school. They belonged to a world which was European and aloof. One met them at Marlborough House rather than at Buckingham Palace, for the Queen lived at Windsor in the seclusion of her widowhood and Marlborough House had become the real seat of the Court.

At Marlborough House one saw not only ambassadors and statesmen but the gay social set which the Prince and Princess of Wales delighted to entertain. It was a cosmopolitan circle, in which Count Albert Mensdorff, the popular Austro-Hungarian attaché, and the Marquis de Soveral, Portugal's Minister to the Court of St. James's, were invariably seen. They were both agreeable, amusing and gay, both bachelors and both courtiers, and both had a fund of good stories and an inexhaustible store of gossip which they imparted with the necessary spice a mischievous delight in certain peccadilloes gives. Count Mensdorff was proud of his Coburg blood and claimed a distant relationship to the royal family. Gifted and discreet, Monsieur de Soveral, who was dubbed the Blue Monkey by those who envied his success, knew more about the affairs of the great than any Father Confessor. He made a point of always addressing the Princess of Wales in the third person, as is customary in France, with whose exiled royal family he was on friendly terms.

In those days fashionable society was to be seen in Hyde Park, where in the mornings we rode thoroughbred hacks and looked our best in classic riding-habits, and where again in the evening, elaborately bedecked in ruffles and lace, we drove slowly back and forth in stately barouches. At a given hour we lined up near Grosvenor Gate to see the Princess of Wales pass, lovely and gracious as she bowed to right and left. Few people had barouches, however, for it was difficult to find a fine pair of seventeen-hand horses, and I regretted the day Marlborough decided we must have one. The *calèche* sprung on C-springs had a swinging motion; the coachman perched high in front obstructed one's view and when one wished to alight one had to wait for the footman to open the door and let down the steps. Circulation in the London streets was rendered dangerous, for the horses with true patrician pride objected to anything as plebeian as an omnibus. Whenever possible I surreptitiously took a hansom and went shopping.

Marlborough, who liked doing things in the grand manner, had ordered himself a cab and, when going for a drive in this beautiful little mail-phaeton, sometimes invited me to accompany him. There was a hood over the seat and behind it a platform on which stood a diminutive groom, or tiger as he was called. To drive in such elegance one naturally wore one's best clothes, and Marlborough had a grey swallow-tailed jacket and a high grey hat. A white gardenia in his buttonhole gave the finishing touch.

A crimson state coach had also been ordered. This was a resplendent affair, with the coachman in a beautiful livery of crimson cloth with silver braid on which were stamped the double-headed eagles of the Holy Roman Empire, of which Marlborough was a Prince. The coachman wore a white wig under his hat and had white plush knee-breeches and silk stockings and a fine red coat with capes. On the platform behind the coach stood two powdered footmen similarly attired. One evening on our way to dinner one of them ignominiously fell off. Knocks behind us called our attention to the fact that something had gone wrong, and when the coach drew up the remaining footman got down to explain that the other had lost his balance at a sudden turn. Fortunately the delinquent arrived at a run, none the worse for the mishap, which, although it annoyed my husband, was to me but a cause for amusement.

In this magnificent equipage I went with my mother-in-law to Buckingham Palace, where I was to be presented at an after-noon function known as a Drawing Room. The Prince and Princess of Wales stood deputy for Queen Victoria, who had withdrawn from such mundane and tedious duties. The Princess of Wales—Queen Alexandra as she soon became—was, as everyone knows, a beautiful woman. Like the Empress Eugénie she had sloping shoulders, and her breasts and arms seemed specially fashioned for a fabulous display of glittering jewels. When she entered the ballroom at Buckingham Palace, her hand lightly resting on her husband's, she always seemed to me the personification of grace and dignity. I can still feel the little thrill of excitement the roll of the drums and the National Anthem gave me as the royal procession entered the ballroom. The great Officers of State were then the Earl of Lathom, the Lord Chamberlain, and the Earl of Pembroke, the Lord Steward. They were both over six feet in height and, being exceptionally handsome men, in their Court uniform looked magnificent as with their staves of office held before them they walked in backwards, facing the King and Queen, I did not realise until told by Lord Pembroke how difficult it is to keep a straight line when walking backwards and to execute a turn in unison without ever looking to right or to left. I could never take my eyes from the lovely Queen as she approached the daïs and bowed proudly and yet with such grace first to the *Corps Diplomatique* on the left, then to the peeresses on the right, of the Throne, and finally to the assembled company. She was most often dressed in white with the blue ribbon of the Garter. On her head glittered a tiara; pearls and diamonds cascaded from neck to waist. The lovely oval of her face, accentuated by a built-up coiffure, the faint smile, the little arrogant nose were so perfect one could not have dreamed of a fairer Queen.

For my presentation, my wedding dress had been cut low and with the court train looked bridal and festive. Around my waist was the diamond belt my husband had given me and on my head a diamond tiara; there were also pearls in profusion. Later I received the following lines signed 'The Patriot' which appeared in an American paper. I include them in deference to their sentiment.

Our Consuelo Outshines the Court

Our fair young duchess far outshone
  The royal dames about her.
In grace and diamonds all her own
  Our Consuelo far outshone
The greatest there, in regal tone—
  How can we do without her?
Three cheers for her who quite outshone
  The royal dames about her.

When my train was taken from my arm and spread I realised the ordeal had begun. In front of me, through the door, I saw a long row of royal personages to whom I should have to curtsy. Sensing that there was a natural curiosity concerning the début of the American bride, I was anxious to acquit myself with dignity since it was no easy task to perform so many curtsies gracefully. I was glad, therefore, when Lady Blandford assured me that I had carried it off in the manner born, adding, "I must tell you that no one would take you for an American."

Always susceptible to criticism of my compatriots, I said rather hastily, "I suppose you mean that as a compliment, Lady Blandford, but what would you think if I said you were not at all like an Englishwoman?"

"Oh, that is quite different," she answered airily.

"Different to you, but not to me," I countered, laughingly; but my mother-in-law then realised that there were certain reflections concerning Americans I would not tolerate.

When we came out of the Palace the band of the Household Cavalry in their beautiful gold uniforms was playing, and as we swung down the Mall in our stately coach with the friendly crowds cheering and waving I felt the little glow of pleasure Cinderella must have experienced when her pumpkin changed into a coach.

That first London season was a hectic time. We dined out nearly every night and there were always parties, often several, in the evening. Indeed, one had to exercise discretion in one's acceptances in order to survive the three months' season which ended with the ball at Holland House, the Earl of Ilchester's house in Kensington. It had been the home of Charles James Fox, and the old brick house with its fine library and panelled rooms had remained much as he had left it. That ball was always an event to look forward to, for there was a huge and lovely garden where couples could roam at will. Whether it was the moonlight, or the end of the season and the dispersal of London society for the summer, no one knew; but it is certain that many marriages were settled at the Holland House balls, and the dimly-lit gardens were more popular than the ball-room.

A ball at Grosvenor House stands out partly because it was there that I first saw Gainsborough's lovely 'Blue Boy', which is now in the Huntington Collection in California, and partly because of a curious incident which only royal prerogative could excuse. Interrupting a dance, an equerry suddenly approached and brought me to the old Duke of Brunswick, the father of the man who later married the German Emperor's daughter. He was blind and asked me if I would object to his running his fingers over my face, since only so could he know what I looked like. It was an embarrassing procedure, but I felt too sorry for him to refuse.

In those days we danced quadrilles, with an occasional polka and the intoxicating Strauss and Waldteufel waltzes played by Viennese orchestras. We took a frantic amount of exercise whirling around until too giddy to continue, for reversing, for some unknown reason, was tabooed in royal circles.

A London ballroom was a sight worth seeing, with the lovely women the British aristocracy has always bred. Lady Helen Vincent, later Lady D'Abernon, was generally considered the most beautiful. Her skin was transparently white and she used make-up to enhance her ethereal appearance. Hers was not a classical beauty. It was the haughty carriage of her tall figure, the poise of her proud head, the arrogance of her up-tilted nose, the blue haze of her eyes, that made her the acknowledged queen. Lady Westmorland, whose sisters Lady Warwick and the Duchess of Sutherland were also considered beauties, had perhaps the most perfect face. I can see her now in a Greek peplum impersonating Hebe at a Devonshire House fancy dress ball. The grey feathers of a stuffed but life-like eagle perched on her shoulder set off the glorious sheen of her red-gold hair. It would be tedious and invidious to enumerate them all, but there was a galaxy of lovely women whose beauty was enhanced by a patrician distinction.

The opera season at Covent Garden owed its success to Lady de Grey and to Mr. Harry Higgins. Lady de Grey, who later became the Marchioness of Ripon, was a tall, remarkably handsome woman and, like her brother Lord Pembroke, had a regal bearing. When she entered a room her presence at once made itself felt not only because of her astonishing beauty, which was haughty and aristocratic, but also because of some strange attraction in her curious eyes and eager lips. She had a bohemian circle of friends in which the de Reszke brothers and Nellie Melba were often seen, and she dominated the frivolous set as Lady Londonderry dominated the political. Her little informal dinners were invariably gay and amusing. She was one of the favourites of the Princess of Wales, who loved practical jokes and so delighted in an informal atmosphere that her hostesses were sometimes put to it to supply just the right touch in the way of amusement. I recall one of Lady de Grey's dinners at which we were all startled by a frightful clatter of broken china. I was amazed to see the Princess in fits of laughter while Lord de Grey, our host, remained unmoved. It appeared that at a previous dinner a footman had dropped a tray of Lord de Grey's valuable china, producing the amusement that the misfortunes of others usually create; since then the incident had been repeated, with the china specially bought for making a noise.

So great was Lady de Grey's social prestige that she inspired an unmusical but snobbish public to attend the opera, a task in which she was assisted by Mr. Harry Higgins. He was a popular member of society, and was married to the former Mrs. James Breese, an American widow whom as a child I used to watch playing croquet with my mother. Thanks to him and to Lady de Grey we had Wagner cycles conducted by Hans Richter; Verdi, Gounod and Meyerbeer operas; *Carmen* with Calvé; and contemporary works by Massenet and Puccini.

The famous Gaiety Theatre patronised by the young bloods had no need of a social Egeria. Mr. George Edwardes had an infallible flair for a potential theatrical star; to him we owed George Grossmith, jun., Edna May in *The Belle of New York*, Gertie Millar, who later became Countess of Dudley, and Joe Coyne, with whom Lily Elsie shared the honours of *The Merry Widow*. The Empire Theatre, which also belonged to Mr. Edwardes, had such outstanding performances that it became the first music-hall to be attended by royalty and the

Prince and Princess of Wales's presence effectually counteracted Lady Lansdowne's admonition against music-halls. Then there was His Majesty's Theatre, with Sir Herbert and Lady Tree in the plays of Pinero, Stephen Phillips, Galsworthy, Ibsen and Oscar Wilde. The latter had lost his lawsuit against the Marquess of Queensberry in 1895 and had been incarcerated in Reading Gaol. When Sir George Alexander reproduced *The Importance of Being Earnest* the author's name was not announced and, although the secret of Wilde's pseudonym was known to many, London society flocked to the first night. The brilliant audience seemed to contain everyone of note and Sir Ernest Cassel, then in the heyday of his financial success, a few days later was dubbed "The importance of being Ernest Cassel" by some wit, who facetiously added, "for God blessed Egypt but Cassel dammed the Nile."

In the afternoons we would drive to Ranelagh, to Roehampton and to Hurlingham. Ranelagh had been the resort of fashion in the eighteenth century, when Richard, Viscount Ranelagh, had built a mansion there and had laid out gardens which in 1742 were thrown open as a proprietary place of entertainment. Its vogue had been shortlived, but in my day it had once again become fashionable, with the addition of modern sports as entertainment. There we watched inter-regimental polo matches, which were slow-motion affairs compared with the international matches. But they were gay, intimate and friendly, and women wore the badges of their husbands' regiments or, in the case of a flirt, sported a more discreet ribbon.

There were serious days when Parliament claimed our attention and we sat behind the grille in the Speaker's Gallery listening to Mr. Arthur James Balfour, leader of the Conservative party in the House of Commons, winding up a debate in the elegant and scholarly manner still in practice; or perhaps in the Peeresses' Gallery, looking down on the Lords, we heard Lord Rosebery castigating the Government and the venerable Marquess of Salisbury's dignified but no less caustic defence. When the Archbishops of Canterbury and York rose to intervene they were listened to with all the respect their lordships owed their spiritual rulers. When the Chancellor on his Woolsack raised a point of order it was immediately subscribed to, for, even in the heat of debate, courtesy ruled in this august assembly. There were so many noble lords that only the ministers or the best speakers attempted to hold the ear of the House, and when a young peer was chosen to move or second the Address at the opening of Parliament, he knew that with his speech he could either make or mar a future political career. A full-dress debate in the House of Lords was an event to be looked forward to, for, whatever the subject, there would be speakers of renowned eloquence and erudition. Experiencing the excitement the Greeks must have felt when matching one orator against another, one strained to hear every word, for it would never do to miss a point or to fail to appraise an eloquent peroration. The English language never seemed so rich and so beautiful as when spoken by these cultivated men who owed their education to the Universities of Oxford and Cambridge. The polished elegance of their phrases, the purity of their diction and the pleasant pitch of their voices made of these debates something more than the mere expression of political loyalties. It was as if a standard of excellence had to be maintained and a forum created for the perfect presentation of any opinion. One of the finest speeches I ever heard was delivered by the old Duke of Argyll against 'The Deceased Wife's Sister's Bill' which sought to do away with the ban on the marriage of a widower with his dead wife's sister. The combined eloquence of the Duke and of the Bishops did not prevent the passing of the Bill, but the debate furnished a flow of oratory reminiscent of the best days of the eighteenth century.

These varied activities in London, to me novel and interesting, but also somewhat of an effort, since I was always meeting strangers who had to be identified and classified, were followed by immense house-parties at Blenheim for the week-ends. Thanks to my mother-in-law, I was able to unravel the relationships of the families I was coming to know. I found her anecdotes at times more amusing than helpful. Once, for instance, when I consulted her about the best cheese to serve with port wine she told me of a dinner-party at which she had had small bits of soap placed among real pieces of cheese. With tears of laughter still rolling down her cheeks she said, "Poor Mr. Hope was too polite to spit this out, so he swallowed the soap and was violently sick, and, fancy, he never forgave me!" She was very fond of practical jokes—an ink-pot tied over a door had at one time dropped its contents on my father-in-law's head as he opened it. There were other such exploits, which, however, I was never tempted to follow in dealings with my husband.

There were always from twenty-five to thirty guests at our week-end parties and they were all considerably older than myself, since it was judged advisable to invite members of the family and people of importance for our début as hosts and for my introduction to English society. Although delighting in the companionship of brilliant men and agreeable women, the sustained effort of a perpetual round of entertaining was considerable. Marlborough had given me the supervision together with the financing of everything pertaining to the house, while reserving the administration of the estate for himself. Unfortunately he was more inclined to criticise than to instruct and I had to trust to observation to ensure the continuity established by past generations of English women.

We would return to Blenheim on Saturday mornings and our guests would follow in the late afternoon. By then I was inclined to resent the amount of trouble their impending visits had given me; for my round of the thirty guest-rooms, accompanied by the housekeeper, was apt to reveal some overlooked contingency too late to be repaired; a talk with the chef more often disclosed an underling's minor delinquency; orders to the butler invariably revealed a spiteful desire to undermine the chef—a desire that, if realised, I knew would jeopardise the culinary success of my party. Menus had to be approved and rooms allotted to the various guests. I had, moreover, spent hours placing my guests for the three ceremonial meals they would partake with us, for the rules of precedence were then strictly adhered to, not only in seating arrangements but also for the procession in to dinner. Since it was then considered ill-bred not to answer all letters oneself, I had no secretary. There was therefore a considerable amount of purely mechanical work to be done—dealing with correspondence, answering invitations, writing the dinner cards and other instructions which appear necessary to ensure the smooth progression of social amenities—which took up a great deal of my time.

It was, I think, at my first big party that I carefully listed in their order of precedence the four earls who were to be our guests, and I believed I had given to each the status due to him. It was therefore a considerable surprise when one of them in-

formed me that on the second evening I had not given him
precedence over Lord B. as I should have done.

I recall a visit to Althorp, the beautiful family seat of the
Earl and Countess Spencer, when for four days I sat next to my
host at every meal and had as my other neighbour the Brazilian
Minister, so strictly were the rules of precedence still adhered to
in certain circles. Fortunately this custom gradually gave way to
an arrangement permitting a discreet observance of the tastes
and personal predilections of one's guests as more likely to
stimulate conversation. On our visit to Althorp I was fortunate,
for my host talked entertainingly of the politics and affairs of his
day, and re-created a picture of a bygone generation. Lord
Spencer, with his great red beard, his fine head and tall frame,
looked every inch a Saxon. He was descended from the Earl of
Sunderland who had married the daughter of the first Duke of
Marlborough, through whom the Churchills for generations
were Spencers.

As our guests arrived, on fine days I would receive them in
the Italian garden, where tea-tables had been laid, and we would
ramble through the pleasure grounds until time to dress for
dinner. In the sumptuous splendour of the state bedrooms,
where the walls were draped with beautiful tapestries depicting
the battles of the Great Duke, it was strangely incongruous to see
a washstand with its pitchers and basins prominently displayed
against the heroic form of a dying horse or a fallen combatant.
The round bathtub placed before the fire with its accompanying
impedimenta of hot and cold water jugs, soap and sponge bowls,
towels and mats always made me shudder as I ushered in my
guests. It was not only their ugly intimacy that offended me. It
was also the lack of bathrooms which troubled my American
sense of comfort and awakened stricken feelings towards my
housemaids, whose business it was to prepare something like
thirty baths a day. But owing to my husband's dislike of
innovations, it was not until my son succeeded to the dukedom
that sufficient bathrooms were built.

Dinner was an elaborate function. The seating arrangements,
to which I have referred as causing me such endless research,
were greatly facilitated when I discovered a Table of Precedence,
and against the name of every peer the number of his rank. I
was glad to know my own number, for, after waiting at the
door of the dining-room for older women to pass through, I

one day received a furious push from an irate Marchioness who loudly claimed that it was just as vulgar to hang back as to leave before one's turn.

Our dinner-table decked with a profusion of huge pink malmaisons was an impressive sight. We had adopted the French custom, also observed in the royal family, of sitting at the centre of the table instead of at its ends, and a massive silver replica of the Duke of Marlborough on his horse after the Battle of Blenheim, writing out the dispatch announcing his victory, hid me from my husband. On the second evening a gilt service would adorn the table and it blended well with the soft mauve and white of a magnificent display of orchids from the hot-houses built by Marlborough's father. We had a good chef, but there had to be perfect co-operation with the butler in order to serve an eight-course dinner within the hour we had prescribed as the time limit. This was not an easy matter, since the kitchen was at least three hundred yards from the dining-room. We had imposed this limit to prevent the prolonged delays that occur between courses. It also appeared to us sufficient time to linger over dinner, since the men spent an additional half-hour over coffee and liqueurs. But such a schedule had at times its draw-backs, and at Lady Londonderry's, where the rule was most rigorously enforced, I once watched with amusement the silent but no less furious battle between a reputed gourmet who wished to eat every morsel of his large helping and a footman equally determined to remove his plate.

Hostesses were prone to vagueness; this consideration rendered me no exception to the rule. When seated between two elderly noblemen who owed their rank to their ancestors rather than to any personal merit I found dinner interminably long and boring.

Two soups, one hot and one cold, were served simultaneously. Then came two fish, again one hot and one cold, with accompanying sauces. I still remember my intense annoyance with a very greedy man who complained bitterly that both his favourite fish were being served and that he wished to eat both, so that I had to keep the service waiting while he consumed first the hot and then the cold, quite unperturbed at the delay he was causing. An entrée was succeeded by a meat dish. Some-times a sorbet preceded the game, which in the shooting season was varied, comprising grouse, partridge, pheasant, duck, wood-

D

cock and snipe. In the summer, when there was no game, we had quails from Egypt, fattened in Europe, and ortolans from France, which cost a fortune. An elaborate sweet followed, succeeded by a hot savoury with which was drunk the port so comforting to English palates. The dinner ended with a succulent array of peaches, plums, apricots, nectarines, strawberries, raspberries, pears and grapes, all grouped in generous pyramids among the flowers that adorned the table.

At the end of the prescribed hour I rose to lead the ladies to the Long Library, where Mr. Perkins, an organist of repute, was playing Bach or Wagner. If our guests were younger, an Austrian orchestra summoned from London played the Viennese waltzes which were then the rage. There were, however, evenings when a guest would dally over the fruit she had piled on her plate— impossible to make her hurry. At one of my first dinner-parties, to my surprise, I found the ladies rising at a signal given by my husband's aunt, who was sitting next to him. Immediately aware of a concerted plan to establish her dominance, and warned by my neighbour Lord Chesterfield's exclamation, "Never have I seen anything so rude; don't move!" I nevertheless went to the door and, meeting her, inquired in dulcet tones, "Are you ill, S.?" "Ill?" she shrilled, "no, certainly not, why should I be ill?" "There surely was no other excuse for your hasty exit," I said calmly. She had the grace to blush; the other women hid their smiles, and never again was I thus challenged!

Sundays were interminably long for a hostess who had no games wherewith to entertain her guests. Golf and tennis had not yet become the vogue, nor would they have been played on the Lord's Day. Instead we trooped to divine service at Woodstock, and in the afternoon to evensong in the chapel. Promenades were the fashionable pastime, and the number of tête-à-tête walks she could crowd into an afternoon became the criterion of a woman's social success. I have known some unattractive women, who, unfortunately for their peace of mind, were as vain as they were self-conscious, to prefer to spend an afternoon in their rooms, pleading a headache, than to acknowledge that they had not been invited to go for a walk. Sometimes I had to find a recalcitrant swain to accompany a fair lady. One never knew where one's duties as hostess would end. It was not astonishing that at the close of my first London season, on going to the seaside to recuperate, I slept for twenty-four hours without waking.

We took a small house for the Ascot race meeting. Marlborough invited five of his friends to stay with us, which, with the thirty we had entertained at Blenheim the previous week-end and the thirty more expected for the following Sunday, implied a terrific amount of work for the staff and a considerable strain for the hostess. The chef quite rightly claimed that he was overworked, and he certainly made us pay for it by ordering quails at five shillings each and ortolans, which were even more expensive, and then serving them for breakfast, an extravagance so *nouveau riche* that I blushed with shame as well as with annoyance. But this was not the only blatant display that shocked me. The racecourse lay only fifty yards across the road from our house, but Marlborough had our coach-and-four sent on to Ascot simply so that he could drive on to the course. It was, moreover, a drive fraught with danger, since there was a sharp turn out of a narrow gate on to a main thoroughfare. A groom had to be sent ahead to hold up the traffic, and fresh horses over crowded roads provided a daily and unpleasant emotional experience.

I found Ascot Week very tiring. After a long afternoon spent greeting acquaintances in the Royal Enclosure there were evening rides in Windsor Forest, which meant changing from diaphanous organdies into a habit and braiding one's hair into a tight bun.

Fortunes were yearly spent on dresses selected as appropriate to a graduated scale of elegance which reached its climax on Thursday; for fashion decreed that one should reserve one's most sumptuous *toilette* for Gold Cup day. Of course there was always the danger that it might rain that day. Meteorological prognostics were not at everyone's disposal and the English climate is proverbially as fickle as a woman's moods, and would sometimes provide an icy wind in midsummer. We spent our mornings donning various dresses in accordance with the vagaries of the weather, and by noon we were apt to be not only cross and tired but also probably attired in the wrong dress.

Sometimes we were invited to lunch in the royal pavilion with the Prince and Princess of Wales. The Guards also provided an excellent meal in their Regimental Tent. The Royal Enclosure was so crowded one could hardly move about, but we walked to the paddock to see the horses saddled and then to our waiting coach better to view the races from its heights.

It was during that summer of 1896 that I had the honour of being presented to Queen Victoria. The Lord Steward's invitation to dine and sleep at Windsor Castle arrived casually on a large printed card without an envelope. On the back of the card I read the following instruction:

Should the Ladies or Gentlemen to whom Invitations are sent be out of Town, and not expected to return in time to obey the Queen's commands on the day the Invitations are for, the Cards are to be brought back.

The reply to this Invitation to be addressed to the Master of the Household.

One was barely given twenty-four hours' notice. As Queen Victoria was nearly eighty and had for years been a recluse, this honour was viewed as something of an ordeal. We travelled to Windsor by train, where we were met by a royal carriage and conducted to our apartment. Lady Edward Churchill, one of the Queen's ladies-in-waiting and a great-aunt of Marlborough, kindly came to instruct me on what I should have to do. She said that there would be but a few guests, and gave me strict injunctions only to speak when spoken to by the Queen and to limit my remarks to answers to hers, for only the Queen had the right to initiate a subject. On being presented I was to kiss the Queen's hand. Her Majesty would in turn imprint a kiss on my brow, which was the protocol for a peeress.

Having heard so much about the Queen's terrifying personality, it was with some trepidation that I awaited her appearance before dinner. When eventually she came in, a little figure in sombre black, I discovered to my dismay that she was so small that I almost had to kneel to touch her outstretched hand with my lips. My balance was precariously held as I curtsied low to receive her kiss upon my forehead, and a diamond crescent in my hair caused me anxiety lest I scratch out a royal eye.

At dinner Princess Henry of Battenberg, the Queen's youngest daughter, sat on her right; Lord Salisbury, her Prime Minister, with members of the household and ourselves made up the rest of the party. I had evidence during the evening of the happy relationship between the Queen and her Prime

Minister. His admiration for her character and her affection for him were seen in the deference and esteem their manner to each other indicated. The dinner itself was a most depressing function. Conversation was carried on in whispers, for the Queen's stern personality imposed restraint. After dinner we returned to the narrow and sombre corridor where we had assembled, and I wondered why, with all the rooms the Castle possessed, we should be confined to this small passage. We were, in turn, conducted to where the Queen sat and she addressed a few words to each of us. I found it most embarrassing to stand in front of her while everyone listened to her kind inquiries about my reactions to my adopted country, which I answered as best I could. I was, moreover, haunted by the fear that I might not notice the little nod with which it was her habit to end an audience, having heard of an unfortunate person who, not knowing the protocol, had remained glued to the spot until ignominiously removed by a lord-in-waiting. It was only twice my privilege to meet Queen Victoria—for again in the following summer we were honoured with a "dine and sleep" command. I confess to a feeling of discomfort on each occasion, her appearance was so severe and sombre. It seemed to me that it was her deliberate intention to emphasise the dignity of her rank and person, and I felt that any warmth she might have possessed must have been buried with the Prince Consort.

Marlborough was a staunch Conservative, and that summer of 1896 he staged a political demonstration at Blenheim to celebrate the union of the Liberal Unionists and Conservatives. Mr. Balfour and Mr. Chamberlain were the guests of honour. Mr. Joseph Chamberlain, leader of the Liberal Unionists, was at that time Secretary of State for the Colonies in Lord Salisbury's Government. I may remind my readers that at the end of the eighties he had broken away from Mr. Gladstone over the Home Rule for Ireland Bill and, with Lord Hartington and ninety-four Radical and Whig members, had joined the Conservative party as Liberal Unionists. It was chiefly due to Mr. Chamberlain's vigorous, ceaseless and unsparing opposition that Mr. Gladstone's second Home Rule Bill was defeated and it was Mr. Chamberlain's influence in the Unionist Cabinet that brought about such measures of social reform as the Workmen's Compensation Act. His tenure of office of Colonial Secretary between 1895 and 1900 proved a turning-point in the history of relations between the British Colonies and the mother country, for in spirit he was an imperial federationist.

Mr. Arthur James Balfour, statesman, scholar and philosopher, who was then leader of the Conservatives in the House of Commons, became one of my truest friends, a friendship I remember with humility and gratitude, for there has, I believe, never been anyone quite like him. When I think of him it is as of some fine and disembodied spirit. The opinions he expressed and the doctrines he held seemed to me to be the products of pure logic. Invariably he sensed the heart of the matter and freed it of sordid encumbrance, and when he spoke in a philosophic vein, it was like listening to Bach. His way of holding his head gave him the appearance of searching the heavens and his blue eyes were absent, and yet intent, as if busy in some abstract world. Both mentally and physically he gave the impression of immense distinction and of a transcendent spirituality. He could talk on nearly every subject with equal distinction and I have heard him baffle scientists, musicians and artists with his intimate knowledge of their subjects. He was gifted with a breadth of comprehension I have never seen equalled. Unemotional and serene, he was rarely disturbed by human strife; but when it was necessary to impose stern measures he could be both tenacious and courageous.

Accompanied by these two great leaders I entered the luncheon tents, where three thousand delegates greeted their appearance with cheers. It was Mr. Chamberlain who received the greater ovation, and I noticed that in spite of his immaculate appearance, the orchid in his buttonhole and the monocle in his eye, he did not seem to mind the enthusiastic and somewhat rough greetings his admirers gave him as he passed through the crowd.

In addition to the delegates who had come from various parts of the country, one hundred Members of Parliament had accepted our invitation. We gave them luncheon in the great hall, after which we proceeded to the north terrace overlooking the courtyard, which was flanked by the two wings of the house. Here the delegates and a huge crowd had assembled to hear the speeches. In the distance, up a grassy slope, stood the high column on which John Duke surveyed the domain a grateful country had by parliamentary grant given him and his heirs in perpetuity, and as we listened to my husband and to Mr.

Balfour's addresses I could almost detect a satisfied smile on John Duke's countenance. It was somewhat different when Mr. Chamberlain spoke of social measures that in the distant future would still leave the Duke on his column but might drive his heirs from the palace the nation had bestowed.

Whatever was said on that day, it was all a great success. Comments in the depleted House of Commons on the absence of a hundred members at what the Opposition was pleased to call the Blenheim Garden Party only added to the savour. In 1899 Marlborough was named Paymaster-General to the Forces, a post his famous ancestor had found lucrative, but which no longer held the same perquisites, unless attending service in Christopher Wren's lovely chapel of the Royal Hospital in Chelsea could be considered such. This was, however, but the first step in my husband's political career. In 1900 he went to South Africa as Assistant Military Secretary to Lord Roberts; and the following year became Under-Secretary of State for the Colonies under Alfred Lyttelton, better known as a great cricketer.

In the autumn of 1896 we were invited to Sandringham by the Prince and Princess of Wales. Partridges and pheasants were plentiful, and since Marlborough was a good shot I realised he would enjoy himself; but for my part I rather dreaded four long days in such august society—for the guests were expected to stay from Monday to Saturday. We sent our servants ahead, and on our arrival I was shocked to hear that my maid had lost a bag containing quantities of small jewels, such as brooches, rings and bracelets, which I prized more for their associations than for their intrinsic value. Luckily the jewel-case with my more valuable possessions had escaped the attention of the thief, who at Paddington Station had disappeared with the loot. Although a full description of every jewel was given to the police not one was ever recovered.

Life at Sandringham was simple and informal and the Prince and Princess proved to be delightful hosts. The more stringent protocol of Windsor Castle and Buckingham Palace was relaxed here and in the intimate atmosphere of family life one might almost forget the prerogatives of royalty. Nevertheless, the Prince's stout but stately presence made rare any such lapse as that of which a friend of mine was guilty: in a moment of forgetfulness she addressed him as "my good man", to which with a somewhat frigid intonation he replied, "My dear Mrs.

B., please remember that I am not your good man." In spite of this, he was always accessible and friendly and knew how to discard ceremony without loss of dignity.

In the mornings we sometimes walked to York Cottage, a small house in the park where the Duke and Duchess of York (the future King George V and Queen Mary) lived with their children, delighting in the rest from functions and formalities. The ladies would join the men for luncheon, which was served in a tent, and afterwards we stayed to admire the skill of the fine sportsmen whom the Prince had assembled. The Duke of York was a beautiful shot, and it was a pleasure to watch the clean way he killed his birds. I hated to see birds maimed, but a high pheasant plummeting to the ground or a partridge winged as it passed was exciting. It was cold, however, sitting behind hedges when the north winds blew straight from the sea and I was glad to walk home to the roaring fires and copious teas that greeted us.

The Princess showed me her rooms, which were cluttered with small tables on which were quantities of photographs in costly frames. A unique collection of bejewelled flowers and animals cut in semi-precious stones, and another of miniature Easter eggs in lapis lazuli, were arranged in cabinets. They had been gifts from the Dowager Empress of Russia to her sister and were the work of Fabergé, the famous St. Petersburg jeweller. These rooms are best described by the word cosy, with its suggestion of nooks and corners. The Princess's good taste was more apparent in her wardrobe, for she was always suitable attired, with a quiet distinction that enhanced her beauty. Her costumes would at her death have supplied a history of fashion for nearly eighty years, for she could not bear to part with a dress.

I grew to love Princess Victoria, the lonely Princess who never married because of loyalty to her mother, to whose selfishness she became a slave. Princess Maud, who had recently married Prince Charles of Denmark, later King Haakon of Norway, was there, and the Princess Royal, already married to the Duke of Fife, lived near-by. They were all simple and kindly and their family life was a model of virtue—though the Prince of Wales, if rumour was to be credited, found many pleasures outside the family circle. He was a shrewd man of the world and longed to have a voice in the politics and destiny of his country. Everyone recognised the fact that, in spite of Queen Victoria's determination to exclude him from all affairs of state, he was the best informed person in the kingdom. Viscount Esher, who was appointed by King Edward VII as one of the editors of the *Letters of Queen Victoria* and who later wrote *The Influence of King Edward* and *Cloud-Capp'd Towers,* has in the latter work an interesting appraisal of Edward VII. He says:

At the age of 22 he showed such independence of spirit that he braved the Queen's wrath by welcoming Garibaldi to London.

And again:

Before he was thirty he was in the habit of requesting interviews from Ministers and begging for explanations of their policy. His intercourse with foreign Ambassadors was no less intimate. When thirty-four years old, in an outspoken talk with the French Ambassador, he had already suggested an Entente with France as the only means of restraining Bismarck and preserving the Peace of Europe. This was anticipating by many years that day when Gambetta said of him, "He loves France gaily and seriously, and his dream is an Entente with us."

It was not therefore surprising to find him, even while still Prince, influencing the affairs of the day, gradually turning the direction of English policy away from the German trend given it by the Prince Consort's influence and towards the *Entente Cordiale* with France.

During our visit the Prince expressed a wish to come to Blenheim, and we at once began the rather onerous preparations such a visit entailed. Our proposed list of guests having been submitted and approved, we became engrossed in plans to make the visit agreeable and memorable. A great amount of staff work was involved and there were endless details to be discussed. I faced this, my first big shooting-party, with trepidation, for I had no experience and no precedent to guide me. Fortified, however, by the thought that American women were considered adaptable I tried to still my apprehensions.

A ball to give the county families an opportunity to meet our royal guests was planned. But an untoward event occurred. My grandmother, Mrs. W. H. Vanderbilt, died suddenly. I first saw the news on a poster in the London streets a few days before the royal visit and realised that our mourning might prevent its taking place. After consulting my father by cable it was agreed that we should receive the Prince and Princess as arranged, but that the ball should be cancelled and replaced by a concert, which was at once a concession to our mourning and to the feelings of our county neighbours, who would have been greatly disappointed had there been no festivities.

There were, I remember, over a hundred people in the house, including thirty guests, among whom were not only the Prince and Princess but Princess Victoria, Princess Maud and her husband, Prince Charles. Our rooms on the ground floor were given over to them, and we retired to crowded quarters upstairs.

Our party lasted from Monday to Saturday, and each day I had the Prince as my neighbour for two long meals. This was a terrible ordeal for one so unversed in the politics and gossip of the day as I was, since he liked to discuss the news and to hear the latest scandal, with all of which at that age I was unfamiliar. The Princess of Wales, gay and animated, with an almost childish interest in everything, was easier to cope with. She was full of fun. Gossip and stories about people delighted her. She made us laugh, telling us how she had to use a ladder in order to get into my bed which was on a daïs, and how she kept falling over the white bear skins that were strewn on the floor.

Years later I was amused to read some of the impressions made by this party on Arthur Balfour, one of our guests. In a letter to Lady Elcho* he writes:

There is here a big party in a big house in a big park beside a big lake. To begin with (as our Toast lists have it) "the Prince of Wales and the rest of the Royal family——" or if not quite that, at least a quorum, namely himself, his wife, two daughters and a son-in-law. There are two sets of George Curzons, the Londonderrys, Grenfells, Gosfords, H. Chaplin, etc., etc. We came down by special train—rather cross most of us—were received with illuminations, guards of honour,

* Mrs. E. C. Dugdale, *Arthur James Balfour* (London: Hutchinson & Co., Ltd., 1936).

cheering and other follies, went through agonies about our luggage, but finally settled down placidly enough.

Today the men shot and the women dawdled. As I detest both occupations equally I stayed in my room till one o'clock and then went exploring on my bike, joining everybody at luncheon. Then, after the inevitable photograph, I again betook myself to my faithful machine and here I am writing to you. So far you perceive the duties of society are weighing lightly upon me.

The "inevitable photograph" can be found in this book.

This visit was a tiring and anxious experience for me, since I was responsible for every detail connected with running the house and ordering the pleasures of my numerous guests. The number of changes of costume was in itself a waste of precious time. To begin with, even breakfast, which was served at 9.30 in the dining-room, demanded an elegant costume of velvet or silk. Having seen the men off to their sport, the ladies spent the morning round the fire reading the papers and gossiping. We next changed into tweeds to join the guns for luncheon, which was served in the High Lodge or in a tent. Afterwards we usually accompanied the guns and watched a drive or two before returning home. An elaborate tea gown was donned for tea, after which we played cards or listened to a Viennese band or to the organ until time to dress for dinner, when again we adorned ourselves in satin, or brocade, with a great display of jewels. All these changes necessitated a tremendous outlay, since one was not supposed to wear the same gown twice. That meant sixteen dresses for four days.

On Friday I awoke with a sense of exultation that the last day of what had seemed an interminable week had finally dawned. I was exhausted and hardly able to face the endless questions that had to be settled for the culminating reception and concert that evening. So much had still to be discussed. There was the Prince to be consulted on the people he wished to meet, the royal procession in to supper to be arranged, and a hundred household details to be reviewed. As I went on a last round of inspection before dinner I thought the state rooms, which we had redecorated in Louis XIV *boiseries* of white and gold, were a splendid setting for such a festive scene, and the long suite of reception rooms filled with orchids and malmaisons looked to me truly palatial. Later, as the royal procession wound its way through the throng of guests, the Prince stopping here and there for a word of greeting, I realised that the Crown stood for a tradition that England would not easily give up.

The Christmas festivities loomed as the next social event. Two of my husband's aunts, besides his sisters, mother and grandmother, formed the nucleus of a party of friends. I felt somewhat isolated in this clannish company, since my family in America could hardly have been expected to take so long a voyage to be with us. The grandmother, the Dowager Duchess, proved somewhat of a trial. It is not always pleasant to look back on a past perhaps less brilliant than the present and to reflect on things left undone from necessity rather than from choice. It was perhaps for this reason that the Duchess's comments were somewhat jaundiced and that, in giving advice, she forgot my nineteen years, expecting me to conform to a dignified decorum even then considered old-fashioned. It was no doubt annoying for her to contemplate that my duties sat so lightly upon me, and that the dignity of my position as her successor did not oppress me. Trailing her satins and sables in a stately manner, she would cast a hostile eye upon my youthful figure more suitably attired in tweeds, and I would hear her complaining to my sisters-in-law that "Her Grace does not realise the importance of her position." She did not perhaps realise that a little relaxation was necessary after my lengthy conversations with her, which were rendered difficult by being conducted through her ear-trumpet. Nevertheless, I was not neglecting my duties, and there were Christmas trees for the schoolchildren and teas for the older people, and every morning, with my sisters-in-law and the housekeeper, I made up bundles of clothing and gifts to be taken to the poor.

Marlborough and the other guns were always shooting, for there were pheasants, rabbits, duck, woodcock and snipe to be killed. I remember a record shoot one autumn when seven thousand rabbits were bagged by five of the best English shots in one day. They had two loaders and three guns each, and every one of them had a violent headache on reaching home. At least for a time the High Park was free of rabbits.

In the first months of the New Year we moved to a small house near Melton Mowbray, since my husband wished to hunt with the various fine packs of hounds Leicestershire boasted. He was a good horseman and looked well in his pink coat, his grey horse—for we had only greys—conspicuously in the lead. As I was then expecting a baby I was unable to hunt, but Lord Lonsdale, who was Master of the Quorn, drove me in his buggy on days when he was not hunting. His knowledge of the lie of the land and the ways of the fox enabled me to see many good hunts and to be present at the kill more often than I would have thought it possible. We drove at a great pace over the ridges and furrows of the grass fields and through gates opened for us by yokels who received his pleasant greeting with a grin and a hand to the cap. The Earl of Lonsdale was as popular a person with the farmer over whose fields he rode as he was in sporting circles, for he was a good fellow and a thorough sportsman, genial, generous and gay. His imagination some-times got the better of his veracity but it always contributed to the fun of the occasion. He had a complete outfit of reindeer skins made up for me as a coat and a carriage rug, informing me that he had shot the lot; but when I repeated the story it was received with incredulous laughter. I found a few days spent hunting the fox on wheels sufficient initiation and decided to discontinue hunting until I was able to ride. Meanwhile, I read German philosophy with a teacher who came from London. This, to my surprise, consigned me to the company of blue-stockings and I realised that I had shown more courage than tact in advertising my preference for literature. Only this interest, however, got me through the first depressing winter, when my solitary days were spent walking along the high road and my evenings listening to the hunting exploits of others. Whenever there was a frost Marlborough went off to London or to Paris, but since it was considered inadvisable for me to travel in my condition I remained alone. From my window I over-looked a pond in which a former butler had drowned himself. As one gloomy day succeeded another I began to feel a deep sympathy for him.

This winter was succeeded by a memorable summer, for it was the year 1897 and the occasion of Queen Victoria's Diamond Jubilee. The number of royal personages assembled in London proved a tax even on proverbial English hospitality. Sumptuous and lavish were the receptions, balls and dinners given in their honour. To the Marquess of Lansdowne, Minister of Foreign

Affairs, fell the brunt of official entertaining and I remember a dinner at Lansdowne House where Prince Ferdinand, who in 1908 became Czar of Bulgaria, was the guest of honour. We had already met at Buckingham Palace and for the second consecutive time he chose to spend the evening with me and to make me the confidante of his disappointment at not having received the Garter, hinting in his cynical manner that the German Emperor would no doubt be more responsive to his advances. I was interested in the ambitious schemes he unfolded, for at that time—and for many years thereafter—the Balkan question was to harass the statesmen of the Great Powers. An ugly man, with the long Coburg nose, he had a passion for decorations and precious stones. Had he not been in uniform scintillating with decorations (all but the Garter), he would have appeared as the rather mean little bourgeois his spiteful resentment against all things British proved him to be.

The fancy dress ball at Devonshire House was a fitting climax to a brilliant season. The ball lasted to the early hours of morning, and the sun was rising as I walked through Green Park to Spencer House, where we then lived. On the grass lay the dregs of humanity. Human beings too dispirited or sunk to find work or favour, they sprawled in sodden stupor, pitiful representatives of the submerged tenth. In my billowing period dress, I must have seemed to them a vision of wealth and youth, and I thought soberly that they must hate me. But they only looked, and some even had a compliment to enliven my progress.

CHAPTER FIVE

Red Carpet and Protocol

ON SEPTEMBER 18, 1897, my first son was born. We had taken
Spencer House, overlooking Green Park, for the event. It was
fitting that Churchills should be born there, since they were
descendants of the Spencer family. The first Duke of Marlborough's two sons having died unmarried, a special Act of
Parliament granted succession through the female line; and the
eldest son of one of the Duke's daughters who had married the
Earl of Sunderland eventually succeeded to the dukedom.

Spencer House was an eighteenth-century mansion partly
decorated by the brothers Adam. As the bedrooms were small,
I occupied a corner drawing-room and from my bed could see
the fine gallery with the vista of a further room painted in the
Pompeian style. There were nights when a sudden cold draught
would wake me; it was as if a presence had glided through the
room. My mother, who had come from American to be with me,
professed to have seen a ghost.

After my son was born, she told me she had been surprised by
what she described as the ineptitude of the obstetrician who
attended me; yet he was then considered at the top of his profession. Comparing the antiquated methods then practised with
the painless births young women now are privileged with, it
seems as if Eve, in spite of the curse imposed upon her, must
have redeemed her original sin. On awakening from a week's
unconsciousness, I found to my surprise the family doctor at my
bedside. He had been summoned from Scotland, where he was
vacationing, and had arrived just in time to order a partridge
and bread sauce for my first meal—a prescription that cost us
dear, since he had the right to charge a pound a mile. It was only
then that I realised that my condition must for a time have been
cause for anxiety, but my recovery was rapid and the joyous
approval of the family intensified the happiness motherhood
brought me.

The Prince of Wales had offered to be godfather to our son who was therefore given the names of Albert Edward (we vainly tried to eschew the Albert), William after my father, and John in memory of the Great Duke. In spite of all these names he was called Blandford, for it was the custom in the family to name the heir by his title.

The christening took place in the Chapel Royal, St. James's Palace. The sun, streaming through the oriel window, touched the gold vessels on the altar, the white lilies round the font and the scarlet tunics worn by the royal choristers. The Prince of Wales in a tight frock-coat had a smile of gracious urbanity; my father, looking too young for his new responsibility, and Lady Blandford, with the baby in her arms, completed the group of godparents. In the pew opposite Marlborough, his sisters and me, sat Lady Blandford's sister, the Duchess of Buccleuch. As Mistress of the Robes to Queen Victoria, she was very much aware of the dignity of her rank and position. When our housekeeper, superb in black satin, was ushered to a seat beside her I viewed with apprehension her surprised reaction; for never could she have supposed that anyone less than a Duchess would share her pew, and vainly did she try to place this new arrival among the twenty-seven ducal families she prided herself on knowing. Her astonishment was so visible that we were all at pains to hide our merriment. Our housekeeper alone, with great dignity, remained unperturbed.

During my convalescence Marlborough had met a young woman named Gladys Deacon, who had come to London on a visit from Paris, where she lived with her mother and sisters. Gladys Deacon was a beautiful girl endowed with a brilliant intellect. Possessed of exceptional powers of conversation, she could enlarge on any subject in an interesting and amusing manner. I was soon subjugated by the charm of her companionship and we began a friendship which only ended years later.

When I recovered, we returned to Blenheim and to the routine of house-parties, and I to do the duties of a chatelaine. The added responsibility of motherhood was made easy by the robust health of my baby; and the happiness he brought me lightened the gloom that overhung our palatial home. But there followed another bleak winter in Leicestershire awaiting the birth of my second child.

Ivor was born the following autumn. We had rented

Hampden House from the Duke of Abercorn and there my mother-in-law greeted me as I lay in my bed, exhausted but content, with, "You are a little brick! American women seem to have boys more easily than we do!" Thus having done my duty I felt I should now be allowed a certain measure of the pleasures of life.

That third winter in Leicestershire I was able to hunt—no more walks on the high road. I shall always remember the first meet with the Quorn hounds when, perfectly fitted in a Busvine habit, a tall hat and veil, I mounted 'Greyling', inwardly trembling with excitement and fear. Marlborough, as I have said, was a fine horseman and it was up to me to follow him. Ladies then rode side-saddle and the Leicestershire people were hard riders. Mrs. Willie Lawson—'Legs', as she was known for the length of them—Miss Doods Naylor, Lady Angela Forbes and a host of others were eyeing me critically and so far, thanks to my tailor and a good seat, had found nothing amiss. But the great test was still to come. Hounds were moving off to covert. Then came the wait with the cold wind blowing me blue and numb, while Greyling trembled, his ears cocked for the find. Suddenly it came with the exciting cry of hounds in chase and we realised we were on the right side of covert. There was a gate through which a crowd was pressing; there was also a fence under arching branches with a drop on the other side. Marlborough chose the fence. With my heart in my mouth I followed. Greyling jumped in perfect form and I ducked in time to avoid the branches. When I looked back and heard Angela Forbes say, "I am not going over that horrid place," I felt my day had begun auspiciously. What a pity that we had a record run, or rather that my strength did not last out. I must have jumped a score or more of those stake and bound fences which Greyling seemed to fly over—just brushing through the unbound tops like the clever hunter he was—when exhausted by such unusual exercise I reined him in and regretfully watched the hunt go by. I remember Lord Lonsdale who, with a passing word of praise for my dashing début, thought it necessary to explain he had been held up by a riderless horse and an un-horsed lady. But it was our stud groom who gave me the most pleasure by his praise and the pride he took in Greyling's performance. "You fairly let him go," he said, "and he's a beautiful jumper."

I never became completely addicted to hunting, and during those Leicestershire winters, bereft of congenial companionship, my chief interest was reading. My babies were too young to spend with me more than the accredited hours an English nurse allows a mother the privilege of her children's company. A horrible loneliness encompassed me. Reports from our agent at Blenheim told of unemployment and of its accompanying train of hunger and misery. When I announced my desire to provide work for the unemployed it was labelled as sentimental socialism; but unable to reconcile our life of ease with the hardships of those who, although not our employees, were yet our neighbours, I dispatched funds to institute relief work. Unfortunately the men, grateful for the help given them, sent a letter of thanks to my husband, who to his indignant surprise discovered that the roads on his estate had been mended and his generosity exalted. It was only then that I discovered how greatly he resented such independent action and that had I committed *lèse majesté* it could not have been more serious. The long winter ended at last and we returned home.

It was in that summer of 1899 that the German Emperor, who was Queen Victoria's guest at Windsor, having expressed the wish to see Blenheim, came to lunch with us. We were given but a few days' notice, the arrangements suffering the constant changes the Queen's wishes decreed. First it was the Emperor and Empress, the Prince and Princess of Wales and the Duke and Duchess of Connaught who would arrive by special train in time for luncheon. Hastily inviting the most important county dignitaries, we laid a long table in the painted saloon, which on occasions we used as a dining-room. The *demi-daumont* with two horses and postilion and the *daumont* with four horses and postilions were ordered to meet our guests. Marlborough, preferring to ride escort, decided that I should accompany the royal visitors. Other carriages for their suites were in waiting. On the morning itself a telegram informed us that the Queen had decided to keep the ladies with her at Windsor and that we should only expect the Emperor, the Prince of Wales and the Duke of Connaught. All the carefully made arrangements were thus upset and we would be short of ladies. The table had to be reset at the last minute and the seating rearranged. But, worst of all, I suddenly realised that if I met our guests at the station, as my husband wished, the

Emperor would have the seat of honour in the *daumont* next to me, and the Prince of Wales would, together with the Duke of Connaught, be seated with his back to the horses. At the time this appeared to me a minor calamity, for I knew that the Prince disliked his nephew and would resent being in a subordinate position during our drive through the throngs who were even then crowding the streets of Woodstock to greet him. I therefore begged Marlborough to let me remain at home and receive them on the steps, suggesting that he should drive in the *daumont* with them, an obvious solution, since the Prince and the Emperor could then share the seat of honour. However, he had made up his mind to ride escort. As we entered the waiting *daumont* the Prince eyed me resentfully while refusing, as I knew he would, the seat next to the Emperor. The arrangement no doubt suited the Emperor, for he beamed approval. As we neared the house and he saw his Imperial standard being raised to our flagstaff, he saluted and then thanked me for that attention.

Just before luncheon, perhaps in anticipation of further discomfitures, the Prince of Wales drew me aside and asked me how I had seated the guests.

"The Emperor opposite Marlborough, myself at his right, Your Royal Highness at my right," I told him.

"And where have you placed my brother?" he asked, stressing the *r*'s in his German way.

"Opposite you, Sir," I said, and when I added, "With your permission I will not come to the station," he smiled his approval. During luncheon I noticed how skilfully the Emperor concealed the uselessness of his withered arm, cutting and eating his food with a special fork to which a blade was affixed. His conversation was self-centred, which is usual with kings and with him seemed to spring from a desire to impress.

Later, during our tour of the house, he gave a lecture on the Great Duke's battles, which are depicted in tapestries that adorn the rooms, capping his remarks with a dissertation on Prince Eugene of Savoy, the Allied Commander who shared in the victories. I was amused by his evident desire to shine, but William II seemed to me no more than the typical Prussian officer with the added arrogance and conceit his royal birth inspired. Indeed I was surprised by his undistinguished appearance, which was perhaps due to the fact that he was not in

uniform, without which Germans usually appear at a disadvantage. Even his famous and formidable moustache which
seemed to bristle in indignation could not confer dignity. He
seemed to have inherited no English characteristics and had
neither the charm nor the wisdom of his uncle, the Prince of
Wales. During the South African War, soon after this visit, his
jealousy and hatred of England became evident.

When we reached the Long Library, Mr. Perkins (a famous
organist) played a selection of German music, which so pleased
the Emperor that he invited him to give a concert in Berlin.
This eventually took place. My sons, aged two and one, were
brought down by their nurses; it was, I felt, just the sort of occasion Nanny enjoyed. Before leaving, the Emperor asked us to
entertain the Crown Prince during the coming summer. He was,
he said, planning some country-house visits for him, since he
wished him to see something of English life. We could but agree.
Then, promising to send us the inevitable photograph, he
departed, accompanied by somewhat disgruntled uncles and a
subservient suite.

The South African War, which began in 1899 and ended in
1902, gave me my first experience of war work when, with Lady
Randolph Churchill and other American women, I helped to
equip and send out a hospital ship to Cape Town. This ship,
called the *Maine,* was the precursor of an endless tide of
American generosity, which reached the high mark in World
War II. Lady Randolph went out on the ship to join her son
Winston. We knew that she was equally anxious to see young
George Cornwallis-West, whom she later married. The resistance
the Boers were putting up proved unexpectedly successful and
alarm at the English casualties and more especially at the loss
of British prestige was becoming general.

In 1900 Lord Roberts went out as Commander-in-Chief and
on his staff went my husband. I was then living at Warwick
House, overlooking Green Park, a stone's throw from St. James's
Palace, and I shall always remember the wild joy of the London
crowds when the news of the relief of Mafeking became known,
for its heroic defence by a small English garrison had awakened
general sympathy. As I was driving home from the theatre my
carriage was caught up in the vortex of the crowds, feathers were
pushed through the windows to tickle my cheeks, and if it had
not been for a male escort in uniform I might have suffered

further indignities, so bent were the people in their infectious high spirits to kiss and be friends with all they met. Under Lord Roberts and Sir Ian Hamilton the war was brought to a successful close, but, to tell the truth, no one was very proud of the campaign and the war was never popular.

My husband returned before the end of the year. Winston's career as a war correspondent for the London *Morning Post* also ended after he had been taken prisoner by the Boers, and later managed to escape. Two brilliant books based on his war service with the Malakand Field Force attracted general attention, but we knew that his ambitions lay elsewhere and were not surprised when he decided to stand for Parliament.

I remember my first experience of a British election with him at Oldham in Lancashire. Listening to his speeches or driving with him in an open carriage through cheering crowds was equally exciting, for already he possessed the flame that kindles enthusiasm. I noted his frequent references to his father, Lord Randolph Churchill, and was struck by his evident admiration and respectful reverence for him; I had a presentiment that inspired with such memories he would seek to emulate him!

Winston was then the life and soul of the young and brilliant circle that gathered round him at Blenheim; a circle in which the women matched their beauty against the more intellectual attractions of the men. Whether it was his American blood or his boyish enthusiasm and spontaneity, qualities sadly lacking in my husband, I delighted in his companionship. His conversation was invariably stimulating, and his views on life were not drawn and quartered, as were Marlborough's, by a sense of self-importance. To me he represented the democratic spirit so foreign to my environment, and which I deeply missed. Winston was even then, in his early twenties, tremendously self-centred and had a dynamic energy. He told me that he had learned very little at Harrow and that he wanted to do a course of the classics. I was then absorbed in Taine's *History of English Literature* and suggested that he read it. How I envied him his marvellous memory! How seemingly without effort he could recite pages he had but scanned! That he has studied the masters of English prose to good effect we know, and as proof of his memory I quote a letter I have received from a friend, Lady Katherine Lambton, while writing these memoirs. She says, "Sir Laurence Olivier and his wife expressed the wish that Mr. Churchill should come to see 'Richard the III' which they are now acting. During the whole play Mr. Churchill recited the words almost putting the actors out. At supper afterward, to the Oliviers' immense surprise he knew the whole of 'Henry IV' and 'Henry V' by heart, and when Sir Laurence Olivier consulted him about how to say a certain speech Mr. Churchill gave his rendering and Olivier thinking it better than his own adopted it." The letter ends, "a great statesman, a master historian, a good painter, who knows perhaps also a master actor had the fates so decreed."

We had an Indian tent set up under the cedars on the lawn, where I used to sit with our guests. We always brought out *The Times* and *The Morning Post* and a book or two, but the papers were soon discarded for conversation. We talked so much more in those days than we do now, when I find my guests stampeding for the bridge table as soon as they leave the dining-room. We talked morning, noon and night, but we also knew how to listen. There was so much to be discussed. Politics were interesting, but so also were the latest novels of Henry James and of Edith Wharton—Americans who had the temerity to write of England and of the English. There were the plays of Bernard Shaw and Ibsen, the psychic phenomena of William James, and the social reforms of the Sidney Webbs and the Fabians. We talked endlessly, for the tempo of life was slow, gentle and easy; there was no radio to tune it up. Sometimes we played tennis or rowed on the lake, and in the afternoon the household played cricket on the lawn. The tea-table was set under the trees. It was a lovely sight, with masses of luscious apricots and peaches to adorn it. There were also pyramids of strawberries and raspberries; bowls brimful of Devonshire cream; pitchers of iced coffee; scones to be eaten with various jams, and cakes with sugared icing. No one dieted in those days and the still-room maid, who was responsible for the teas, was a popular person in the household.

Our endless discussions on politics fostered a sense of civic responsibility, and I began to look beyond the traditional but superficial public duties expected of me. Opening bazaars and giving away prizes with a few appropriate words could be successfully done by a moron—indeed, I realised that my dress and appearance were more important than any words I could utter. The cinema star had not yet eclipsed the duchess and archaic welcomes were still in line: one day at a bazaar presided over by a clergyman I found myself greeted as typical of his favourite fruit; he alluded, he explained, to the strawberry leaves of a ducal coronet. So perhaps it was not surprising that I became inspired to turn to more serious efforts, and accepted an invitation to go to Birmingham to speak on technical education to a club of blinded men. It was, I think, my first real speech and I took endless trouble with it; Winston, who was kind enough to criticise it, laughingly added no professor could have done better! It was the kind of audience I liked—working men who would not doubt my sincerity. I immediately felt in touch with them. And when, at the end, they greeted me with a storm of applause it made all the nervous anticipation worth while and encouraged me to continue. Indeed, I never minded the endless trouble that preparing a speech required, but the twenty-four hours that preceded its delivery were always pure agony.

And so the summer sped its uneventful days. There were agricultural and horticultural shows and the giving away of prizes that claimed my presence. There were school treats for the various villages to arrange. There were cricket matches, which I never learned to appreciate. There were mothers' meetings, and women's organisations to address. I even wrote a sermon for a young curate who was shy and pressed for time. In spite of endless duties, I never missed my daily ride, weather permitting. I remember an ignominious toss in full view of a concourse of people I had previously addressed. The hunter I rode was fresh and as I dug my heel into his side I lost my stirrup. A series of buck-jumps sent me flying—sufficiently damaged to be driven home in the hastily summoned electric car. The Press made a great to-do. It was midsummer, which newspapers dubbed "the silly season", so that minor events became welcome diversions. I was amused by the telegrams Marlborough received from various mamas whose daughters were ready to fill my place. Their professed anxiety contained a note of hope, but not for my recovery.

The electric car to which I referred was a present sent by my mother from America. It was my only escape from the household and from an irksome form of surveillance. In the house I was followed by a black boy Marlborough had brought from Egypt to be my page. In his Oriental costume and turban he looked picturesque, but he was a perpetual cause of irritation, for his garbled messages in broken English caused endless misunderstandings. When he threatened an old lady who sold toys in the village, brandishing a knife and shouting that he would kill her if she did not reimburse him for the objects he had broken and wished to return, I was glad of an excuse to send him back to his native land. Indeed, with a page in the house, a coachman or a postilion to take me for drives and a groom to accompany my rides, my freedom was quite successfully restricted. Even driving a pair of spirited cobs lost its charm when Marlborough, galloping past on a dangerously narrow road, caused the horses to take fright; only my presence of mind in throwing the end of the reins to the groom behind and our combined strength avoided a serious accident.

The electric car, which I was allowed to drive unaccompanied, and the long solitary walks I took in the High Park provided welcome respites from household cares and personal problems. The royal forest of Woodstock was rich in legend, and I loved to wander through the bracken among the great oaks with the lake shimmering below and to day-dream of past centuries and of the persons who then had haunted those green glades.

In January, 1901, Queen Victoria died. We were invited to attend the state funeral in St. George's Chapel in Windsor Castle. We were all in deep mourning and the ladies wore crêpe veils like widows. Going down in the special train, Marlborough paid me one of his rare compliments when he said, "If I die, I see you will not remain a widow long." I remember how impressive the service was. The stalls of the Knights of the Garter, where each had his escutcheon emblazoned and his standard overhead, were occupied by the German Emperor, by foreign Kings, Heads of State and Ambassadors Extraordinary. Indian Princes, Colonial dignitaries, Ministers of State, Court officials, generals and admirals with their ladies filled the benches on either side facing the procession as it moved in silence up the aisle. Looking at the brilliant assemblage, I thought that no country had ever possessed so fine an aristocracy or a Civil Service so dedicated. As the great doors were thrown open one saw the royal cortège slowly mounting the steps; only the boom of distant guns and the clangour of swords were heard above the muffled notes of the funeral march. But I was shocked to hear the voice of Margot Asquith, who even at that moment was unable to resist a quip.

Once the service was over we went up to the Waterloo

Chamber, where a collation had been laid, and I found myself so sought after by many public men—Arthur Balfour, George Wyndham, a man of great personal charm who was then Secretary of State for Ireland, St. John Brodrick, George Curzon, Mr. Asquith and others—that I felt that Marlborough's compliment had perhaps been deserved. I was having a wonderful time. The only fly in the ointment was that Lady Dudley, who seemed preoccupied, interrupted all my conversations and never left me a moment alone with those who wished to speak to me. I discovered later that she was anxious to have her husband appointed Lord Lieutenant of Ireland and, knowing that Marlborough was spoken of as a candidate, she feared that I was pleading his cause with the political personages present. It was, on the contrary, a relief to me when Lord Dudley became Lord Lieutenant and Marlborough was given the Garter, for any political aspirations I might have had were more gratified when my husband became Under-Secretary for the Colonies with Alfred Lyttelton as Secretary of State.

After the Queen's death a period of mourning was proclaimed. Wearing black depressed me, and I had an insane desire to don bright colours during that spring in Paris. Discipline, however, prevailed, and my only departure from the prescribed black was to wear white gloves. How well I remember those white gloves and the lecture they cost me, for, as ill luck would have it, the first person I met at Longchamps, where I had gone with my father to see one of his horses run, was the old Duchess of Devonshire, in the deepest mourning. A renowned character and virtually dictator of what was known as the fast set as opposed to the Victorian, Her Grace was a German aristocrat by birth. She had first been married to the impoverished Duke of Manchester, and when he died had improved her status by marriage to the rich Duke of Devonshire, who waged an undisputed influence in politics. Rumour had her beautiful, but when I knew her she was a raddled old woman, covering her wrinkles with paint and her pate with a brown wig. Her mouth was a red gash and from it, when she saw me, issued a stream of abuse. How could I, she complained, pointing to my white gloves, show so little respect to the memory of a great Queen? What a carefree world we must have lived in, that etiquette even in such small matters could assume so much importance!

My father had an apartment on the Avenue des Champs

Élysées, where I frequently visited him, and together we raced at Longchamps and at the more intimate meetings of St. Cloud and Maisons-Lafitte, which combine the pleasures of the country with those of sport. He was in the initial stage of a successful racing career which culminated in his owning the finest stable in France, a position he maintained for many years. He looked so young no one could have taken him for my father, and on one occasion when we were, owing to my grandmother's death, lunching in a private room at Voisin's, Marlborough was refused admission by a discreet *maître d'hôtel*. In those days, not so long past, mourning required that one eat in private; had one been seen in a restaurant it would have been considered bad taste. What would then have been thought of the widows who now with a graceful gesture throw back their veils as they follow their husband's coffin down the aisle?

How gay were those years at the turn of the century when in Paris there gathered a cosmopolitan society come from Rome, Berlin, St. Petersburg, Vienna and London, with the sole object of spending money and finding amusement! There were parties every night, and the days were crowded with sightseeing, racing and shopping.

It was then I met the artist Paul Helleu, who has made so many gracefully alluring etchings of American women. He asked me to sit for him, which I did until I discovered he was doing a thriving trade on the side with the numerous pastels, etchings and drawings he refused to let me pay for. Helleu was a nervous, sensitive man with a capacity for the intense suffering that artistic temperaments are prone to. He thought himself something of a Don Juan, and with his black beard, his mobile lips and sad eyes he had the requisite looks, but he was too sensitive for the role. Seeing his tall, thin, wiry frame cramped and bent over a dry-point, one realised that he would be more at ease on the deck of the yacht he loved to sail. He had wanted to be a sailor almost as fiercely as to be an artist, and at the end of his life spent most of his days on a chair in the Avenue du Bois, his melancholy eyes eager for the sight of the beauty he could not live without.

It was through Helleu that I met Boldini, who was in every respect so different from him but for whose talent he had the highest regard. Boldini was short and squat and square. Sem's caricature in which he looks like an elderly Silenus gives an indication of his moral as well as of his physical nature. Helleu took me to his studio and Boldini expressed the wish to paint me. Such a compliment could not be easily refused and I agreed to sit for him provided his behaviour remained exemplary, for he had a salacious reputation with women. In the sittings that followed it was difficult for him to restrain the sallies that his bohemian nature inspired. When the temptation became too strong he would look at me with a humorous smile and, wagging his monstrous head, ejaculate, *"Ah, la Divina, la Divina!"* As the portrait was a good likeness we decided to acquire it and to have the canvas enlarged to include my younger son, so that it might hang in a space allotted for it in the dining-room at Sunderland House. Boldini came to London to finish it. He had difficulty in getting my left arm on which my weight rests in the proper position, and at one time I resembled a Hindu goddess, with no less than three arms protruding at different angles. The portrait is considered one of his best, and now is in the possession of the Metropolitan Museum.

I often saw Helleu, Boldini and the caricaturist Sem, but the caricature Sem did of me dining in a café with the three of them was not founded on fact. Their conversation was witty, often caustic, and they were no respecters of persons. In the midst of the Dreyfus case Sem published a brilliant but cruel caricature of the Baron and Baroness de Rothschild walking on the beach at Deauville shunned by the crowd of elegants, while even the tide was leaving them high and dry.

On one of my visits to Paris I was delighted to find my cousin Adele Sloane, then married to James A. Burden. Her sympathy, humour and understanding had always made her my favourite cousin and, lost as I was among foreign in-laws, it was pleasant to re-live childish scenes and to resume family ties. The accident of one's birth has always appeared to me no adequate reason for personal pride; though it is pleasant to realise that cause for shame in one's forebears is non-existent, still the achievements of others lend one no special glory. Nevertheless, to search for the facts, fortuitous or otherwise, that confer distinction on one's name is interesting, and Adele and I, while indulging in this pursuit, brought to light the feud that had caused a rift between our grandfather and his sisters. It appeared that our great-grandfather, the Commodore, had left the major part of his considerable fortune to my grandfather, each of his daughters receiving

legacies that, as I remarked to Adele, would have been considered
colossal as well as unnecessary in England. However, the Commodore's daughters, having already in the mid-nineteenth century acquired a decidedly American conception of women's
rights, thought otherwise. Visiting their rancour on their more
fortunate brother, they became estranged from him, and so formidable was their reputation that not one of his progeny had
ventured a reconciliation.

A child of one of these daughters, who strongly resembled
the Commodore, was married to Mr Meredith Howland and
lived in Paris. She was a widow—very handsome—very arrogant
—very headstrong. She had, I was told, a circle of distinguished
friends and was herself considered *une femme très distinguée.*
We wondered, Adele and I, what she was like, for since neither
of us had known our great-grandfather, we felt a natural
curiosity about this lady. "Let's go and see her," I suggested,
and with one of those unpremeditated acts young people indulge
in we told the chauffeur to drive to her apartment. A dignified
maître d'hôtel opened the door. He seemed surprised to see two
young and elegant women instead of Mrs. Howland's usual old
beaux. She had three with whom she played bridge daily.
Raising his eyebrows and showing us into a salon he said, "And
who am I to announce?" "Tell Mrs. Howland her great-nieces,
Mrs. James Burden and the Duchess of Marlborough, have
called to see her." We waited a long time, but the salon was
beautifully furnished and we found much to admire. Suddenly
the double doors were thrown open by the butler and in its
portal stood our great-aunt. She was immensely tall and straight
in spite of her fourscore years. Her iron-grey hair was piled in
curls on her proud head. She had on a lovely silk dress, a fichu
of lawn crossed over her breast. "And to what do I owe this
pleasure?" she said, fixing her large eyes upon us. For a moment
Adele and I felt like intruders, but recovering our composure
we managed to state the reasons that had brought us, adding
the flattering comments that our aunts who lived in Paris had
made. We were happy to see her relax and become gracious
and charming. As we left, the beaux trooped up the stairs, and I
recognised three of the older members of the French Jockey Club
known for their wit and gallantry.

This same cousin Adele, some years after the death of James
Burden, married the Honourable Richard Tobin, for long our

distinguished and popular Minister at The Hague. I was then married to Jacques and when she told me of her intended marriage I was overjoyed, realising that with her literary and artistic tastes she would find an ideal companion in such a cultured and charming man. He is indeed in every sense an example of the perfect diplomat who, with flair and tact, knows how to skirt an almost unavoidable pitfall. A voracious reader, he ranges through the centuries, from which he culls romances and episodes that please him, and when he speaks of them one experiences the delight of an intimate acquaintance with characters long since dead. No wonder, I thought, when I first succumbed to the charm of his wittily told tales, that Queen Mary should have said, "That is the type of American I like to have as a neighbour at a dinner-party!" Many others less exalted have thought the same.

On another visit to Paris I was tempted to consult a fortune teller who blended science and psychic phenomena to a strangely convincing degree. Ledot lived on the top floor of one of those old houses on the left bank of the Seine and one had to toil up endless flights to reach him. I was impressed when I saw him, for he seemed almost from another world, so frail, ethereal, did he appear. But when he summoned me to sit opposite him and when his eyes looked into mine I felt an emanation of surprising strength. It seemed as if time were standing still, or rather as if time no longer existed, and that past, present and future were one. He told me that misfortune threatened me; he prophesied that for many years I should be thrown on my own resources but that eventually I would reach happiness. I was taken to see him by Sir Edgar Vincent, whose own past Ledot had correctly interpreted, also prophesying an important and successful future for him.

Sir Edgar Vincent, when first I knew him, was a strikingly handsome man. His presence carried with it a suggestion of larger than life. With the head of a Greek statue he had the beard, the wide eyes and fine forehead of the type. An amateur of the arts, a great reader, a sardonic and at times brilliant talker, he combined all the attributes needed for social success. His mind was logical, his views definite, his wit pointed—he had, I thought, the balanced judgment we associate with the Greeks —and was in fact the author of a modern Greek grammar.

The picturesque *sans gêne* of the artist appealed to him—in

the country his collar was always open, his huge flannel trousers
were perpetually being tucked into a belt, his tousled hair stood
on end in ruffled curls. After a particularly gruelling tennis
match he would wind a scarf around his throat and throw a
sweater about his shoulders, and someone would rush at him
with a big white coat and a towel or two. At such moments
there was something about him irresistibly challenging. He was
like a large St. Bernard that puppies delight to badger.

With his love of beauty it was not surprising that he should
have married the most beautiful woman of her day, and if their
union had been childless it had been productive in many other
ways. They were outstanding figures in the social world—invariably to be pointed out—Lady Helen for her beauty, Sir Edgar
for that indescribable quality that attracts others. Much simpler
and kinder than his hard and polished surface indicated, he
radiated vitality—the temperature of his environment was invariably ten degrees higher than anyone else's. He had made
his considerable fortune while still young, and was busy spending it on works of art and good living. They had a beautiful
home at Esher Place, a short drive from London. Built on a hill
with England's park-like countryside to view, it had a short golf
course, a perfect grass tennis court, and in the house a real tennis
court, where Sir Edgar, in spite of increasing corpulence, challenged younger and better players.

Week-ends there were invariably busy and gay. The set known
as 'The Souls' predominated, with the Marquis de Soveral
and Count Mensdorff as the foreign element. The Souls were a
select group in which a high degree of intelligence was to be
found happily allied to aristocratic birth. Their intellectual
tastes, their æsthetic manner and their exclusive aura tended to
render them ridiculous to those whose feet were firmly planted
in the prosaic walks of life, and also proved a source of irritation
to others who were not admitted to their circle. It was at a big
dinner given by their friends in honour of Lord and Lady
Curzon of Kedleston on his appointment as Viceroy of India in
1898 that I first floated on to their Olympian heights. In a
photograph I possess I see myself with a sad and pensive air
sitting next to the hero of the evening. Looking at the assembled
company, I think there is some justification for the name of
Souls, since many have since become immortal. There are
present two future Prime Ministers—Asquith and Balfour—

John Morley, the future Lord Haldane, Minister for War, and countless other Cabinet ministers. It is a brilliant company assembled to do homage to one of their own. I felt even then the prevalent spirit of patriotic dedication. It could be sensed in their optimism and in that joyous fraternity bred in public schools and universities which echoed in their speeches. At Esher there was usually a sprinkling of rising young men or lovely women, so to speak, on trial. Sometimes they became initiates—more often they disappeared.

In 1914 Sir Edgar was made Lord D'Abernon, and after the war he went to Germany as Ambassador. His views eventually became so pro-German that our friendship nearly ended. On one occasion, after a particularly acrimonious passage of arms over the relative merits of French and German partisanship, driven to unsuspected bitterness I exclaimed, "I hear the Germans so appreciate your policy that they are taking the nails out of Hindenburg's statue to put them into one for you." He shook himself rather as a dog would have done, and I felt that I had gone too far, for strangely he made no answer.

It was through Sir Edgar that I got to know the rising generation of painters. I always felt that he wanted to use me as an experiment before trusting his beautiful wife to their brushes. It was in this way that McEvoy came to do his three portraits of me—of which, however, I kept only one.

My visits to Paris were rare, alas, for I loved the lovely lights and shadows of its sun-flected scenes. The warm humanity of French lives, so simple and gay, appealed to me. There was no false shame in their frank acceptance of life's joys. Lovers strolled arm-in-arm, mothers held babies to their swelling breasts, and as one passed one shared their happiness. When speeding homewards over the golden wheatfields to the white town of Calais I invariably felt sad at leaving a people whose civilisation I believed had truly assessed the values of life.

Returning to Blenheim I would become once more engulfed in the whirlpool of political life. Among the Members of Parliament who were friends of Winston and who often met at Blenheim in the early 1900s were Ian Malcolm, who later became the secretary of Lord Balfour, to whom after his death he wrote a tribute addressed "To one fearless—resolved and negligently great"; F. E. Smith, who became the Earl of Birkenhead and Lord Chancellor; Lord Hugh Cecil; and Lord Eustace Percy.

These young and able back-benchers were by no means satisfied
to remain such, but the Conservative party was then rich in
middle-aged men distinguished for the services they had
rendered and under-secretaryships were hard come by.
Although a Conservative by tradition, Winston was, with his
cousin Ivor Guest and other young rebels who later joined the
Liberal party, at that time fanning insurrection against the
reactionary elements of Conservatism. Marlborough's affection
for these his favourite cousins was in no wise affected by their
political views, which were freely discussed around our dinner-
table, at which we often lingered until midnight, carried away
by Winston's eloquence and by the equally brilliant and sophisticated defence of Conservatism offered by Hugh Cecil.

These were indeed stimulating guests, but we were not always
so privileged and there were many days given over to the entertainment of visitors who were simply glorified tourists. From
Windsor, royal guests could easily come the forty miles in a
special train, and, after the German Emperor, the King of
Portugal spent a day with us. King Carlos was a rotund little
man who in spite of the preternatural dignity he assumed did
not suggest kingship. I remember his telling me that among
royal personages he was the least likely to be murdered because
he was an admirable pistol shot and always carried a weapon he
prided himself on producing with lightning rapidity. Nevertheless he was assassinated a few years later, in 1908, together with
the Prince Royal. The Queen and her younger son, who were in
the same carriage, miraculously escaped. After his visit to Blenheim, his Minister to the Court of St. James's, the Marquis de
Soveral, brought me two royal photographs, one with a diamond
crown on its frame as a mark of special favour.

How different from the red carpet and protocol of the usual
royal visits was the impromptu appearance of the Crown Prince
and Princess of Roumania. It was Tourist Day and I had taken
refuge near the Indian tent, where I was reading under the
cedars when the Groom of the Chambers found me. "I thought
Your Grace should know," he informed me, "that the Crown
Prince and Princess of Roumania accompanied by Mr. Waldorf
Astor are touring the Palace." 'Oh bother,' I thought, 'it is now
one o'clock and they will want luncheon, and there is only the
light meal prepared for Marlborough and myself.' Resigned but
flustered, I hurriedly ordered a more ample repast and went to

find my uninvited guests. They were in fits of laughter, for the housekeeper, unaware of their identity, was describing the royal personages in the photographs which adorned the tables. The Crown Princess, later to become Queen Marie, was, as everyone knows, a very beautiful woman. Dazzlingly fair, with lovely features, the bluest of eyes and a luscious figure, she was at that time at her zenith. Remembering that she was Queen Victoria's granddaughter, I was not prepared for the disconcerting bohemianism she affected; nor did her evident desire to charm successfully replace the dignity one expected. Accustomed to the restraint of the English royal family, I thought her eagerness indiscreet, and was conscious of a theatricality usually associated with a prima donna rather than with a bona-fide princess. It seemed to me that she overacted the part. That I did her an injustice I later discovered on reading her letter to a young American who succumbed to her beauty but whom, it is rumoured, she never met, and whose identity is undisclosed. After her death her letters to him were published. In one, quoted by Hector Bolitho in *A Biographer's Notebook*, she writes:

> Especially I am grateful that you should sense that nothing in me was acting. . . . The stage was always set. I was always the one who had to appear, who was expected, awaited. Why disappoint them when I came? Why not my most radiant smile, my prettiest dress, my most becoming hat? Why not a gesture of appreciation towards the eager Mother showing off her child; why not a kind word to the old Granny who was clapping hands in excitement; why not a helpful word to a man with one leg; a look of appreciation for a young girl's new Spring gown? There was no acting in all this, only a real desire to spread joy around me, good understanding and a happy atmosphere of good will. . . . My so-called acting was in fact unselfishness, because one is no more self-conscious when one thinks of others instead of oneself. Besides, I also had this feeling: the crowds are waiting for you in sunshine or rain. . . . Then do your best, do not disappoint them; look as well as you can, let it be worth while having you as Princess, as Queen.

The Crown Prince, on the other hand, was a most unprepossessing person. He was ugly, and his ears protruded at an

E

extraordinary angle. Waldorf Astor, who accompanied them, was my childhood friend. With his curly hair and flashing smile, he was as opposite to the Crown Prince as an Adonis.

Luncheon was served at a small table in the bow window of the little dining-room, where Marlborough joined us half an hour late, as was his habit. I have always disliked hospitality of the pot-luck variety, but on this occasion I could not be held responsible for the simple fare. It was in any case better than the sandwiches which they had brought with them.

But to return to less impromptu visits—indeed one might say to imposed visits—the German Emperor, wishing his son to see something of English life, sent us the Crown Prince accompanied by Count Eulenburg and his tutor, Kurt von Prittwitz. Little did the Emperor suspect that his son would spend his visit in the company of a beautiful and alluring American girl. We had not invited a party; there were at Blenheim only a few friends who usually spent the late summer with us, and the German Ambassador, Count Metternich. I still feel a certain sympathy for him when I think of the harrowing week he spent anxiously preening a stiff neck in vain endeavour to follow a flirtation his Prince was happily engaged in pursuing. It was useless to remonstrate with the mischievous lady whose vanity was at stake. But, at all events, nothing came of the flirtation, so that the result was different from the case of another American who was later to marry an English King.

The Crown Prince was tall and slight, and gave one an impression of shyness and indecision. Very fair, with prominent blue eyes, and a silly expression that accentuated the degeneracy of his appearance, he nevertheless had charming manners and took infinite pains to please. Only a few years my junior, he seemed to me still a collegian when he told me how much he disliked the thought of succeeding the Emperor, whom he greatly admired, and modestly disclaimed any capacity for continuing the tradition the Hohenzollerns had established as Kings of Prussia and German Emperors.

Signing the visitor's book on his last day, our royal guest gratuitously added, "I have been very comfortable here!" He then expressed the wish to drive our coach to Oxford station, where he was to entrain for London. Count Metternich, who was afflicted with a nervous twitch, shook his head more vehemently than ever, protesting that H.I.H. knew nothing

Mrs. Vanderbilt with her three children, William, Harold and Consuelo

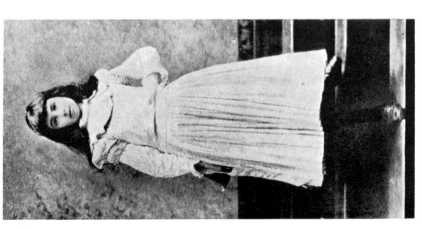

About ten years old (*Brown Brothers*)

At sixteen

At the age of five

EARLY PICTURES
OF CONSUELO VANDERBILT

Mrs. William K. Vanderbilt, in the costume she wore at her famous fancy dress ball in 1883

William K. Vanderbilt in 1900

CONSUELO VANDERBILT'S PARENTS

The Vanderbilt houses on Fifth Avenue, opposite the present site of St. Patrick's Cathedra
Left to right: first, home of W. H. Vanderbilt, the author's grandfather; second, the house
built for his two daughters; third, home of the W. K. Vanderbilts, the author's paren
Beyond are St. Thomas Church and the Fifth Avenue Presbyterian Church (*Brown Bros., N.*

The entrance to Marble House, the Newport, R.I., home of the W. K. Vanderbilts

House party at Blenheim during the visit of the Prince and Princess of Wales in the autumn of 1896; picture taken at high lodge, Blenheim Park. Left to right: back row, Earl of Gosford, Lady Emily Kingscote, Hon. Sidney Greville, Mr. George Nathaniel Curzon, General Ellis, Countess of Gosford, Mr. A. J. Balfour, Mrs. William Grenfell, Sir Samuel Scott, Marquess of Londonderry, Lady Helen Stewart, Lady Lilian Spencer-Churchill, Mr. William Grenfell, Prince Charles of Denmark, Viscount Curzon; middle row, Earl of Chesterfield, Lady Randolph Churchill, the Duchess of Marlborough, the Princess of Wales, Mr. H. Chaplin, the Prince of Wales, Mrs. George Nathaniel Curzon, Marchioness of Londonderry, Princess Victoria, Princess Charles of Denmark; front row, Lady Sophie Scott, Duke of Marlborough, Viscountess Curzon (*Country Life*)

THE DUCHESS OF MARLBOROUGH

The Duchess of Marlborough as canopy bearer to Queen Alexandra at the coronation of King Edward VII in 1902 (*Photograph by Lafayette*)

The Duchess of Marlborough in 1901

Winston Churchill with the author at Blenheim in 1901

The Duchess's bedroom at Blenheim (*Country Life*)

The Room in which Winston Churchill was born (*Woman's Journal*)

The Salon at Blenheim (*R. A. Photos*)

The Duke of Marlborough as a young man (*Brown Bros., N.Y.*)

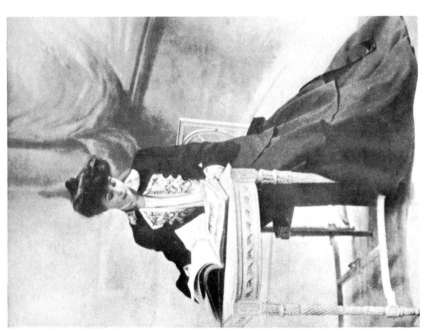

The author in 1904

With her son Ivor, painted by Boldini, 1905 (*Metropolitan Museum, N.Y.*)

A royal shooting party at Elveden, country seat of Viscount Iveagh, 1912. Left to right: back row, Lord Acheson, Sir Charles Frederick, Major Clive Wigram, Lady Cooper, Lord Valletort, Mrs. E. Guinness, Mr. Rupert Guinness, Lord Iveagh, Mr. E. Guinness, Hon. H. Stonor, Sir Derek Keppel and Marquis de Soveral; front row, Lady Gwendolen Guinness, Lady Iveagh, Duchess of Marlborough, Lady Linlithgow, H. M. King George V, Lady Valletort, Countess Hochberg, Lady Acheson and Count Mensdorff

Colonel Jacques Balsan during World War I (*Photograph by G. L. Manuel Freres*)

The Château at Saint Georges-Motel, Normandy, summer home of the Balsans from 1930 to 1940

Consuelo and Jacques Balsan on the terrace of Saint Georges-Motel

Consuelo Vanderbilt Balsan in 1942 (*Photograph by George Hoyningen-Huene*)

about driving four horses and that there would be an accident. 'Nevertheless,' I reflected, 'he has been sent here to study English country life, and although it is not usual to drive about the country in a coach-and-four, if he wants to do so I suppose he must.' Resigned, I climbed to the box seat beside him, primed to seize the reins in an emergency, though I had never driven more than two horses in my life. As our American guest sat behind us between Metternich and Marlborough, the Prince spent more time gazing back at her than at the road and we had several close shaves. The groom, with repeated blasts of the horn, did his best to clear the way of vehicular traffic, and English sportsmanship considerably abetted our safe arrival at the station. I heaved a sigh of relief as the train bore our guest away, his silly face protruding from the window to catch a forlorn and parting glimpse of the lady he was leaving.

A week later a letter from the Emperor's chamberlain informed me of His Majesty's indignation at the fact that the young American had accepted from the Crown Prince a ring which had been given him by his mother on the occasion of his first communion; he requested me to order her to return the ring at once. So ended a foolish and completely futile conquest.

The incident, however, was not forgotten by the Emperor, nor was he taking any chances of its renewal. When I went to Berlin with the lady in question some months later, we were no sooner settled in our hotel than an Imperial aide-de-camp was announced. He informed us politely but firmly that the Emperor had deputed him to show us the sights of the city, "and that," with a click of the heels, "I am at your command". We were, alas, to discover that we were at his command, for he never left us. His evident boredom at our raptures over the Palace at Sans Souci, his preference for the *Beergarten*, his stilted conversation and his Prussian officer mentality spoiled our sightseeing. I can see him now, uncomfortably seated on the *strapontin* of our *fiacre*, sadly reflecting on the hours he was wasting with us. Unaccustomed as we were to so little success, for we were both young and pretty, we consoled our vanity by remarking that the Emperor had wisely chosen a man impervious to woman's charm. No chances of our seeing the Crown Prince were taken; he had been banished from Berlin during our entire stay.

The day we shed our escort and entrained for Dresden stood out as a day of deliverance and we were in high spirits. Our talks, so long interrupted, were taken up with renewed vigour; life, art and philosophy were discussed with youthful enthusiasm. The beautiful city of Dresden, its opera and picture galleries were a joy. I gave myself to art with the *élan* and concentration of my twenty-four years and spent hours on a camp stool writing descriptions of favourite pictures while suspicious attendants lurked around, doubtful of my intentions. In the evenings we sat entranced at the opera and on sunny afternoons we took the little steamer that chugged down the Elbe, delighting in the scenes of rural life along the river-banks. Germany would have been pleasant had it not been for the Germans. I disliked them intensely. In the streets they stared offensively, in queues I was invariably pinched and, hemmed into a train compartment, we were embarrassed by officers who did not hesitate to tell indecent stories that they realised we understood by the blushes that reddened our cheeks.

I looked forward to returning home to my children. Aged four and three, they had developed into definite personalities—Blandford, audacious and wilful, for ever rebelling against authority; Ivor, gentle and sensitive, already displaying a studious trend. Indeed, it is Blandford who can claim credit for the only time I ever saw my mother at a loss. I had left him and Ivor sitting in the barouche with her while I went into Goode's in South Audley Street to choose some china. I was absent only a few minutes, but when I came out I saw a small crowd and my mother, for once, nonplussed. My eldest son was happily and busily engaged in throwing my card-case, my pencil and various other gew-gaws into the street, where a harried footman in red knee-breeches, tall hat and powdered hair, who should have been the picture of dignity, was running to collect them from under buses and pedestrians. As I reached the carriage I heard Blandford singing "Gentle Jesus meek and mild loves this little child", greatly to the amusement of the assembled company.

Besides Nanny and her staff, the children had a French governess whose life was enlivened by incidents I believed were often provoked by Nanny, to whom rebellion against Mademoiselle's authority was welcome. Mademoiselle had rooms at the end of a long and solitary passage to which one gained access by a single door. One day on which the key had been left on the outer side it was mysteriously turned in the lock and hidden. It was some time before Mademoiselle's screams from the window were heard below, and much later that the lock was removed and the door opened. It did not take me long to spot the delinquent. The punishment to administer was a greater problem. Blandford, whenever spanked, reflected, as I let him go, "You have hurt your hand much more than you did me," so that a variety of deprivations had to be found, which in turn he said he did not mind. Racking my brain for an ethical approach to this child of four, I spoke of the omnipresence of God and was very much startled when, pointing to a large easy-chair, he asked me, "Is He in that chair?" An appeal to his affection was, I found, the easier way. I had definite ideas concerning discipline, but had difficulty in overcoming Marlborough's stubborn opposition to any form of punishment. Claiming that he had been bullied by his father, he refused to exert any control, and punishments became for me a doubly painful duty in view of his critical disapproval. Never a strict disciplinarian, for a sense of humour and the love I bore my children rendered punishments hateful to me, I nevertheless believed that a certain standard of behaviour had to be maintained. That my children recognised this obligation our tender and loving relationship testified. Later, when a tutor replaced Mademoiselle, their training became easier since he had a greater authority. A devout priest, a man of high integrity, his influence proved invaluable during the difficult years when I shared my children with their father after our separation.

Looking back on the last years of the Victorian era, I see a pageant of festive scenes. But pomp and ceremony were becoming tedious to one who, as my husband complained, had not a trace of snobbishness. The realities of life seemed far removed from the palatial splendour in which we moved and it was becoming excessively boring to walk on an endlessly spread red carpet. Even now I can evoke the linkman in his drab and faded suit as he opened the carriage door and with a sweep of a battered top hat bowed me to that red carpet. I remember a dinner in honour of the Prince and Princess of Wales at which I wore a diamond crescent instead of the prescribed tiara. The Prince with a severe glance at my crescent observed, "The Princess has taken the trouble to wear a tiara. Why have you

not done so?" Luckily I could truthfully answer that I had been
delayed by some charitable function in the country and that I
had found the bank in which I kept my tiara closed on my
arrival in London. But such an incident illustrates the over-
importance attached to the fastidious observance of ritual.

There were more intimate dinners where a diamond crescent
could be worn without rebuke, since they were not graced by
the Princess's presence. These were given by what was known
as "the Prince of Wales's Set", a small cosmopolitan coterie in
which for a while we were included. Lady Paget and Mrs.
Cavendish-Bentinck vied with one another in providing rare
wines and delicacies, but the list of those invited brought no
surprises and Monsieur de Soveral was an outstanding, if somewhat constant, guest. While the Prince enjoyed his game of
bridge with Mrs. George Keppel, the general company awaited
his good pleasure for permission to retire. The Honourable
George Keppel was one of those tall and handsome Englishmen
who, immaculately dressed, proclaim the perfect gentleman, and
in bringing his wife into the somewhat cloistered family circle
of the Earl of Albemarle had introduced a note of gaiety and
Gallic bonhomie that previously had been lacking. Alice Keppel
was handsome and of genial and easy approach; nevertheless
she knew how to chose her friends with shrewd appraisal. Even
her enemies, and they were few, she treated kindly, which, considering the influence she wielded with the Prince, indicated a
generous nature. She invariably knew the choicest scandal, the
price of stocks, the latest political move; no one could better
amuse the Prince during the tedium of the long dinners etiquette
decreed. How intolerably boring they were, with everyone else
twice my age and the few Court officials who attended them
chosen for their discretion rather than for their brilliance. Little
by little we found excuses for absenting ourselves and the last
link was severed when Marlborough gave up racing, an interest
the Prince had stimulated by making him buy a horse named
Barabbas, trained by Marsh, the Prince's trainer. I was thankful
when I no longer had to attend the races at Newmarket and
those dinners in London.

On Queen Victoria's death there came with the Edwardian
era a greater freedom, but it was accompanied by a greater circumspection than had been expected by those who had known
the King as Prince of Wales. The red carpet was still there,

although the linkman's manner grew bolder and he was heard to murmur, "Make way for the beautiful Duchess"—causing one to wonder whether a new Restoration had dawned. Americans then became popular at Court. Mrs. Keppel had many among her intimates. Financiers such as Sir Ernest Cassel occupied niches that in the past had held statesmen such as Palmerston and Beaconsfield. The Court became cosmopolitan. Gone were the German stiffness and formality, gone the stern interpretation of a life lived purely as a duty, gone the perpetual mourning that had for so long obscured the Crown.

CHAPTER SIX

The Queen is Dead, Long Live the King!

THE Queen is dead, long live the King! The unpopular South African War is over. The Coronation of King Edward VII is to take place on June 26, 1902.

That winter we went to Russia for the great Court functions which then ushered in the Orthodox New Year. Two years later Russia was at war with Japan and these functions never regained their former splendour. My husband, who had a weakness for pageants, wished to play a fitting part in festivities renowned for their magnificence. No preparation appeared too elaborate to ensure the elegance of our appearance. Every detail had to be subjected to his exacting scrutiny. Court uniforms had to be refurbished, and in Paris I bought some lovely dresses. A diamond and turquoise dog-collar was ordered as a special *parure* to be worn with a blue satin gown. We had heard much about the fabulous furs of Russian nobles; it is true my sable coat was fine, but I had only one. To ensure an added prestige we invited the beautiful young Duchess of Sutherland to accompany us, as well as Count Albert Mensdorff, then attached to the Austro-Hungarian Embassy in London, and also Mr. Henry Milner, a friend, who had expressed the wish to join us. The usual number of valets and maids and a private detective to safeguard our jewels made an imposing retinue.

As we travelled through Russia, the strange eeriness of her white plains as seen under the pale light of the moon depressed me. In St. Petersburg, then Russia's capital, at the Hôtel de l'Europe a suite fit for foreign potentates had been reserved. The enormous high-ceilinged rooms were somewhat gaudily furnished with stiff chairs and gilded tables. A strange and stuffy smell caused me to fly to the window, but the manager explained that with the coming of winter they were sealed tight, a system of hot air providing the only ventilation. I felt imprisoned. The hotel could not compare with those of Paris and my first view of the city when driving through its streets revealed little of the Oriental splendour I had anticipated. The wide wind-swept avenues were lined with modern buildings in doubtful architectural taste; only here and there a vast palace presented a façade of some distinction. The Orthodox churches with their domes and spires, the grim fortress of St. Peter and St. Paul, were, however, distinctly Russian.

We were introduced to Russian society at parties in the British and Austrian Embassies. I remember the British Embassy, a fine house on the quay from which one overlooked the frozen River Neva. The Ambassador and Lady Scott received us with the genial kindliness they were noted for and seemed pleased to welcome English visitors, of whom there were far too few.

The Austrian Ambassador, Freiherr Alois Lexa von Aehrenthal, a typical suave and polished diplomat, also gave a dinner in our honour at which he greeted the English Duchesses by expressing his thanks for the compliment we were paying his country in wearing the Austrian national colours. It was only then that we observed that the Duchess of Sutherland's black satin and my yellow velvet did in fact represent the Austrian colours, and I realised that diplomats sometimes read more than is meant into a fortuitous circumstance. In this diplomatic world, so sensitive to social reactions, the undercurrents of the secret diplomacy then prevalent were inspired by Count Lamsdorff, Minister for Foreign Affairs in the Czar's government. He struck me as a smooth and sinister personage, an Oriental at heart. I was told that he never spoke to women, so I was flattered when he spent the evening with me.

It was not until we went to a supper-party at Countess Shouvaloff's in her great palace, with its private theatre and endless reception rooms, and were entertained by the Orloffs and Belosolsky's, that we penetrated into Russian homes. However, these families were, in fact, cosmopolitan rather than Slav. There were evenings when we drove in open sleighs to the islands on the frozen Neva and supped and danced to *tzigane* music. Russian days were short, but their nights were endless and we rarely went to bed before the early hours of morning. At the opera the ballets were Tchaikovsky's; Diaghileff had not yet revolutionised the classic dance. The *danseuse-en-tête* had been the Czar's mistress, according to tradition, and others had

E*

been assigned to the Grand Dukes as part of their amorous
education. As the intrigues and scandals of society became
familiar to us, we felt as if we had plunged into an eighteenth-
century atmosphere, so different was it from the rigid Victorian
morality of England.

We were privileged to attend three glorious Court functions.
For the first, a great ball of three thousand guests which was
given at the Winter Palace, Milly Sutherland and I donned our
finest dresses. Mine of white satin was draped in lines of classic
simplicity and had a tulle train held by a belt of real diamonds.
A tiara of the same stones lightened the dark waves of my hair
and cascades of pearls fell from my neck. I looked very young
and slight in that shimmering whiteness and my maid
delightedly exclaimed, *"Comme Madame la Duchesse est belle!"*
Thus encouraged I felt ready to face the more critical scrutiny
of my husband, who wore the Privy Councillor's uniform with
white knee-breeches and a blue coat embellished with gold lace,
the feathered hat under his arm. He smiled and said, "At least
we look distinguished," which from him was indeed a compliment.

At the Winter Palace the stairs were adorned by a magnificent
display of gold plate fixed to the walls. There were hundreds of
footmen in scarlet liveries and Cossack guards in flowing robes,
who gave an impression of barbaric splendour. In the great ballroom innumerable chandeliers threw a glittering radiance on the
handsome men and graceful women assembled there. On my
return to England I was asked by Lady Dudley whether the
Russian women were beautiful, and when I answered, "Not as
beautiful as your compatriots," I was amused by her dry retort,
"You must have been relieved!"

With the entrance of the Imperial family to the inspiring air
of the Russian anthem—the procession of Grand Dukes in
splendid uniforms, the Grand Duchesses, lovely and bejewelled,
the beautiful, remote Czarina and the Czar—the ball took on
the aspect of a fairy tale. With the first strains of a mazurka, the
Grand Duke Michael, the Czar's younger brother and heir
since the Czarevitch had not yet been born, invited me to
dance. It was a very different affair from the mazurkas I had
learned at Mr. Dodsworth's class. "Never mind," he said,
when I demurred, "I'll do the steps," and he proceeded to
cavort around me until I was reminded of the courtship of birds.

But he was young and gay and, carried away by the increasing tempo, I found myself treading the Russian measure with the best. He was killed by the Bolsheviks in 1918.

At the more select *Bal des Palmiers,* so named because of the palms around which the supper-tables were built, I had a chance to talk with the Czar. Count Mensdorff, who had been told that I was to be the Emperor's supper companion, bade me wear my prettiest dress and seemed satisfied when I appeared in blue satin with the turquoise dog-collar to match. As one entertainment had succeeded another, Milly Sutherland and I were somewhat chagrined to notice that Russian women had a *parure* of jewels to match each dress, so it was with some satisfaction that I could produce the blue necklace. The *Bal des Palmiers* was much smaller and seemed gayer and more intimate than the first Court ball. Flirting mildly with my cavaliers, I awaited the moment of my meeting with the man in whose hands lay the fate of millions.

Supper was served to the Imperial family and the Ambassadors on the daïs. The general company was seated at small tables of eight. At my right was a vacant seat which, so my escort whispered, was destined for the Czar, who, with his staff, was making a tour of the rooms. In a moment he was there and unobtrusively took his place. My first reaction was to notice the extraordinary likeness that he bore to his cousin, the Prince of Wales, later George V. He had the same kindly smile, half hidden by a beard, the same gentle blue eyes and a great simplicity of speech and manner. I was also struck by his youthful appearance, for he was only thirty-two, having come to the throne at the age of twenty-six. As he talked I began to realise the enormous difficulties he had to face. There was at that time a constant and increasing agitation for reforms that he contended could not be granted without danger. When I asked him why he hesitated to give Russia the democratic government that was so successful in England, he answered gravely, "There is nothing I would like better, but Russia is not ready for democratic government. We are two hundred years behind Europe in the development of our national political institutions. Russia is still more Asiatic than European and must therefore be governed by an autocratic government." He went on to explain that his power was absolute, but that he saw his ministers every day in separate audiences. I gathered that even a Cabinet did not exist. He

seemed fearful of any one minister's becoming too powerful—
the fear that haunts autocrats the world over. He also seemed
to fear the great millions that were Russia—their ignorance,
their superstition, their fatalism. As he sat there at my side he
struck me as pitiful; he, the Emperor of all the Russias, the Little
Father, anxious and afraid—a good man, but a weak one. He
was dominated by the Empress whose fears for the health of her
son later induced in her a state of religious exaltation and
brought her under the influence of Rasputin, whose mystic
powers often helped to cure the sufferings of the Czarevitch, a
hæmophiliac.

Supper was a lengthy affair with almost as many courses as
a dinner. There were soups, caviar and monster sturgeons, meats
and game, *pâtés* and *primeurs*, ices and fruits, all mounted on
gold and silver plate fashioned by Germain—chased and
beautiful in shape and colour.

The Emperor had been talking simply and seriously like a
man face to face with grave issues, when with what seemed to
me childish pleasure he remarked, "I know everything you have
done since your stay in Russia, for my secret police send me a
dossier on the movements of foreigners; but will you tell me
why the Duchess of Sutherland goes to see Maxim Gorky when
she knows he is in temporary exile?" I found it difficult to
explain that in England people have a right to their own
opinions even if those opinions are not shared by the Ruler of
the State. When he left me to return to the Empress he asked
for my photograph and promised me his, which I duly received.
I never saw him again, but I am firmly convinced that he was
fundamentally good; that it was his desire to make his people
happy, and that if he failed it was because he was weak and
Russia was not ready for democratic government. Surely Lenin,
Trotsky, Stalin and their ilk have proved the truth of what he
told me.

The Czar and Czarina lived quiet domestic lives. The
Emperor's uncle, the Grand Duke Vladimir, with his German-
born wife, a Princess of Mecklenburg, were the leaders of
Russian society and the head of a cabal which, like the Orléans
group at the French Court, sought to wield political power. We
were invited to dine with them, and during the evening I had
occasion to note the shrewd questions with which the Grand
Duchess Marie Pavlovna sought our impressions of her adopted

country. She had a majestic personality, but could be both gracious and charming.

After dinner the Grand Duchess showed me her jewels set out in glass cases in her dressing-room. There were endless *parures* of diamonds, emeralds, rubies and pearls, to say nothing of semi-precious stones such as turquoises, tourmalines, cat's-eyes and aquamarines. It was on the proceeds from these that she lived after her flight abroad during the Revolution, having first handed them over to an English friend, Albert Stopford, who was able to smuggle them out of the country.

The Dowager Empress received Milly Sutherland and me in her palace and talked of her sister, Queen Alexandra, with great affection. The Czar's mother was not beautiful, but she had the same innate dignity and kindness that made her sister so beloved. Her courtesy to us was favourably compared in Court circles with the Czarina's failure to give us an audience, and we realised how unpopular the latter's unsocial nature was making her.

Bad weather prevented a visit to Tsarskoe Selo, but there was an unforgettable supper in the picture galleries of the Hermitage. It was indeed a beautiful scene, looked down upon by Titians and Van Dycks of the Imperial collection. The evening had opened with a ballet in the Hermitage theatre built for the Empress Catherine. In its small and intimate circle were gathered the Imperial family with the great nobles of Russia, the Chevalier Guards, the *Corps des Pages*—Cossack officers in their picturesque uniforms and lovely women, a brilliant company. We found the places allotted to us and the curtain rose. I cannot remember the ballet, but whether by mischievous command or fortuitous chance the air *'Malbrouck s'en va-t-en guerre'** suddenly floated out and the Emperor and the audience smilingly turned to us. It was as if we were being taken into the small world which this Court represented—a world so self-sufficient, so sure of its destiny, and yet, alas, so blind to the evils without, that even in that moment of flattered elation a premonition of tragedy came to me and I thought of how Beaumarchais' *Figaro* had been acted at Marie Antoinette's command at Versailles shortly before her undoing. Such moments

---

* This air was sung by French nurses and children and is found in collections of such songs. It refers to the first Duke of Marlborough's departure for war against the French King Louis XIV.

of psychic foreboding sometimes assail me and on this occasion the feeling was enhanced by my ability to visualise the other side of the picture, for that other side was only too visible in the long cordons of hungry housewives in the decimated markets, in the beggars freezing in the streets, in the persistent clamour for representative government.

We had a more democratically staged evening when we dined with the Minister of Finance, Count Witte. He struck me as a European rather than a Slav, and amused me by saying that what Russia needed was some enterprising American magnates to open the country and its resources, "for," he added, "we have no business acumen." In illustration he mentioned that the government had at one time received an extremely favourable prospectus from certain mines and had been so impressed that a railway leading to the mines was built at great expense, also a village to house the miners; but when the mines were further exploited they were found to be so poor that the venture turned out a colossal loss. I thought at the time that he merely wanted to say something agreeable to me, knowing that I was American by birth and the great-granddaughter of what he described as a magnate. The Russo-Japanese War soon disclosed the general inefficiency of those in power.

For our visit to Moscow we required visas. To Europeans accustomed to travel untrammelled by passports, this necessity struck a sinister note suggestive of secret police and surveillance. We realised that not all strangers were welcome when we heard of what had happened to the Ephrussis, who had left Paris with us. Madame Ephrussi was a daughter of Baron Alphonse de Rothschild, the French head of that great banking family. She was a beautiful creature with a small head which, like a bird, she tilted slightly to one side, looking up with soft mischievous eyes framed in delicately pencilled brows. Her finely chiselled features, her lovely colouring and prematurely grey hair gave her the alluring look of an eighteenth-century pastel. While in Paris we had been told of the fortune she was spending on jewels and gowns for her anticipated conquest of the Russian Court, and we were surprised that during our fortnight in St. Petersburg we never set eyes on her. Years later the Czar's chamberlain, who like so many White Russians found refuge from the Revolution on the French Riviera, disclosed that he had had the disagreeable task of informing Madame Ephrussi that she could not be received at Court since her husband was a Russian Jew, a fact that had been withheld from the Ambassador in Paris and unearthed only on the arrival of the Ephrussis in the Russian capital. "I never had a more disagreeable task," Count X added feelingly, "and I thought she was going to die of hysterics."

When we arrived in Moscow, Russia enveloped us. Left behind was the cosmopolitan society of St. Petersburg which spent its winters gambling at Monte Carlo, its springs racing in Paris, its summers at "cures", impressing the whole world with its air of fabulous opulence. Moscow was Asiatic rather than European. The Kremlin behind its immense walls was Oriental. It had colour and grandeur—spires which like minarets pierced the sky, and churches which, with their gilded domes, looked like mosques.

In St. Petersburg French art and Italian architecture had inspired the rather baroque palaces built for the rich. Like Catherine the Great, her nobles had acquired pictures and furniture from abroad, and the works of famous French painters, sculptors and cabinet-makers were to be found in the best collections. But to me these palatial interiors, in which the ikon with its flame and the steaming samovar were the only distinctly Russian features, lacked the perfect taste one finds in France. One could not imagine oneself in a French house any more than one could mistake a Fabergé jewel for one set by Cartier. It was evident that the Russian genius had found expression in music and literature rather than in the plastic arts; just as the rivers of France recall a Sisley, her villages a Pissarro, Russian scenes evoked description by Turgeneff or the echoes of a well-known folk song.

The few days we spent in Moscow were busy with sightseeing. We dined with the Grand Duke Serge and his beautiful wife, the Grand Duchess Elizabeth, sister of the Czarina. As Governor of Moscow, the Grand Duke lived in the Kremlin. One of the handsomest men I have seen, he was well over six feet tall, and in his uniform a most imposing person. He had, however, a cruel and arrogant air, and in spite of his undoubted charm he suggested something evil. As he was doing the honours I thought what a magnificent Mephistopheles he would make, and the self-satisfied gleam I caught in his eye made me realise that he sensed my thought. He was bitterly hated in Russia; assassins dogged his steps and had it not been for the constant attendance of the Grand Duchess, who was greatly loved for her charity and goodness, the fatal bomb would have found him years before it finally did.

Despite the interest of our visit we left Russia with no regrets. The wastelands of its plains where every sign of life was muffled in snow chilled me and I was happy to return to the scenes of domestic contentment that the little villages and fields of England bespoke.

My thoughts turned to the imminent Coronation, for Queen Alexandra had honoured me by selecting me as one of the four duchesses who were to be her canopy bearers during the ceremony. The Duchesses of Portland, Montrose and Suther-land were the others. We were summoned to Buckingham Palace for our first rehearsal. Colonel B., a tall, distinguished officer in command of the Guards, informed us he had been deputed to drill us and confessed that our task would be difficult since the canopy was both tall and heavy. We were well matched in height, but our strength was unequal to the effort of holding the canopy taut while walking and I ventured to observe that with trains three yards in length those behind would surely step on the trains of those in front. It was decided therefore that the canopy should be carried by pages and placed over the Queen, and that then only should we take our places.

London was in a ferment of excitement. Patriotic crowds come from the outermost parts of the Empire filled the streets. Every day the arrival of a new foreign potentate increased the tension. The metropolis was gay with royal equipages in which the King and Queen, princes and maharajahs drove in state accompanied by military escorts. Never had London been so festive, so beflagged, so impressively the capital of a far-flung Empire.

There were state dinners at the Palace and every night we were bidden to a reception or a ball given by those whose rank entitled, and whose fortune permitted, the entertaining of royal personages.

Then suddenly, like a thunderbolt, came the news of the King's illness and of an emergency operation. The great tide of popular rejoicing changed overnight to one of anguished anxiety. The same cheering crowds now stood outside the Palace in woeful solicitude awaiting the hourly bulletins, discussing the ominous presage. It was said that the King would never be crowned. One heard that Sir Frederick Treves, the royal surgeon, overcome with emotion, had not been able to complete the operation and had turned to his assistant. No one knew what to believe but everyone gossiped, while foreign princes and special ambassadors departed and London once again became normal.

In due time we heard that the appendectomy had been entirely successful and that the Coronation would take place on August 9th in a shortened form, to spare the King's strength.

On the appointed day we dressed early in red velvet robes trimmed with miniver and put chocolate into our pockets, for it was said we would be five hours or more in the Abbey, including the wait before and after the ceremony and the crush of getting away. The Marlborough colours are crimson, not unlike the royal scarlet, and as we drove in our state coach from Warwick House to the Abbey we were cheered by the assembled crowds who had spent the night camping there to have a better view. When we reached the Abbey, Marlborough left me, for he was to take part in the royal procession. The long length of the Abbey stretched before me with spectators ranged in tiers on either side of the aisle. A page spread the velvet train of my robes; and with head held high and eyes straight before me, lost in the sense of solemn splendour the scene evoked, I reached my place in the transept, where, massed in scarlet, flashing with diamonds, England's peeresses sat.

It seemed hours before the trumpets announced the royal arrival. We had been riveted to hard chairs, rising occasionally as some royal personage passed to his appointed place. As the peers came to their seats on the right of the throne opposite to us they provided the laugh that always greets a dog lost in a solemn procession. There were those whose ancestral robes were much too big and long. Quite unconscious of the merriment they created, they passed, solemn and disdainful, holding their coronets and their robes tucked up under their arms. But the most hilarious moment came when the King was crowned and, as tradition decreed, the peers placed their coronets on their heads. For in some cases the coronets—made for ancestors with larger heads—slid down to the chin of the unfortunate peer, completely hiding his face behind the velvet cap with which the coronet was lined! I had taken the precaution to have a very small coronet made to fit inside my tiara, so that when the Queen was crowned I fitted it deftly to its place and watched with amusement the anguished efforts of others whose coronets were either too big or too small to stay in place.

But now the trumpets were blaring, the organ pealing and the choir singing the triumphant hosannas that greeted the King and Queen. The long procession was in sight—the Court officials with their white wands, the Church dignitaries with their magnificent vestments, the bearers of the royal insignia, among whom was Marlborough carrying the crown of King Edward on a velvet cushion, the lovely Queen, her maids-of-honour holding her train, and then the King, recovered, solemn and regal. I felt a lump in my throat and realised that I was more British than I knew.

The beauty of the service was heightened by the fine traditional liturgy, the piercing sweetness of the choristers' notes, the gorgeous vestments, the sacramental vessels of gold and precious stones, the jewels and scarlet robes of the assembled company. When the Queen left her throne to kneel before the aged Archbishop to be anointed, we rose to hold the canopy over her. From my place on her right I looked down on her bowed head, her hands meekly folded in prayer, and watched the shaking hand of the Archbishop as, from the spoon which held the sacred oil, he anointed her forehead. I held my breath as a trickle escaped and ran down her nose. With a truly royal composure she kept her hands clasped in prayer; only a look of anguish betrayed concern as her eyes met mine and seemed to ask, "Is the damage great?" I shall always remember that look of gentle resignation and then later the great peal of acclamation that rose from the assemblage as the King was crowned. It shocked my sense of fitness, for it seemed almost as if the earthly symbol of majesty had superseded the divine—but then I was not English and could not feel the same pride in the tradition of unbroken lineage the act of crowning symbolised.

That same summer of 1902 Marlborough was made a Knight of the Garter and we were invited to spend a week-end at Hatfield, the ancient seat of the Cecil family, where Queen Elizabeth had spent part of her childhood in the care of Prime Minister Cecil. There was again a Cecil as Prime Minister and the Marquess of Salisbury was no mean successor to his ancestor; indeed he seemed to me the finest type of Englishman and his family a perfect example of the best English tradition. His eldest son, Viscount Cranborne, was in the House of Commons; Lord Hugh, the Benjamin, later became Provost of Eton College; Lord Robert Cecil, in diplomacy, was to become identified with the League of Nations; Lord Edward's career lay in the Army; and Lord William was soon consecrated Bishop of Exeter. There were many amusing anecdotes concerning the latter's vagueness, and I was told that once while travelling to a Church conference he lost his railway ticket, and much perturbed apologised to the guard. "Never mind, my lord, we know you and trust you." To which the Bishop answered, "But don't you realise, my good man, that I have not the faintest idea where I am going!"

On the first night of our visit Lord Salisbury took me in to dinner and I succumbed to the charm of his courteous and polished discourse. There was indeed something very like a benediction in the ancient and serene ritual of that house to which I must unconsciously have subscribed, for he told someone that my language had a Biblical turn. With a twinkle in his eye he approached the reason for our visit—"I am, I believe," he said, "to present the Order of the Garter to the Duke, but I have not the slightest reason wherefore." Sorely tempted to reply with the old quip, "We know there is no damned merit to it," I nevertheless abstained.

With my husband embarked on a political career it seemed advisable to have a permanent establishment in London rather than to lease a different house every year. I only had to mention our wish for my father to promise its fulfilment. Unable to find a building to suit us, we acquired one of the rare real estate sites in the market. The West End of London where the "best people" lived belonged to the great landlords, the Duke of Westminster, the Lords Portman and Cadogan, whose policy was to lease their lands, sometimes for as long as ninety-nine years, but never to sell. To find a freehold, however small, was therefore an achievement. There was a chapel on the site, which in the eyes of the superstitious it was considered unlucky to demolish, but there was a wine cellar situated in the basement. The rhyme "spirits below—spirits of wine, spirits above—spirits divine" gave us hope that by abolishing the temptations in the cellar we might conciliate the spirits above; and as the chapel was demolished, neighbouring clergymen, whose congregations had been attracted by the more popular preacher of Curzon Chapel, thanked us for causing deserters to return to their folds.

Curzon Street was close to the slum known as Shepherd's Market, and we built a grey stone house sixty feet wide and one hundred deep, linking the street to the Market. It was designed in eighteenth-century style by Achille Duchêne, a French architect, better known as the landscape gardener who, with his famous father, had restored many of the ruined gardens of France to their former glories. We had not yet decided on a name for the house when, during a dinner at Marlborough House one night, the Prince of Wales with a malicious smile inquired, "What name are you giving your house—since you cannot very well call it Marlborough House?" I ventured Blandford or Sunderland House as other family names it could bear, but he was not to be denied his *bon mot* or his criticism for an ill-chosen site, and with a chuckle, referring to one of John Duke's famous battles, he asked, "Why not Malplaquet?"

When we settled in Sunderland House the first floor with its long gallery and two salons had not yet been decorated. The entrance hall with a white and red tiled floor, a small morning-room, Marlborough's sitting-room and a dining-room were decorated in the Louis XVI manner. Later, when I lived there alone and Sunderland House became mine to dispose of, I finished decorating the reception rooms on the second floor. The architect wished to place bas-reliefs at either end of the long gallery, and in a spirit of bravado, not untinged with humour, I had one made of the Great Duke and one of my great-grand-father, the Commodore, who just one hundred years later founded my family's fortune. The shocked sardonic glances of my English guests provided a certain relish as I realised what their caustic comments must be; and when, in the numerous crusades undertaken on behalf of social reforms, I stood on the platform with my back to John Duke and my eyes on the Commodore, I wondered which of the two would most radically have disapproved of my speeches.

When Marlborough became Under-Secretary for the Colonies and a member of the Government, my duties as hostess included entertaining guests from overseas. Long lists of important officials and guests had to be memorised, for Colonials were proverbially touchy and had Mr. Smith from New Zealand been presented to Lady Snooks as coming from Australia, or vice versa, the result would have been disastrous. These receptions were by no means a pleasure, and I turned to debates in the House of

Commons with interest and relief. Occasionally, I had the privilege of a seat in the Speaker's Gallery. The debates known as full-dress were very particular occasions. One knew that one would hear the chief protagonist of whatever legislation was to be discussed and that Parliament's most eloquent orators would take part in the debate. The Liberal party's espousal of Home Rule had brought that furiously contested measure again to the fore. At that time Irish Nationalist members were a formidable and strong minority in the House of Commons. John Redmond was then leader, with Timothy Healy and John Dillon as able lieutenants. They never lost an occasion to harass the Conservative Government in their tactics to secure Home Rule. Mr. Balfour, as leader of the Government in the Commons, was ably seconded in the Home Rule debates by Sir Edward Carson. He was the member for Dublin University and also chief advocate for the continued union of Ireland with England. How well I remember those exciting debates and the roars of anger emitted by the Home Rulers whenever Sir Edward touched a vulnerable spot. He was a brilliant and practised counsel at the Bar and never rushed his kill. On the contrary, he seemed to play with his opponents as he restated their case and freed it from bias; then with ruthless thrusts and bitter scorn he would castigate the Home Rulers as traitors to England and to Ireland as well, since they spoke for but a part of that distraught land. There were times when, sitting in the Speaker's Gallery between Lady Londonderry, whose sympathies were for Ulster, and Margot Asquith, an ardent Home Ruler, I found it difficult to keep an impassive neutrality. It was a relief when Mrs. Lowther, the Speaker's wife, imposed the silence it was the rule to observe.

Lady C., as Lady Londonderry was still called by those who had known her as Lady Castlereagh, should have been born in the eighteenth century. Descended from England's first Earl, impressed by her splendid lineage, she made great play of those rights which the governing classes still possessed, and sought to impress others with the importance of her position. Intelligent and ambitious, she exploited her husband's position in the Conservative party in order to influence the trend of politics. Pre-eminently the Egeria of the Unionist Cause, she made of Londonderry House the rallying point of all Conservatism. It was a fine mansion with suites of drawing-rooms overlooking Hyde Park. As is the fashion in English homes, flowers were massed on every table, together with an array of autographed photographs. Political receptions were numerous and so crowded that when Lord and Lady Londonderry and the Prime Minister received, the staircase which led up to the handsome picture gallery had to be supported by scaffolding, so great was the weight of the crowds. This scaffolding and the revolting tripods placed about for the stubs of cigarettes and cigars spoiled for me the elegance of the scene. I imagined that the great Lord Castlereagh, handsome and stately in his Garter robes in Lawrence's portrait, looked down from the walls with equal disfavour on such practical concessions to our times.

Some years later, after my separation, I was better pleased to wait upon my hostess alone in those friendly rooms while she dispensed tea and counsel. She knew that my life was a lonely one and her shrewd worldly wisdom proved a wholesome antidote to any sentimental tendencies on my part. At times her frank materialism shocked me, for, to her, social and political power were all that mattered.

Her friendly attempt to reconcile me with my husband proved abortive, but on one occasion we both attended a dinner she gave in honour of King Edward and Queen Alexandra. Since separated couples were not received at Court, this tacitly created an exception in our favour. It was at this dinner that the following incident so typical of a past century occurred. The ladies had moved up to the drawing-rooms, leaving the men below. Coffee was about to be served when Lady Londonderry suddenly seized the royal cup from her astonished butler and with a sweeping curtsy presented it to the Queen. Startled as we all were by this curious departure from precedent, we with difficulty suppressed our amusement; but quite unperturbed our hostess explained that it was a tradition in her family thus personally to serve one's sovereign.

Lord Londonderry was as ardent a champion of the prerogatives of birth and position as his wife, and I remember a dinner at the German Embassy when I managed to avert what might have become a diplomatic incident. In the controversy over Home Rule which reached its heights in the years preceding World War I, Lord Londonderry, who was a Unionist in the family tradition, since his ancestor, Lord Castlereagh, had brought about the Union, bitterly opposed the Prime Minister's policy of Home Rule. When Prince and Princess Lichnowsky, who were friends of mine, gave their first official dinner at the German Embassy, in honour of King George and Queen Mary, I was among those invited, and in the circle awaiting Their Majesties I found Lord and Lady Londonderry. Suddenly the doors opened and the Prime Minister and Mrs. Asquith were announced. With a snort of indignation Lord Londonderry turned to me, his face crimson with rage, and announced that he was leaving, since the Ambassador had insulted him in asking him to meet Mr. Asquith. It was with the greatest difficulty that I made him realise that at a dinner given in honour of the King a foreign Ambassador would have to invite the Prime Minister, that he himself should have been aware of this and that more-over he could not expect a foreigner to realise how deeply he felt the partition of Ireland. Thus was the scandal of his leaving prevented at a time when relations between Germany and England were already strained. Such incidents, revealing the idiosyncrasies of friends I loved, can in no wise detract from their sterling qualities, in which courage, loyalty and kindness predominated. I have related them because they seemed to portray the modes and manners of a vanished past. They lived in another era, and if their conceits now awaken a smile let us remember all they gave to their country in public-spirited service.

The year following the Coronation we were invited by Lord Curzon, the Viceroy of India, to be his guests at the Durbar which was to be held in celebration of King Edward's accession. Although I had known Lord and Lady Curzon only for two short years before he was, at the age of forty, appointed to this exalted position, they had always evinced a warm friendship for me which I particulaily cherished. Lord Curzon's wife, Mary Leiter, was a compatriot of mine, and a dazzling beauty. I thought that she had shed her American characteristics more completely than I was to find myself able to do. Wholly absorbed in her husband's career, she had subordinated her personality to his to a degree I would have considered beyond an American woman's power of self-abnegation. I was moved by the great love they bore each other. Her admiration for her brilliant husband's conspicuous attainments, her strong partisanship, her sympathetic understanding of his faults, the humour with which she accepted the secondary role he assigned her, even in the domestic duties usually delegated to women, were altogether admirable. Indeed, as she sometimes confessed to me, her only reproach was that he would not allow her to take on the burdens that should by right have been hers alone, for the insistent and meticulous attention he gave to minor and prosaic chores often robbed him of the rest he owed his health. It was a weakness he never learned to cure. It stemmed from a deficient sense of proportion, perhaps originally due to his strict upbringing in the atmosphere so vividly described by his friend and secretary Harold Nicolson in his sympathetic book on Curzon:

> It is often forgotten that Curzon was nurtured in what essentially was a mid-Victorian vicarage; its floors may well have been of opus alexandrinum and its columns of alabaster; yet Kedleston was none the less a vicarage; there was more than a breath of Calvinism in the air; and Curzon's childhood was thus disciplined, narrowed, intimidated, uncomforted and cold.

It may also have had roots in the tortures he so gallantly suffered from curvature of the spine, for the hourly nag of pain breeds a nervous irritability that may well find an outlet in constant if unnecessary work. Be that as it may, even in the days of his hardest political battles he would choose the bill of fare and go over the household accounts.

In 1917, after Mary's death, he married another beautiful woman, Grace, the widow of Alfred Duggan of Buenos Aires. I well remember my amusement, visiting Hackwood for the first time after his second marriage, when Lady Curzon pointed to a neat pile of books near my bed and laughingly remarked, "George has chosen them, so you will like them. I had myself," she added, "selected the books to be placed in every visitor's room, but when George inspected them he decided that I had not correctly assessed the literary tastes of our expected guests and after sending a footman with a tray to collect the books he made a new selection."

We travelled out to India in a P. & O. liner—some sixty guests, friends of the Curzons. Among others were the Duke and Duchess of Portland, Lord and Lady Derby, Lord and Lady Crewe, Mr. and Mrs. Laurence Drummond, Lord Elcho and a host of other pleasant and agreeable people. From the moment of our arrival in Bombay, where Marlborough and I were guests of the Governor, events as glamorous and gorgeous as those narrated in the tales of *The Arabian Nights* enchanted us. His Excellency the Viceroy had surpassed even royal tradition in his desire to impress the native rulers and princes. Pomp and splendour were visual signs of the trouble he had taken to stage the pageant; but when one considers the difficulties which, in India, the provision of fresh meat, chickens, milk, butter and eggs represented, one realises the miracle of organisation such a camp for sixty guests, supplied as they were with every luxury, must have been. For the actual Durbar a special train brought us to a great camp which had been built near Delhi to accommodate the Viceroy's guests. A double row of beautiful tents lined a central avenue. We had a salon as ante-room, two bedrooms behind, and a smaller room which held a round tub. Marlborough's valet and my maid lived near-by and a native servant brought hot water for our ablutions, and breakfast hot and delicious at any hour. But there was little privacy and I remember our coolie's cry of despair one morning when, bringing an extra jug of water, he found me in my tub. I was rather perturbed by his squeal of agony until told that his punishment would have been severe had he broken in upon an Indian lady in similar straits.

The Viceroy lived in secluded grandeur. Even Their Royal Highnesses the Duke and Duchess of Connaught, who were among his guests, were never allowed to forget it was Lord Curzon and not the King's brother who represented the King-Emperor. We usually dined in state with him, and on one occasion there was a ball for which we donned our most sumptuous gowns and wore our finest jewels. Lady Curzon was a vision of beauty in a marvellous dress embroidered in a design of peacock feathers emblazoned with semi-precious stones, but I heard ominous whispers of the bad luck associated with those feathers. It was only a few years later that she died in the prime of her youth and beauty. We had been told not to dance with the native princes, since their wives were not allowed out of purdah and such intimacy might be misconstrued, but I heard complaints from the maharajahs that the Viceroy disdained them. They also resented his numerous legislative reforms, which curbed their power.

At the Military Review, Bikaner's Camel Corps with its fine discipline and the beauty of the well-groomed, perfectly appointed beasts impressed me most. The procession of native princes who came to do obeisance, fantastically gorgeous in dress and jewels, was another unforgettable sight. There was a moment of shocked surprise when one of the maharajahs, with an insolent turn, refused the obeisance he owed his Emperor. Lord Curzon paled, but with the studied diplomacy the English invariably show on such occasions he continued the ceremony, which was completed without further incident.

There was also a purdah party to which Lady Curzon summoned the European women to meet the native maharanees and princesses; men were rigorously excluded. The young women were lovely, with the pure beauty of a Persian cameo, and seemed to me like a bevy of imprisoned children or a swarm of bright butterflies who were destined never to fly. When one reflects that it was only in 1829 that suttee was abolished under Lord William Bentinck's administration, one realises how precariously their lives depended on their husbands. Further measures for their welfare were taken by Lady Dufferin in providing better medical treatment, which Lady Curzon in turn fostered and encouraged.

One of the Viceroy's aides-de-camp invited me to a falcon hunt and I was given a mount on a spirited horse. I still remember that early morning gallop on the Indian plains with the sun rising in the distance. Above my head an unhooded falcon soared in circles, waiting on her game. I watched as she climbed immense heights to get above the bird she wished to strike. It seemed remarkable that a falcon should have the power and speed to travel 150 miles an hour, and that the distance between Fontainebleau and Malta, which is not less than 1,350 miles, should have been covered by one in twenty-four hours.

I have one overpowering memory of India. It is not of the lovely rose-coloured town of Jaipur, where the Maharajah's immense pink coral palace stands seven storeys high and stretches for half a mile through the town. It is not of Benares, or of its burning ghats, or of the funeral processions with the dead carried on open litters. It is not of the corpses of babies floating down the Ganges with men, women and cows all bathing in happy proximity. It is not of the lepers who thrust their mutilated hands at us. It is not of the fortress palaces built in red sandstone or in marble, or of their high cool rooms, or of the inner courts where streams are channelled through marbled ways and arabesques of flowers. Nor is it of the Taj Mahal under the moon's silver light nor of the Queen's tomb covered with freshly strewn tuberoses.

The unforgettable memory India gave me is of the intensity of human emotion produced by mass psychology. It was on the night of the Durbar during a display of fireworks. I was taken to a high seat, if I remember rightly, in a tower of the great Mosque in Delhi. It was so still up there I knew nothing of the crowds below. But with the flash of the first rocket an immense sigh was wafted up to me, and looking down I saw a multitude so closely packed that only their dark up-raised faces framed by their brightly coloured turbans could be distinguished. As far as the eye could carry they were massed, their faces upturned in ecstasy as each new light blazed in the sky. The restraint of their pleasure, the depth and dignity of their emotion, were truly impressive. And those multi-coloured turbans framing dark faces suggested a great bed of tulips with their black hearts upturned to me.

A few days later we took our leave of our hosts and embarked on a P. & O. for Marseilles. On reaching home I was overjoyed to find my children. I had never been away from them for so long, and often in India I had longed to be with them. Christmas especially had seemed a sad time, parted from them as well as from my family in America. Blandford was now six and Ivor five, and although still in the nursery they had lessons with their French governess, with whom they also went for walks, talking French all the while. What between the governess, the head nurse and the groom with whom they rode their ponies, there seemed little time left for mother. Nevertheless they came down while we breakfasted. My mornings were always occupied with household duties and village affairs and there was also a voluminous correspondence to maintain, for in those days we wrote letters as we now talk on the telephone. The children joined us for luncheon, and if free of more serious duties I would take them for drives in my electric car, a perilous performance, with one eye on the road and another on Blandford to watch that he did not fall out. They learned to wield a cricket bat and also how to box. In the evenings, dressed in velvet suits, they came down to tea and I read to them or we played games of the Old Maid variety, for having changed into a lace tea gown I could hardly romp and run. But the best part of the day came at six when together we went to the nursery, where a bath and supper awaited them; then they said their prayers as I tucked them into bed.

During our visit to Russia the year before, I had caught a cold that had left me slightly deaf. Recently I had begun to notice that the deafness was becoming more pronounced. I was finding it difficult to hear conversations, which the English are apt to carry on in subdued voices. There are certain people who consider any tone above a whisper ill-bred, especially when addressing a more exalted person, and in spite of my repeated requests to speak louder they would drone on quite oblivious of the fact that I did not hear them. This was not only tiring but also exasperating, not to say humiliating, and was causing me a great deal of anxiety, for to be cut off from human inter-course at so early an age appeared to me catastrophic. When an English specialist advised me to learn the lip language I felt doomed. I decided to try a cure I had been told about in Vienna and set out on the long journey accompanied by my children, their two nurses and my maid.

The Austrian specalist informed me that the cure would take six weeks and did not disguise the fact that it would be painful. Social distractions were therefore welcome, and pro-vided with the letters of introduction kindly given me by Count Mensdorff I was received into the younger cosmopolitan set with utmost friendliness. Frequent visits to the opera, or to one of the numerous gay operettas Vienna was famed for, and supper at the Hotel Bristol after the performance were pleasant episodes in a gay informal life; the Vienna season with its balls and receptions had not begun. There was, however, a party at the Hofburg given by the Emperor Francis Joseph in honour of the engagement of one of the Archduchesses. When I was presented to the Emperor, he welcomed me to his capital in French, for he did not speak English. Small and insignificant next to the tall, good-looking Archdukes, he seemed sad and withdrawn, with a chilling manner which I ascribed to the murder of his wife and the loss of his only son.

On Maundy Thursday I saw the Emperor once again, at the medieval function known as the *fusswaschung*. Only the Pope, the King of Spain, and the Emperor of Austria, as titular head of the Holy Roman Empire, continued this act initiated by Our Lord. Originally intended as an act of humility, it had become, when I saw it, a scene of splendour in which arrogance mas-

queraded in spurious simplicity. Twelve of the oldest and
poorest men in Vienna were seated on a bench just in front of
the tribune from which, clad in prescribed mourning, I watched
the scene. They had been carefully washed and scented so that
no unpleasant odour should offend the Imperial nostrils. I was
told that on one occasion such precautions had been neglected,
and that the Emperor of the time had been nearly overcome as
he knelt to wash the filthy feet extended to him. The feet now
were faultlessly clean—one might almost say manicured—and
each man in turn placed a foot in perfumed water. When the
Emperor reached the last man he raised his weary eyes, in which
I saw disillusion shine cold and bleak. Then rising he returned
to the Archdukes, who were dressed in gorgeous uniforms and
stood in line facing us. The great doors were flung open and a
procession of lackeys entered bearing twelve trays heaped with
delicious viands which the twelve Archdukes ceremoniously deposited before the twelve elders. But to my dismay the trays
were then immediately removed by the lackeys. My escort
reassured me that the food would be sent to their homes,
explaining that when they used to eat it at the ceremony the
Emperor and the Archdukes grew weary of waiting and the men
themselves invariably suffered from indigestion. It saddened
me that an act of Christian humility such as the washing of the
beggars' feet should have become an operatic scene shorn of
all spiritual meaning.

I remember a very different occasion when I was shown the
Emperor's famous cream-coloured horses in the Imperial Riding
School. As we stood around admiring them, one of the horses
relieved himself and a groom rushed forward extending a basket
to receive the offering—whether out of respect for the
immaculate tan that covered the ground or to teach the horse
better manners I never knew. I remember blushing scarlet,
much to the delight of the blasé Viennese.

In 1904 Vienna was still an eighteenth-century capital. It had
an antique elegance and an archaic respect for tradition and
birth. The *beau monde* was still that of the rich and the well-
born. World War I had not yet taken its holocaust of lives;
its levelling process was in the future. Breeding gives a distinction perhaps beyond its value. A thoroughbred, be it among
animals or men, is generally more physically favoured, and the
aristocratic Austrians I met looked like greyhounds, with their

long lean bodies and small heads. A polished education tends to bestow a certain ease of manner, and this these Viennese possessed to an eminent degree. It sometimes helped one to forget that they were as a rule more educated than intelligent. It was, I thought, a pity that they could express their thoughts in so many different languages when they had so few thoughts to express.

I returned to Vienna for repeated treatments but they never effected a cure, and I was beginning to find conversation exhausting. There were so many hiatuses that had to be filled in, so many half-tones that had to be divined, so much intensive guess-work towards significance, that even when the purport had been grasped the end barely justified the trouble. And later, when loved voices grew dim and I saw the flicker of annoyance that follows an unappreciated jest, I became withdrawn and lived in a world peopled with characters of my own choosing, at once apprehensive and apprehending. Solitude can become fiercely possessive, and I loved to walk alone, for then nature spoke to me through the soughing of wind in the trees and the songs of birds and the hum of bees, which, though unheard, created in my consciousness a lovely harmony, as with musicians who can no longer hear but in whom melody is still conscious. It became a solace for me to remain what Lord Curzon called "a black swan", aloof in soundless shadowed waters where I could choose the mirrored scene.

I have often been asked how I could sit on committees and do the work I did, handicapped as I was. I had some help from an instrument I wore under my hat, but it was mainly an effort of concentration. In preparing a subject on which I was to speak I invariably had answers ready for the questions that I thought might be asked. When I went to live in France the dry air improved my hearing; French voices are clearer, their accents sharper, and I could once again join in conversation. But it was only with the perfecting of modern electrical instruments that I enjoyed normal hearing again. Surely a monument should be erected to the patient scientists who have achieved what no aurist has so far accomplished—to give hearing to the deaf.

And so the years went by—in England coping with my work and private problems, in France on visits to my father. I loved France, that country of changing lights, of smiling plains, of innumerable rivers. I loved the poplar-lined canals, the discreet villages where life was lived behind walls. I loved the wheat-fields where peasants garnered life's sustenance. I never tired of her varied landscapes, from the orchards of Normandy to the dour hills of Auvergne, from the lazy Loire to the rapid Rhone. I loved her acacias and planes and lindens, the tapering cypresses and squat grey olives of Provence. I loved the scent of flowering lavender and thyme and the sweet grey smoke of woodland fires. I loved Brittany, with its verdant landscape and cloistered domains. I loved the orchards and lovely towns of the Ile-de-France. And oh, the excitement after a night on the train to waken on the Côte d'Azur with the snow-capped Alps behind and the sea before, glittering like a gigantic sapphire in the brightest of all suns, and its rich red earth which seemed to hold the tenseness and ardour of life. But I lived in England, a land of half-tones and shades, of mists and fleecy clouds, of damp and rain.

Visits to my father were particularly pleasant, for I rejoiced in the happiness he had found in his second marriage. My step-mother had a gay and gentle nature. Entirely engrossed in her husband and the four children two previous marriages had given her, she lived the life that suited my father. It was a quiet and domestic life within a small circle of devoted friends. In Paris or in New York my stepmother worked in the clinic my father had founded, or at some other philanthropic enterprise. My father had his racing stable and a small house at Poissy, a short motor drive from Paris. We sometimes spent the night there and in the early morning went out to his private track to see his horses gallop. As my father clocked them I would visualise them winning the Grand Prix, the Prix du Jockey Club and the other classic events he successfully competed in. His judgment was good and when after his death the stable was bought by Mr. McComber, Duke, his trainer who went with them, said to me, "Those horses will never run again as they did for Mr. Vanderbilt." And they never did.

During the summer of 1905 Marlborough decided to have our portrait painted. He wished to have a family group as a pendant to Sir Joshua Reynolds's portrait of the fourth Duke and his family. In the first years of the twentieth century John Singer Sargent had gained a distinct ascendancy over con-temporary artists in England; his portrait of Lord Ribblesdale, his groups of the three lovely Wyndham sisters—Lady Elcho,

Mrs. Adeane and Mrs. Tennant—and of the Wertheimer family were shown at the Royal Academy. They were always the most startling and most discussed pictures, and were usually surrounded by crowds in violent disagreement over their merits. In spite of the fact that he was an American, Sargent had become a resident of London and had taken a studio in Tite Street, where Whistler had painted before his time. When Sargent came to Blenheim at my husband's invitation and was told that he was to paint a pendant to a picture in which there were eight persons and three dogs, he seemed in no wise daunted. "But," he exclaimed, "how can I fill a canvas of this size with only four people? I might, of course," he added facetiously, "add a few Blenheim spaniels!" When, however, he realised that there was no choice he began to study a composition that would place us advantageously in architectural surroundings. We were therefore depicted standing in the hall with columns on either side and over our heads the Blenheim Standard, as the French Royal Standard captured at Blenheim had become known. I was placed on a step higher than Marlborough so that the difference in our height—for I was taller than he—should be accounted for. He naturally wore Garter robes. For me Sargent chose a black dress whose wide sleeves were lined with deep rose satin; the model had been used by Van Dyck in a portrait in the Blenheim collection. For my elder son he ordered a costume of white and gold. Ivor in blue velvet played with a spaniel at my side. Sir Edgar Vincent, who took great interest in the portrait, asked Sargent whether he was going to accentuate the slightly Japanese or Spanish Infanta accent of my type. "The Infanta, of course," Sargent answered, for he was a great admirer of Velasquez. He had, moreover, a predilection for a long neck, which he compared to the trunk of a tree. For that æsthetic reason he refused to adorn mine with pearls, a fact that aggrieved one of my sisters-in-law, who remarked that I should not appear in public without them.

Sargent had been Carolus Duran's pupil, and he often talked of him and of Boldini, for whose work he expressed great admiration, claiming that his Italian rival had been more successful with me than he himself was. During the sittings, which were numerous and took place in his studio, he was always agitated and smoked endless cigarettes. He was very self-conscious, and his conversation consisted of brief staccato remarks of a rather caustic nature. Viewing his sitter from afar, he would cock his head to one side, screw up his eyes, and with poised brush and extended palette would rush at his canvas and paint in short jerky movements. Children made him nervous; he had no idea how to manage them. Since mine were temperamental and mercurial, I had to supervise all their sittings. And as I got to know him better, I came under the spell of his kind-heartedness, which not even his shyness could disguise.

CHAPTER SEVEN

Deed of Separation

WE HAD been married eleven years. Life together had not brought us closer. Time had but accentuated our differences. The nervous tension that tends to grow between people of different temperament condemned to live together had reached its highest pitch.

Desiring to be free, we contemplated divorce, but in England the divorce laws then existing required a man to prove unfaithfulness in his wife; a wife, however, had to prove physical cruelty as well, or else desertion and non-support. It was not until years later that a new legal code removed much of the stigma of divorce. In 1906, separation appeared to be the only solution. We were given equal custody of the children, which was considered a concession in my favour, since they were boys and Blenheim was their home. The public interest then centred on this affair now seems excessive, but can more readily be understood by those who remember that in Edwardian social circles divorce or separation was not recognised as a solution for marital discord. Husbands and wives who could not get on together went their separate ways and in the great houses in which they lived practised a polite observance of the deference each owed the other.

Our separation accomplished, Sunderland House became my home. My mother-in-law and many of my English family and friends gathered round me, and I was deeply touched by the innumerable letters I received, even from people unknown to me, expressing hopes for my future happiness.

To the present generation the disgrace then attached to divorce will seem strange—indeed even a legal separation presented difficulties and made life alone in a great house, with a great name, a complicated problem for a young woman still in her twenties. During the next London season a splendid concert, at which John McCormack, Emmy Destinn and Fritz Kreisler performed, provided an opportunity to test the *beau monde*'s reactions to one living as I did—separated and alone. Standing with my father at the head of the staircase to welcome the flow of guests, I realised that although separated couples were not received in Court circles, London society would not so be governed. My mother-in-law's kindly observation, "It is a tribute to the dignity of your behaviour," added to the pleasure my English friends had given me.

Nevertheless, I was grateful for the visits my father and mother paid me. My mother came from America to be with me; her sympathy was precious, but the realisation that my life must be a lonely one, since my children would spend but half the year with me, and far less when once at school, underlined my need for some absorbing interest. A purely social life had no appeal, and in considering the future my thoughts turned to Prebendary Carlile, who, as head of the Church Army, had already aroused my interest in various philanthropic activities. One of the most selfless persons I have known, strongly convinced of the inherent goodness of humanity, he so instilled his belief into others that while under his influence they lived, as far as their natures allowed, according to his hopes. He now wished me to help him in a new venture—an attempt to reinstate first offenders, to prevent their return to the criminal world, and to induce them to become useful members of society. He used to say, "I have seen men come out of their first imprisonment determined to go straight, but when they find their homes broken up and their children in public institutions, and realise that the consequence of their crime has fallen upon their innocent families, their good intentions break down and they take again the easy course of a criminal career."

To be punished for the guilt of others is essentially unfair, yet our vaunted civilisation has done nothing to assist the wives of first offenders during their husbands' incarceration. Left without means of support, and often with several children to provide for, these unhappy women have difficulty in finding employment. With a view to helping them, we leased two adjoining houses in Endsleigh Street, London, which we equipped with laundries and sewing-rooms, where they were able to earn a standard wage; their babies were cared for in our day nursery. At Prebendary Carlile's request, I closed our day's work with prayer, and I can still feel the emotional tension with which those sorrow-laden souls filled our simple service. "We like the Duchess to read to us," they said, "but she always makes us cry." For me there was comfort in feeling that for once their tears were not bitter.

Their experiences at times had the inherent greatness of inescapable tragedy. I remember a young and lovely creature who had the virginal sweetness Murillo gave his Madonnas. Her husband had been imprisoned for theft, and while she sewed in our work-rooms we cared for her child. As the time approached for her husband's release she appeared to be anxious, and when she told us that the child she was bearing was not her husband's I realised that his release might bring about a tragedy. Then came the miserable tale of his cruelty to her. He had driven her into the streets to earn money to support him, and when sent to prison had asked his best friend to look after her and his child. Then life changed for her; she was well cared for and she and her husband's friend grew to love each other. "And now he is going to leave me," she sobbed. "He says he has betrayed the trust my husband placed in him, and that he cannot bear to face him!" I told her to send her lover to see me, but it was too late. On returning home she found a letter in which he told her that he had insured his life in her favour and was going to drown himself in the Thames. He also left a pitiful letter for her husband in which he asked his forgiveness, and begged him to look after his child. On the husband's release I asked him, "Are you going to care for your wife?" "Yes, and also for his child," he answered. I saw that for once he was deeply moved and hoped that a better future awaited his wife.

With the intention of finding work for the prisoners I used to interview them on their release. Comedies as well as tragedies resulted—and sometimes at my expense. There was the presentable young man who in the course of our interview boasted that he could easily earn his living could he but afford to buy the necessary tools. I must have been more anxious to help than I was either vigilant or wise, for I advanced him the money he said he needed. The very next day his wife turned up.

"What are you doing here?" I asked.

"My husband has returned to prison, and told me that you would surely take me back."

"But what has he done?" I gasped.

"Why, you gave him the tools, and he broke into a house last night and the police got him."

She was indignant when I explained that my homes were for first offenders only and seemed to think I had done her a mean trick in becoming an accessory in the crime.

When one plunges into philanthropy it is not long before one becomes submerged. The National Commission appointed to inquire into the declining birth-rate, on which I was the only lay member in a conclave of clergy, doctors, eugenists, economists and social workers, presided over by Dean Inge of St. Paul's ('the Gloomy Dean'), was at once a relaxation and an interest, since I had no responsibility other than that of a humble member. Our meetings were enlivened by the most divergent views, but it seemed to me that any opinion could be supported by the same statistics if differently presented. The men, who predominated, maintained that the declining birth-rate in the middle classes was entirely due to the higher education of women, an argument so conspicuously prejudiced that I immediately determined to champion that cause. Dr. Marie Stopes, whose books on the Science of Married Love were startling us all, asked pertinent questions which often reduced an eminent divine or a recalcitrant medical man to an embarrassed silence. The only immovable person, as it was in the tradition he should be, was the Monsignor representing the Roman Catholic Church. When the use of contraceptives was being argued, he stated irrevocably that no concession from that quarter would be considered.

One thing has a way of leading to another, I found, and during a visit to America in 1908 I made my début as a speaker in New York. The occasion was a dinner in the Waldorf-Astoria in honour of Mrs. Humphry Ward, who had come from England to launch an appeal for playgrounds for children. It was Colonel George Harvey who persuaded me to address this, to me, memorable gathering at which seven hundred citizens had assembled to render homage to England's leading authoress. I had returned to my native land deeply impressed with the civic service English men and women so wholeheartedly gave their country. It was, I thought, the truest patriotism, unstinted and unselfish, and I felt it almost an obligation to tell my country-women what I had learned. A sense of duty overcame my fears, although I suffered agonies of apprehension. The following day there were headlines in the papers: "Consuelo in Dinner Talk Criticises U.S. Women", "Duchess of Marlborough Delivers an Eloquent Speech", with verbatim reports. Admittedly extremely gratifying, they, together with a carrying voice—an important asset in the days before microphones—provided a strong incentive to further public work.

On my return to England I threw myself wholeheartedly into various activities chiefly concerned with the welfare of women and children. Sir Edgar Vincent gave me a house in the lovely grounds of Esher Place where I opened a recreation home for working girls. The Mary Curzon Lodging House for Poor Women as well as my Home for Prisoners' Wives were other permanent interests.

Always interested in the higher education of women—an interest recently stimulated by the discussions on the birth-rate commission—I accepted the post of Honorary Treasurer of Bedford College, a women's college incorporated in the University of London. Here I was fortunate in securing the magnificent donation of 100,000 guineas from Sir Hildred Carlyle, which enabled the college to be moved from its cramped quarters in Baker Street to a beautiful site in Regent's Park.

An amusing repercussion to a speech I made on behalf of the college was a poem which appeared in *Punch*, written by Sir Owen Seaman, a well-known English humourist, at that time editor of the magazine:

To Sophonisba, of Bedford College

(The Duchess of Marlborough, in advocating a scheme for the removal of the Bedford College for Women from Baker Street to Regent's Park, is reported to have said that "it was difficult to comprehend why there should be such rooted objection on the part of Englishmen to the higher education of their wives. There must be some secret fear that, hard as they found it to understand a woman now, it would be absolutely beyond their ken were she highly educated." The way to conquer opposition was for women to be "tactful enough not always to worst their husbands in argument.")

Ere the vows at which the bravest falter
Make you my irrevocable bride;
Ere I feel the nuptial noose or halter
Round my throttle permanently tied;
While the hour is open for repentance,
Hear the following prayer which I despatch!
Else, before the priest pronounces sentence,
I propose to scratch.

I implore you not to be too sniffy
Should my lack of culture cause you pain;
Do not petrify your Albert if he
Fails to fathom your unusual brain;
Promise you will temper your ideas
To the taste of just an average man;
Promise, Sophonisba, not to be as
Clever as you can.

Fostered at the fount of higher knowledge,
You enjoyed a chance denied to me;
I was never schooled at Bedford College,
I was nursed at Balliol's homely knee;
Therefore make allowance for the mental
Lapses which invite your lips to laugh,
And, as you are strong, be very gentle
To your feebler half.

Epigrams, in private, I could swallow;
If you make my manly pride to flinch
From a wit too fleet for me to follow,
I could always smack you at a pinch;
But in public, when you take the trophy
For the finest table-talk in Town,
Do not knock me sideways, O my Sophie;
Let me softly down.

O.S.

The speech also brought in the sum of twenty-five pounds
from the editor of the American periodical, *The Outlook,* and the
honour of being quoted in 'Today's Notable Sayings' in the
Westminster Gazette. It proved, I felt, that a sense of humour

is indeed an asset and with ridicule, as a weapon, can stimulate reforms. But there were other causes which required stronger measures.

I admit that such activities provided greater interest than the frivolities of a London season, but these too were still a part of my life. In the fragments of a 1908 diary I found the following appreciation:

> The London season is at its fag end. Conscience-stricken hostesses with unpaid social debts are sending out belated invitations in a vain effort to fulfil neglected obligations. Every night one is bidden to three or more balls. Today there were six parties, and at one of them a monkey called 'Peter' for whose services in entertaining her guests a hostess paid £150. The puns and *bon mots* of the season are stale, as are also Mr. Spooner's Spoonerisms, but to these are added gaffes of a special brand, made by old Lord M. His latest offence concerns me, and was committed during a visit to Blenheim. Approaching the house he remarked on the beauty of the park; and turning to another peer, Lord G., who has himself married a wealthy American, he added, "There are uses for American heiresses and their money after all!" Lady G., who was present, had the sense to laugh, but Lord G., furious at the insult, immediately repeated the insult to Marlborough, setting everyone wondering who had committed the greater *faux pas*. To cap it all, shortly after his return from Blenheim I met Lord M. at a dinner where the seating arrangements separated me from my cavalier; whereupon in strident tones he shouts out at me, "Have you ever been separated from your man before, my dear Lady?"

It was astonishing how he could always be relied upon to give one a shock!

On another page of this old notebook I find:

> This year I have frequently had the new Prime Minister, Mr. Asquith, as my neighbour at dinner, and in the course of conversation he has suggested that I should keep a diary, adding word pictures of the brilliant men it is my good fortune to meet. To encourage me, he quoted an excerpt from his his wife Margot's diary which he considers supremely amusing.

It concerns Viscount Haldane, who was Minister for War in Sir Henry Campbell-Bannerman's Cabinet, and has continued in the same post under Mr. Asquith. Margot wrote: "It took Henry and me a long time to get over his (Lord Haldane's) appearance, but when we did we found in him many good qualities to command our admiration." She insisted upon reading his appreciation to Lord Haldane, who, in spite of the effective reorganisation of the British Army on which he was engaged, was with difficulty prevented from resigning his office.

It is perhaps Mr. Asquith's suggestion which has given me the courage to write these memoirs. I should, however, have remembered that he was invariably kind to the young, for whom he ever had an encouraging word, and that he might not have regarded these belated efforts with the same indulgence.

But it was not every day that I sat next to men of Mr. Asquith's calibre, although invariably placed with much older people, and I longed to see something of another set. So when the Sidney Webbs invited me to dine in their little house on the Embankment, I was overjoyed, for I was curious to meet the Fabians. The success of this new party in the General Election of 1906 had startled the country into realising that socialism was a coming factor in politics; at the same time H. G. Wells attempted to hasten its coming by reorganising the old Fabian Society, thus engaging in a controversy with Bernard Shaw which attracted much public attention.

My hosts Sidney and Beatrice Webb were famous economists and sociologists and had together published three standard works, *History of Trade Unionism, Industrial Democracy* and *English Local Government.* They figured prominently on the Royal Commission on the Poor Law and were active in securing constructive measures for the improvement of industrial conditions and labour relations. When I knew Beatrice Webb she had the beauty of an eagle, with finely chiselled features, while in her eyes one saw the soaring, searching quality of her mind. She was a socialist and an ardent reformer, and when later her husband became one of the Labour Government's first peers she refused to be known as Lady Passfield.

It was a compliment to be invited to join her circle. At that first dinner I had Bernard Shaw as my neighbour. Rather shy of such august company, I turned to him with diffidence, for he had,

F*

I felt, not yet decided whether to treat me as a frivolous out-
sider come to view the lions or as a serious young woman intent
on social reform. He was, notwithstanding, utterly delightful
and his sallies left me wondering whether I was laughing at
myself or at the world in general. He looked like Jupiter, I
thought, with his classical brow and red beard, and his words
could be likened to thunderbolts, for they totally demolished
whatever he disapproved of. We became friends, and both he
and his wife, whose translation into English of one of Brieux'
plays I saw in London, where it had but a *succès d'estime*,
frequented the literary dinners I instituted every Friday during
the following winter.

They were delightful dinners, with many of 'The Souls',
politicians and writers as guests. A judicious mixture of a more
frivolous element provided the froth. Brilliant men are not
insensible to a beautiful woman, even when her beauty surpasses
her wit, and in England they are free to indulge in more serious
conversation with other men once the ladies have left the table.

One of my favourite guests was Lady Frances Balfour, the
daughter of the eloquent Duke of Argyll, from whom she had
inherited a superior intelligence and an easy flow of talk. She
was a stimulating person and it was my good fortune to work
with her on several committees, and at meetings to share the
honours of public speaking. Invariably she was amusing, shrewd
and witty, leaving the boring marshalling of facts to my patient
chairmanship. She held my views on women's suffrage,
believing in the more conservative approach rather than in the
distressing exhibitions of martyrdom which were shocking
society, typified by Mrs. Pankhurst in gaol, being forcibly fed,
and the young woman who hurled herself in front of the King's
horse and was killed as the field swept round the Epsom course
to the Derby's finish.

When first H. G. Wells dined with me he was unknown in
London society, though his books were creating a furore. I had
assembled a brilliant company. Lord Rosebery, at my request,
was host and sat opposite me at the long table laden with silver,
crystal and flowers. His favourite Mouton Rothschild stood at
his side. As he rarely dined out, I had provided not only two
charming women as his neighbours but a galaxy of intellect as
a challenge to his own. There was Bernard Shaw, John
Galsworthy, whose 'Forsyte' novels and plays were the talk of

London, and Sir James Barrie, whose gentle humour was delighting playgoers with his *Peter Pan* and *What Every Woman Knows*. Barrie was a little man with pensive eyes and a deep fund of sentiment and pity. He told a friend of mine, "I would stand all day in the street to see Consuelo Marlborough get into her carriage," which shows that the days of high romance were still alive in the hearts of those who, like Barrie, were chivalrous and kind. I heard that he had once described his business in life as 'playing hide and seek with angels', and one could not talk to him without realising how near he was to Hans Andersen's world of fairies. I had also invited H. S. Chamberlain, just back from Germany. His book, *The Foundations of the Nineteenth Century*, in praise of German institutions, as my readers will remember, caused resentment among his English compatriots, and in 1916 he became a naturalised German and married Eva Wagner, a daughter of the composer. All this, however, was then in the future, and Chamberlain was still English though pro-German, an attitude which at that time he shared with a considerable company. The Charteris family was well represented, with Lord Elcho, later the Earl of Wemyss, a caustic wit, his brilliant wife whom Sargent had painted in his portrait of the Wyndham Sisters, and the Honourable Evan Charteris, whose versatile charm as a conversationalist, whose skill as a shot, a golfer and a bridge and tennis player placed him in the first ranks of *personae gratae* at any party. I placed H. G. Wells between Mrs. Rochfort Maguire and Lady Desborough, without whom no dinner was complete, for they had the most agreeable salons in London. They were thrilled at meeting him, but Lord Lovat, an incorrigible tease, later told them that the Wells I had invited was not the H. G. whose books were challenging the future. The following morning several friends rang me up to congratulate me on "the most brilliant dinner", adding, to my amusement, "but what a pity the right H. G. Wells could not come!" It was not long, however, before I saw the same H. G. Wells in their company, although he refused to be lionised.

Men of letters are not as a rule good at small talk, for there are better ways of investing their capital. I found Galsworthy stiff and ill at ease. R. S. Hichens, on the contrary, perhaps because he was a less distinguished writer, shone in social circles. His *Garden of Allah* and *Bella Donna* were then bestsellers and every new novel of his was eagerly awaited. He was a habitué of my godmother Consuelo Duchess of Manchester's salon, where I often listened to his amusing talk, which she knew well how to stimulate. He was also no mean musician and with my godmother, who herself played delightfully by ear, monopolised both conversation and piano. It is difficult in such brilliant company to award the palm, but to Bernard Shaw or W. B. Yeats or George Wyndham I would give pre-eminence as the best conversationalists. They were not only brilliant, but also possessed physical beauty to an eminent degree—Bernard Shaw, a veritable Zeus; George Wyndham, "outrageously handsome," as he was described in the days when, as Secretary for Ireland, he played so conspicuous a part in rendering palatable an unpopular policy; and W. B. Yeats, an Irish Lord Byron. In 1907 Yeats's *Deirdre* had taken London by storm and brought Irish literature and the Abbey Theatre, with J. M. Synge, Lady Gregory and George Moore, much to the fore, causing their English contemporaries Pinero, Stephen Phillips, Galsworthy and Barrie to look to their laurels.

How cultured and polished was that generation of scholarly men! Looking back on them I cannot imagine a more gifted company in any country. No matter what the subject, the talk was never heavy, for there was always a flash of British humour to enliven it, and with Maurice Baring, Harry Cust and Evan Charteris to add fuel to the fire we were often privileged to assist at a marvellous display of pyrotechnics. Alas that I did not record them, and that I am too honest and also too modest to attempt to invent them!

While reminiscing on authors, I must not forget my meeting with Michael Arlen, for it produced one of the *bon mots* for which Lady Cunard, the former Maude Burke, was famous. Dragging a somewhat reluctant young man across the room (did he already fear the devastating introduction it was her habit to make?), she triumphantly cried, "This is Michael Arlen—the only Armenian who has not been massacred!"

On another occasion she asked me to bring the Grand Duke Dmitri to one of her political luncheons. He was the son of the Grand Duke Paul and the grandson of the Emperor Alexander II. An exceptionally handsome man, fair and sleek with long blue eyes in a narrow face, he had fine features, and the stealthy walk of a wild animal, moving with the same

balanced grace. According to the story he told me, the monk
Rasputin had been murdered in his presence in the house of
Prince Youssopoff. Afterwards the Czar sent for Dmitri and
asked him why he had countenanced so foul a deed. The Grand
Duke replied that his nobles had wished to rid the Emperor of
the baleful influence of a man who was execrated by the Russian
people. The Czar, unappeased, ordered Dmitri to leave the
country, and it was to this order of exile that he owed his later
survival of the Bolshevik Revolution. Eventually he came to
England, where he was befriended by Lord and Lady Curzon.
As the Grand Duke and I arrived at Lady Cunard's luncheon,
she faced the assembled company and shouted, "And here is the
Grand Duke Dmitri, the murderer of Rasputin." Shocked
beyond belief, I looked round to see his reaction, but with a turn
on his heel and a short bow he had already fled—which made
us thirteen for luncheon. Such were my hostess's social gifts
that she managed to laugh it off and we had as usual a most
stimulating meal. Nevertheless, she combined good sense with
nonsense to an unprecedented degree, and in time learned how
far she could go.

Maud, with her marriage to Sir Bache Cunard, had become
the wife of a fox-hunting squire, but such a life was not to her
liking. On returning one day to her home in Leicestershire she
found an iron railing enclosing a garden and on it inscribed
in Sir Bache's unmistakable script (he was something of an iron-
smith) the legend, "Come into the garden, Maud". Having no
taste for such dalliance she took a house in London, for it was
her ambition to have a political salon in the tradition of the
eighteenth century. Ruthlessly determined to succeed, she bent
a conspicuous talent to this end. When first I met her she looked,
I thought, like a little parrakeet, with a golden coxcomb on her
head, a small beak and a receding chin. That chin was the bane
of her life, and with a despairing insistence she had it massaged
and given electric treatments, but nothing succeeded in giving
it the character she desired. Why, so greatly caring, she never
resorted to plastic surgery remains a mystery. Again like a
parrakeet her plumage was brilliant; her startling clothes were
always in the height of fashion, the exaggerated type of fashion
that dressmakers launch at the beginning of a season and later
discard. She loved jewels, especially emeralds, and her small
rather claw-like hands were usually adorned with a fine ring or

two. She appeared to dispense a tremendous energy, but her enthusiasm cloaked an ingrained pessimism. As I grew to know her I realised that it was her need for friendship that caused her to indulge in absurd superlatives. I used to wonder why she did not herself realise that it was the wrong approach, especially in England. She did, however, in time achieve the success one associates with an *enfant terrible*. Her luncheon-parties were famous—few refused an invitation. They rarely comprised more than ten, for she insisted that conversation be general. However, it invariably became a monologue on her part during which she launched sallies at everyone's expense, which everyone took in good part. Somehow it seemed entirely natural that she herself should strike the high note of fun, and that our defects should become a source of amusement to others. In middle age she grew tired of her name Maud and demanded that she be called Emerald. It annoyed her when one forgot. Like a restless child she flitted from one interest to another, lacking stability and repose. Her ambition to foster grand opera in London, to which she gave her unstinted energies and her fortune as well, should have received more generous recognition. After her death instructions were found that her ashes be strewn in Grosvenor Square, the scene of her splendid hospitality. One of her most constant guests performed this macabre task, and afterwards complained that the wind had blown the ashes back into his face, his eyes and his hair, and that he was now full of his former hostess.

Every year at Whitsuntide I spent unforgettable days in the brilliant company Lord Curzon invited to Hackwood. Our host dominated us all, and yet how graciously he knew how to extract from each the quintessence of personal contribution. In 1914, shortly after the invasion of Belgium by the German armies, I went to Hackwood for a night on my way to a meeting. As I entered the living-hall, where in the past I had witnessed so many gay parties, I saw a lonely little figure seated at a table bending over a map. Near her stood a British general in uniform. It was the Queen of the Belgians sadly following the rout of her armies. Lord Curzon had offered her the hospitality of his home until such time as she could with safety return to her country.

Whitsuntide at Hackwood was often followed by a week-end at Taplow Court, where Lord and Lady Desborough dispensed a gracious hospitality. No one had a choicer circle of friends and admirers than Ettie Grenfell, as she was when first I knew her, and no one entertained more delightfully. There was the Thames, lovely in summer, where Lord Desborough punted in professional style, delighting to recount the while how he had twice swum Niagara Falls. There were shady walks in the woods and always an agreeable cavalier as escort. There was general conversation around the tea-table on the lawn—and after dinner the inevitable game of bridge. Time passed all too quickly. Sometimes we motored to Cliveden near-by, that palatial house that had been owned by the Dukes of both Sutherland and Westminster before being bought by the first Lord Astor when he became an Englishman. He had given it to his son Waldorf on his marriage to the lovely and versatile Nancy.

She was, as everyone knows, the first woman to sit in the House of Commons, where she represented Plymouth for many years. During her parliamentary career she defended women's interests with a courage that compelled admiration even from those who opposed her views. She made a great many speeches on her feet and still more interjectory remarks from her seat; she could answer the Labour members in banter or in anger and be equally effective in either mood. She was adored by her constituents but disliked by the classic parliamentarians, who considered her repartees undignified. Her genuine courage and optimism were seen at their best during the dark days of World War II in which Plymouth was so heavily bombed.

Much has been written about the political atmosphere of Cliveden during the 1930s. It was then the headquarters of the circle known as the Round Table which, headed by Philip Kerr, later Lord Lothian, was working for a closer understanding between England and Germany. With my strong pro-French sympathies, I resented the propaganda spread by this political group. I felt strongly that their theories were founded on a false estimate of the Gallic character, which to them was undependable when compared with the honest intentions of the trustworthy German. Even in the winter of 1938–9 when Lady Astor came to Florida she was preaching the surrender of the Sudetenland to Germany and assuring her hearers that Hitler would never encroach on the liberties of the Czechs. It is curious how personal prejudice can blind even intelligent people to the most evident conclusions.

Looking back on the little circle I knew of American women married to Englishmen, there are, I realise, very few who remained definitely American. Nancy Astor was one of these. Her high spirits, her sense of humour, her self-assurance, her courage, her independence are all of the American variety; and also her beauty. I met her when she first came to England and have ever since valued the friendship she gave me, but there were moments when, conscious of her mischievous appraisal, I used to quail, wondering what pertinent consideration her sharp tongue would utter.

Lady Astor's vivid personality made her many friends, but there were those whose dislike was equally marked. She and Winston Churchill were actuated by a strong antipathy one for the other, so much so that one never invited them together, dreading the inevitable explosion bound to occur. It was therefore unfortunate that on one of Lady Astor's visits to Blenheim, when my son was host, Winston should have chosen to appear. The expected result of their encounter was not long in coming; after a heated argument on some trivial matter Nancy, with a fervour whose sincerity could not be doubted, shouted, "If I were your wife I would put poison in your coffee!" Whereupon Winston with equal heat and sincerity answered, "And if I were your husband I would drink it."

Outstanding parties were also given by the Duke and Duchess of Portland at Welbeck Abbey, a princely domain near lovely Sherwood Forest. It was an impressive mansion both above ground and beneath it, for one of the Dukes had like a mole built innumerable underground rooms and galleries in which vast receptions were often given. To me the most memorable of these occasions was a tenants' luncheon which revealed the almost feudal point of view of my host. The Duke's speech to his tenants was charming and kindly in all intents, but would have been more appropriate had it been made before the Reform Bill of 1832. I grew more and more uncomfortable as he proceeded, but no one else seemed to find it at all strange. Indeed, the company at Welbeck impressed me as rather eighteenth-century in character. It had all the style of a princely court. Entering the huge living-hall one found the Duchess, beautiful and elegant in satin and lace, presiding at a tea-table while a younger woman dispensed coffee and chocolate at another. Grouped around the chatelaine might be the Archbishop of York (Cosmo Lang), the Duke of Alba, the Austro-Hungarian Ambassador, a Belgian countess, and innumerable peers and peeresses of the old school. Winnie Portland, as she was known to her many devoted friends, was a gracious and lovely woman who spent her life in well-doing; but she was, as it were, enshrined in a hyper-aristocratic niche where sorrow or want or fear were unknown. It was all very well to spend a few days in such a rarefied atmosphere where the problems created by modern economic conditions and the restless upward striving of twentieth-century socialism were hardly realised. But I would have felt stifled had my stay lasted longer.

I wanted a small house not too far from London, and on a wonderful summer day I found it. It was called Crowhurst and was a little Tudor manor house lost in a fold of the North Wolds. With its high roof of Horsham stone, its walls half-timbered with silvered oak, its stone chimneys and leaded casements, it had the charm of an old engraving. It was, I thought, a dream come true. Crowhurst belonged to the Reverend Mr. Gainsforth, whose family had owned it for four hundred years. By a strange coincidence it had once been leased to Sarah, Duchess of Marl-borough, to lodge some veterans of Marlborough's campaigns. Mr. Gainsforth refused to sell, but the glamour of my predecessor weighed the scales in my favour and he consented not only to let me have the house but also allowed me to add to it. The hall reached from the ground to the raftered roof, in which an open-ing still showed that it had been built before the days of chimneys. Out of the hall an oak stair led up to the great chamber, and opposite the stair a lovely oriel window with diamond panes looked out on the barn and garden. The walls were of creamy plaster and on the oak beams that spanned the roof a family of owls sometimes perched, gazing at me below with impersonal eyes that seemed to hold a hidden menace. The floor was flagged with large grey stones on which were spread rushes and rugs. Crimson velvet curtains shut out the night. There were comfortable chairs in flowered chintzes and the old oak dressers and tables were polished to a honeyed sheen. Coming down from London after a long week's work I would find a tea-table laden with scones, cakes and jams, and when my maid, Hatherly, brought in the golden tea and the fire flared in welcoming spirals I could, in a deep contentment, forget the

worries of committees. And how lovely to wake to the smell
of honeysuckle and roses and to doze to the lap of waters, while
swans sailed their rounds. The farmyard was paved, and on the
far side there was a long tithe barn with walls of mellowed
brick and a roof of stone. It gave access to a sunken garden with
a pool which was surrounded by terraces in three flowered tiers.
Beyond were other gardens cloistered by tall yews and filled
with the scent of herbs and roses. A grass walk through
herbaceous borders led back to the house. Delphinium, phlox,
stocks and Canterbury bells grew in riotous profusion of pinks
and blues and purples. Irises in masses bloomed at the water's
edge, and in the spring the garden was gay with flowering shrubs
and the blossom of peach and plum.

It was not difficult to entertain my guests, for they preferred
working in the gardens. This, in other people's gardens, can,
however, be dangerous, and at times enthusiasm overran discretion and there were unfortunate massacres of favourite trees.
On the other hand, when I wanted an unsightly barn
demolished, union workers would have been aghast at the few
hours it took us.

I used often to sit in the herb garden where the splash of the
fountain tinkling near-by and the lowing of cows in the fields
were the only sounds to be heard. And during the war I would
sit there possessed by the anxiety that besets all mothers who
have sons at the front, and when Hatherly would come out
waving a telegram it seemed as if my heart would stop.

Crowhurst was the scene of many happy week-ends with my
friends. A frequent and welcome guest was Ethel Higgins, later
Mrs. Arthur Fowler. An American by birth, one of the lovely
Cryder triplets, she was a gay and delightful visitor. During the
war we worked together for our American Hospital and she
organised the volunteer workers both for the hospital and for
the Y.M.C.A. that we opened for our troops. I looked forward to
our peaceful week-ends and deeply resented being robbed of
them by clamorous outsiders who wished to be invited. Nevertheless Margot Asquith's insistence prevailed and, in spite of my
protests that the house was much too small for a party, she
suggested that she herself, the Prime Minister and their daughter
Elizabeth should each come on a separate week-end. This
necessitated organising three parties, each to pivot around an
Asquith. They were, I admit, rather special personalities in

their way, but a party for each of them at little Crowhurst had to be chosen with care.

It is difficult to give an idea of Margot's personality to those who never knew her. It is far easier to describe her appearance. Small and phenomenally thin, as she grew older she looked, I thought, rather like a witch. With her grey hair in corkscrew curls, her hawk-like nose and shrewd eyes, one rather expected her after one of her mordant sallies to fly away on a broomstick, her deep voice still screaming invectives. When sometimes she performed skirt dances, delighting to prove the suppleness of her sixty years, one forgot her old Voltaire-like face. But her glance expressed so much wit and understanding that when she smiled, even maliciously, in response to one's quip, no compliment could have pleased more.

On the other hand it was difficult not to feel oppressed by her assumption of superiority, which on occasion even prevented the progression of friendships she wished to cultivate. For in recounting her conversations with celebrities, she invariably capped their most brilliant sallies—a forensic victory few can forgive. Her powers of observation were indubitably shrewd, and she had a quick wit which she exercised freely, regardless of ruffled feelings. But if tempted to estimate her critical faculties one need look no further than her family circle. Indeed, in her stepdaughter, Lady Violet Bonham Carter, she found a rival whose brilliant mind and balanced judgment enabled her with gentler methods to probe deeper. Impatient and intolerant of stupidity, Margot often reduced people to an embarrassed silence, failing to appreciate the genuine qualities they might have possessed. She liked few women and showed a particularly virulent dislike for my compatriots, claiming that American men were greatly to be pitied. Even friends such as Lady Ribblesdale (who had been Ava Astor) and I were viewed with at most a kindly condescension.

I could not help being amused by such an attitude, accompanied as it was by a total imperviousness to any criticism of her own person. At times she reminded me of Lady Astor in the ruthless and castigating way she dealt with her adversaries, but I never ventured to tell either of them so, knowing how deeply each would resent the comparison. Margot had a disarming manner of imparting what we women call a "dig". I once heard her say to a perfectly harmless female whose affectations were nevertheless boring us all, "Darling, must you always be so self-consciously refined?" It was so funny we all had to laugh, but it had a cruel sting.

Margot found it difficult to listen. She would shoot forth exclamations that soared like rockets, and loved to throw in pointed criticisms or to scold satirically. She had a mania for pigeon-holing people and kept a list of possible house guests with letters beside their names to describe their qualifications. Against my own I discovered B. T. & G. and later found that these mysterious initials stood for bridge, tennis and golf. She and her daughter Elizabeth both loved bridge, but when one played with them, their perpetual flow of talk proved very distracting. On her return from an American lecture tour she complained bitterly to me that Americans took no interest in sport. "Perhaps not the sporting episodes of amateurs like yourself," I answered, for she had lectured endlessly about a grey hunter she had once owned.

At her first appearance at Carnegie Hall in New York Mr. Henry White, a former Ambassador to France, took the chair. The suave eloquence of this practised diplomat invariably succeeded in creating the friendly atmosphere a chairman attempts to establish between his audience and the speakers. Mrs. Asquith had been well advertised, and the hall was packed. After being introduced she remained seated and read her lecture in low tones which did not carry. When cries from the gallery "Louder, please" interrupted her, she calmly answered, "I have no intention of raising my voice; I am talking quite loud enough if you will listen." Alas, very few stayed to listen. After this unhappy event Mr. White drove her back to her hotel.

When Margot came to Crowhurst, I invited to act as foils Lord Hugh Cecil and Lytton Strachey. The latter had just published *Eminent Victorians*, the first of his books in which he set a precedent for ironic and detached biography. As I remember him, Strachey then was an overgrown young man with a red beard. Thin and of an æsthetic appearance, he gave the impression of delicacy and asceticism. Watching him and Lord Hugh playing tennis was like seeing figures in an Italian primitive come to life. Their racquets might have been instruments for self-flagellation and the ball always seemed to elude the rushes and passes they made for it. But their conversation was brilliant and under far greater control than the game of tennis. What a pity there were no dictaphones to record such talks—the flow of eloquence—the quick thrust—the tone of voice—the subtle blend, persuasive or perverse—the laugh of glee or scorn—the dialogue of two minds attuned, each qualified to expound the wisdom and follies of the ages.

After such week-ends of talk and bridge, I was glad to have Mr. Asquith come to stay, for there was no need to search for bridge players who were also brilliant conversationalists. Besides Mr. Asquith I had invited a few friends, among whom were the Grand Duke Dmitri, lovely Pamela Lytton and Jacques Balsan. During dinner Mr. Asquith criticised the German Emperor with the pungent acumen he at times indulged in, and it was agreed that he should be hanged. Dmitri remained silent, but on leaving the room he turned to Balsan, and with an air of indescribable hauteur said, *"De quel droit ces gens-là se permettent-ils de nous critiquer?"*—"What right have such people to criticise us?" I thought of Lord Randolph Churchill's remark to the Marquis de Breteuil on seeing in the Breteuil dining-room a portrait of Louis XVI in which a placid stupidity of countenance was allied to an arrogant pose: "Now, at last, I understand the French Revolution!"

The various elements of this house-party which took place during the war—an English ex-Prime Minister, a Russian Grand Duke, a French Colonel—had mingled more successfully than might have been expected. The simple charm of Crowhurst, the fact that one lived as if in a garden, the roses and honeysuckle climbing into one's windows, the flowers at one's feet as one opened the door, awakened in everyone a gentleness sometimes wholly unexpected. I have heard my guests say of each other, "I have never known so-and-so could be so nice!" Crowhurst had that atmosphere only to be found in a happy house, as if kindness had always lived there. Thus Mr. Asquith had brilliantly displayed his versatility without extinguishing our own small sparks of conversation, and, as a hostess, I felt grateful to him that he should have made us all appear at our best.

CHAPTER EIGHT

A New Life Unfolds

DURING THE long years that followed my separation I became gradually more and more immersed in philanthropic and political work. What had begun as an answer to a need for a new interest in my life became eventually my main way of life and gave it a meaning it had hitherto lacked.

I have already mentioned some of the activities in which I engaged, but one that fairly early absorbed a large part of my time and interest was an attempt to do something about the shameful conditions under which women worked in the sweated industries. In response to an appeal by Miss Margaret Laurence and Miss Gertrude Tuckwell, who were influential trade union officials, I helped them organise a meeting at Sunderland House in November, 1913, to call public attention to that social evil. It was an all-day conference at which I took the chair at the morning session, with the Bishop of Oxford as chairman in the afternoon. A contemporary paper gives the following description of the conference:

The sweated women's conference which was organised recently by the Duchess of Marlborough has probably done more to advance the cause of female suffrage in Britain than the violent combined efforts of the militant suffragettes. It is evident that the Duchess of Marlborough understands the British public. She is in closer touch with the thrifty spirit of the nation, which abhors the house-burning and window-breaking methods of illuminating grievances, than any of her radical co-workers. Quite lately she convened a conference of sweated women at Sunderland House, and secured the presence there of the Press and of representative leaders of every section of society. We must take leave to doubt that a soul would have attended had the British public suspected the noble lady's little game.

In all probability the great array of bishops, politicians, butterflies of fashion, industrial captains and bigwigs that assembled went to Sunderland House in the expectation of passing a pleasant hour or two exchanging trite moral reflections over tea and strawberries and gratuitous champagne. We can picture their discomfiture, their horror, on discovering that the Duchess had successfully arranged a trap for the capture and destruction of the national complacency. There was no opportunity provided them of platitudinous discussion. When the conference was opened they found they were to listen, not to talk. Twelve old women occupied the stage. Twelve poor but respectable old women, who had each spent from 20 to 50 years of a long life bearing the yoke of industrial slavery in its cruellest form. They did all the talking. One after another they came forward and related the stories of their miserably cramped and sweated lives. One was a shirt maker. She showed her gilded audience a shirt she had made. "A dozen of these right out before earning 9d. Last week me and my husband sat from 5.30 till 11 at night and made fourteen dozen shirts, which came to ten shillings, and ten pence for cotton." And such had been her daily grind for more than twenty years. A widow in the confectionery trade had worked for twenty years in a factory for eight shilling a week, out of which she had had to provide for the support and education of her child. For twenty years she had never eaten a dinner costing more than a penny. And thus ran all the tales the silent and confounded conference was forced to hear.

Little is the wonder that all England is muttering today of the Sunderland House Conference.

In consequence of this conference, trade boards were opened to about eight more sweated industries.

I loved my work, but it was tiring. Returning to London from Liverpool, where I had addressed two big meetings, and where as the principal speaker I had made an impassioned plea for a Municipal Lodging House for Women, I experienced the repercussion of weariness and deflation such efforts produced. In the cold of my reserved compartment, a hot-water comforter to my feet, a gas jet burning overhead, I viewed the lonely future which seemed to stretch endlessly before me. My thoughts went to my mother, who, seeking distraction from the sorrows of widowhood —for her husband died in 1908—had found comfort in the all-engrossing interest the suffrage movement was to her. To this end she sacrificed her time, her wealth, even her personal feelings. There is a photograph in which I see her valiantly leading a parade up Fifth Avenue. I did not realise what such a conspicuous public act must have cost her until she later confessed, "To a woman brought up as I was, it was a terrible ordeal!"

It was through her that I met many noted leaders of the movement, of whom I chiefly recall Emmeline Pankhurst. I sometimes saw her during her visits to Paris, which were secret and surreptitious, for she was wanted by the police and at that time spent many days hunger-striking in prison. A fine undaunted woman, her delicate body held the flame that animates crusaders, the spirit that willingly endures suffering and pain for an ideal. Forcible feeding even for the doctor who administers it is a gruelling experience; for a sensitive woman it meant torture and long periods of ill-health.

Her daughter Christabel often stayed with my mother. Once suffrage had been secured, she turned her active mind to an exhaustive study of the Book of the Revelation, from which she emerged with the prophecy that Armageddon would soon be upon us, leaving me to contemplate that, if so, women should don armour rather than exercise a futile vote. With my mother she shared a common hatred for the genus man although they both delighted in men's company. An extract from a letter written by my mother to a friend explains her reasons for this prejudice:

> My first experiences in life gave birth to my belief in militant woman suffrage. I found even at the age of seven that boys looked down upon girls. I can almost feel my childish hot blood rise as it did then in rebellion at some such taunting remarks as: "You can't run." "You can't climb trees." "You can't fight." "You are only a girl." But no young would-be masculine bravado ever expressed twice such slurring belittlements of me.

As a specimen of my mother's method of attack, I quote the following extract from a letter written in April, 1913, to the secretary of the Committee on Criminal Courts in New York:

I am in receipt of your circular letter of April 11th containing the question: "What Shall We Do With the Young Prostitute?"

That the victims of man's recognized and accepted vices need protection none can deny; but why call upon the general public to furnish the necessary funds? Why collect money for the benefit of State and City and then divert it into channels for succouring human beings whose viciousness and undesirability were forced upon them by a class of self-indulgent criminals of the male population who have the power to vote against every decent measure brought before the electorate?

No, gentlemen, do not ask the Governor to use his influence in securing a bill such as you refer to, but simply look the situation squarely in the face and ask his help in the interest of another bill which should be sent to the Legislature that shall place the burden of this monstrous sin on the shoulders of those who have created the necessity for such institutions. Arrest every man, rich or poor, young or old, who traffics in human bodies; fine him heavily according to his means, and the $700,000 necessary to provide an enlarged refuge for his victims will soon be raised.

There is no difficulty in arresting the woman of the streets or the inmate of the house of ill repute; therefore the task of detecting men of the same caliber should not be among the impossibilities, and according to statistics, they outnumber women probably twenty to one. Find a means of haling these men into court, see that man-ruled courts and man-made laws can bring them to justice. Can you not realize the effectiveness of such a proceeding?

In the same year, 1913, she went to Budapest as a delegate to the Biennial Convention of the International Woman Suffrage Alliance and I accompanied her. The Hungarian government gave the delegates an outstanding reception. My most vivid remembrance is of a service in a great church where Dr. Anna Shaw of the American delegation had the honour of preaching a sermon from the pulpit. She was a Doctor of Divinity and of Medicine and gave us a remarkably fine discourse.

The following summer I went to America on a visit to my mother at Marble House. She had by then become a leader of the suffrage movement and under the auspices of the Political

Equality Association organised an open-air meeting at which the speakers were Miss Rose Schneiderman, vice-president of the Women's Trade Union League; Miss Mary M. Bartelme, assistant judge of the Chicago Juvenile Court, Mrs. Maud Ballington Booth, of the Volunteers of America; Miss Katherine B. Davis, Commissioner of Correction of New York; Miss Julia C. Lathrop, Chief of the Federal Children's Bureau, in Washington, D.C.; Mrs. Florence Kelly, secretary of the National Consumers League; Mrs. Helen Ring Robinson, a Colorado State Senator; and Miss Kate M. Gordon, of New Orleans, La., president of the Southern States Women's Suffrage Conference. I was impressed by their speeches and by the fine type of American womanhood they represented. My mother opened the meeting in an excellent introductory address and like a good showman presented one 'great woman' after another—until with a horrible thrill of apprehension I trembled lest by error my humble person should be so identified. When in the company of suffragettes a perverse desire to condone all men's errors possessed me, for I found female self-sufficiency somewhat ridiculous. To hear Christabel Pankhurst orate against the male sex, as if their presence in this world were altogether superfluous, made one wonder how far prejudice could contaminate a brilliant intellect.

During this visit, with the threat of a European war imminent, I found it difficult to focus my thoughts on women's suffrage. A return passage to England on the *Kaiser Wilhelm der Grosse*, one of Germany's super-luxury liners, had been booked for me. She was to sail on August 3rd, but on the 2nd news reached me that because of the English destroyers in her path her departure had been delayed. Unable to get in touch with the *Lusitania*, which at the dead of night put out like a phantom ship for an "unknown destination", I left on an American steamer three days after the declaration of war. Brilliantly lighted, with the American flag well to the fore, we sailed through submarine-infested seas, passing ships that like dark and silent ghosts showed neither lights nor colours.

My imagination had pictured an England grim and tense in the throes of a general mobilisation. I was surprised to find how little people had reacted with my foreboding of a long and terrible war. To me the future loomed frighteningly, for my sons were at Eton and Blandford was nearly seventeen. Already I sensed the tragic lot of that doomed generation. Most of them went straight from public school to the Army; the fortunate returned to take a course at Oxford or Cambridge.

Blandford went from Eton to Sandhurst, the Military College, at eighteen, for the short course of training which was all they could afford to give officers in those hard-pressed days, and then straight into the regiment of the First Life Guards as a second lieutenant. It semed to me as I went down to spend a day with them that a shadow already obscured the happiness of our times together, for one had to hide one's apprehensions in that young world of high expectancies.

On the very evening of my return to England I had been rung up by the Austro-Hungarian Ambassador, who in a sad voice and speaking French asked, "May I come to say good-bye? I am leaving tomorrow." "English, please," interrupted the operator. Poor Count Mensdorff—how unhappy he was to leave England, where all his sympathies lay! He had tried against impossible odds to preserve peace, even after the assassination of the Archduke Francis Ferdinand, and if it had not been for the German war lords he would have succeeded. His Embassy in Belgrave Square had been the gayest in London and as a bachelor he managed to avoid the pomp that like a pall enveloped the German Embassy. His dinner-parties were charming and chosen with care among the prettiest women and most entertaining men; and his chef contributed in equal measure to a perfect evening. He usually had an Austrian band and we danced those entrancing Viennese waltzes until early morning. Sometimes he asked me to act as his hostess, and I did so when he entertained the Archduke Francis Ferdinand, and also the young Archduke Charles, who would be Emperor now were he alive and Austria still a monarchy. He was very young then and talked with the greatest enthusiasm of the lovely Princess he was engaged to marry. "She is one of a very large family," he told me, "which is good, for I want ever so many children." He had them, but the Empress Zita lives, widowed and poor, in exile—and the children are scattered throughout the world.

Count Mensdorff came to say good-bye and I realised that he still hoped that the *status quo* might be restored after the war and that he might return as Ambassador. I, however, felt convinced that the war would prove the end of an era. The next day a British man-of-war took him to France, where a special train carried him to his country. It was very different treatment

from that accorded Monsieur Jules Cambon, the French
Ambassador to Germany; there women spat on the windows of
his compartment as he travelled through in an ordinary train,
and every courtesy—even a glass of water—was refused him.
French has been well chosen as the language of diplomacy, but
the Hun will never learn its meaning.

Another call that I received on my arrival in England was
from the American Women's War Relief Fund asking me to be
their chairman and to make an appeal for funds at a meeting
that was to be held in Mrs. William Leeds's house the following
day. During the first year of that war $303,740.28 were sub-
scribed by my countrymen and women.

We organised and ran a military hospital of four hundred
beds in a splendid house in Devonshire given to us by Mr. Paris
Singer, a hospital for officers in London and work-rooms for
needy women whose husbands were at the front. Thanks to the
generosity of our compatriots these activities never lacked support, but if on occasions we envisaged a new departure, Mrs.
Whitelaw Reid would say, "How much do you want?" and, without waiting for an answer, "I will give it." In fact I had to
remonstrate, pointing out that our work should not depend
altogether on the generosity of one of its members. Ambassador
and Mrs. Reid's daughter, Lady Ward, was also on the committee and, with Viscountess Harcourt and Mr. and Mrs. Walter
Burns, was the most active member. Lady Harcourt, as honorary
secretary, proved that she had inherited her uncle Pierpont
Morgan's business acumen. She carried the brunt of the work
and, when decorations were forthcoming, was made a Dame of
the Order of the British Empire.

English women were forming a 'Women's Emergency Corps',
with Lady Tree and Miss Lena Ashwell, two leading actresses,
as guiding spirits. At their request I spoke for them at their first
meeting at the Shaftesbury Theatre a few days after the outbreak of war. So many women responded to this call that an
overflow meeting was held at the Little Theatre. Ten thousand
offers of personal service were received from doctors, dispensers,
trained nurses, interpreters and others; while bus drivers and
sportswomen who understood the care of horses volunteered to
assist in transport work. Mrs. Pethick-Lawrence urged all
volunteer workers to refuse any kind of work in which they
would compete with women who had their livelihood to gain. As

honorary treasurer of the Corps, I realised what splendid work was done in registering and training women to take the place of enlisted men and to carry on such activities as collecting food, feeding Belgian refugees and making toys to supplant those formerly imported from Germany.

I remember the first day the German planes came over London. It was during the morning, and my secretary was taking letters when suddenly the zum of planes overhead became formidable. Dropping everything we rushed down and into the streets—apparently everyone else had done the same—and craning our necks we saw a company of German planes sail over in perfect formation. They had come to challenge our defences and not a shot was fired in answer. All we could do in the instinctive gesture of vengeance was to shake our fists at the blue of that brilliant sky.

During the Zeppelin raids the basement of Sunderland House became the refuge of my neighbours, who all lived in small, old, rather frail houses. The following letter is typical of many I received:

> 69 Curzon Street
> Mayfair
> September 5, 1917

Your Grace:

I feel I cannot help letting you know that your kindness in opening the basement of Sunderland House saved our lives last night.

We sheltered there, and during our absence our drawing-room windows were shattered and a very large piece of shell-casing came into the room which we had only left ten minutes before.

Pray believe I am very grateful

> Yours faithfully,
> (signed)   Maude M. C. Foulkes

I preferred to sleep quietly in my bed and had forbidden my maid to wake me, being a sound sleeper. Last-minute repentances are to my mind rather cowardly, and if I was doomed to be blown up I thought it better not to anticipate it.

The days were full of work; I retired early, and very rarely dined out, not having the heart for it. There was, however, one evening when, while Lady Essex, my two sons and I were at dinner before going to the opera, the siren sounded, to be succeeded by the distant thud of bombs and, quite close, the ack-ack from the guns in Hyde Park. The parlourmaid with perfect composure finished serving the meal and we debated whether or not to go to the opera. Unnecessary circulation during raids had been forbidden; nevertheless, because the opera was a favourite we decided to go. The streets were empty and we reached it in no time. There had been a lull in the bombing, but no sooner were we installed in our box than another raid was upon us, accompanied by such noise that Sir Thomas Beecham, who was conducting, shrugged his shoulders in annoyance and the soprano sang louder than ever. The police came in to evacuate the upper tiers while the rest of us sat it out. The only other raid that caught me in a theatre was at His Majesty's, when the manager came out to announce, "The iron curtain will be let down for the safety of the actors; the audience is requested quietly to remain in their seats." A general laugh was, however, followed by a general exodus.

In the year 1915 it became fashionable to offer one's London house to the War Office as a nursing-home. Sunderland House was not adapted to this purpose and was, moreover, the only house left free for public meetings, for which it was particularly suited since it had a long gallery where three hundred people could be seated.

On investigating hospital accommodation I found that the labour wards were in many cases being given over to the more important work of caring for the wounded and that there was an increasing demand for a lying-in hospital. I decided to meet this demand by closing my Home for Prisoners' Wives, the need for which no longer existed. After being fitted with eighteen beds, it became an annexe to the Royal Free Hospital. Lady Barrett and Dr. Aldrich Blake, two prominent gynæcologists, headed the staff of women doctors and students.

Our patients often postponed arriving until the very last moment, and on one occasion a taxi driver came in to inform us the baby had been born in his car. At that time unmarried women were finding it difficult to gain admittance to the general hospitals, so that we had a great number of these unfortunate girls, whom we also tried to help with the difficult problem of their future. Going round the wards one day, I saw the mother of a lovely baby in tears, and I inquired the cause of her unhappiness. "He's white," she answered, pointing to the baby, "and my husband when he sees him will not believe he is his." Then the English nurse in charge told me that the husband was an American negro, and added, "I told her babies were always born white even if they become black later on, but the girl will not believe me!"

During the war immorality among girls in their teens assumed disturbing proportions, for they were the chief carriers of disease and ignored the serious consequences. The echoes of Victorian morality were still vibrant and any enlightenment had to be given clandestinely. When I was asked to give the Priestley Lecture, which that year, 1916, was to deal with 'Infant Mortality, Its Causes and Preventions', I prepared a comprehensive survey based on medical facts and public health statistics which it took me three weeks to write and an hour to read. One could not ignore the prevalence of venereal disease and its disastrous effects, but when I mentioned the fact, I saw several old ladies rise in dignified disapproval and with horrified glances at my scarlet face turn their backs and walk out of the hall. Not until the next day, when an editorial in the London *Times* thanked me for the courage shown in unveiling unpalatable truths, did I regain my composure. In spite of the fact that my predecessors as Priestley Lecturers had been men of the calibre of Professor Sir Ray Lankester, K.C.B., F.R.S., and Professor Metchnikoff of the Pasteur Institute, an excerpt from a London newspaper will show that I did not acquit myself too badly:

The Duchess of Marlborough always fascinates her hearers by the combined simplicity, persuasiveness and logic lighted by quaint little flashes of humour of her speeches, and her choice as the first woman to deliver a Priestley Lecture was more than justified.

As honorary treasurer of the Medical School for Women in connection with the Royal Free Hospital—at that time the only hospital where women students were accepted and allowed to practise—I was fortunate in securing donations which enabled us to establish and equip additional premises. In recognition of my services the Council of the School of Medicine for Women

(University of London) did me the honour of attaching my name to the extension of the Physics Department.

Public work had little by little absorbed me. The interest of tackling a new subject, of making out a good case, of arousing sympathy, and of furthering a cause overcame the nervousness public speaking always engendered. My interests were varied, but my chief concern was the welfare of women and children and the extension of pre-natal as well as post-natal care for them. For this I spoke all over the country, and in time came to be called the "Baby Duchess", which in view of my height and advancing years was thoroughly misleading. But my biggest thrills were speaking at meetings at 10 Downing Street with Mrs. Lloyd George in the chair; at the Mansion House, where the Deputy Lord Mayor presided and I was sandwiched between two Cabinet Ministers as the only woman speaker; and again at the Guildhall, when the Lord Mayor presided.

I was also writing articles for the Press and thinking out ways and means to extract donations from an impoverished and war-weary public. One untapped source occurred to me and we launched an appeal to women to give a jewel to save a baby's life. Thus 'The Children's Jewel Fund' was born and had instantaneous success. We raised nearly fifty thousand pounds in the fourth year of war—an astounding display of British generosity. Gifts great and small poured into Cartier's sumptuous premises in Bond Street which they generously lent us as head-quarters. Great ladies ransacked family heirlooms and brought out cameos, chatelaines, diamond brooches, bracelets and rings, stomachers in their old-fashioned settings and diamond tiaras and necklaces. Yet more touching were the offerings of the poor who gave us trinkets and treasures of gold and silver; even wedding rings were parted with by those who had nothing else to give. We had a most successful auction at Christie's, at which Mr. Lloyd George's pearl and diamond scarf-pin was put up for auction again and again amid scenes of great enthusiasm.

In addition to these philanthropic activities I had formed a Women's Municipal party with the express purpose of getting women elected to municipal councils; for if it was left to the tender mercies of the Conservative and Liberal parties it was evident that women would be given seats to contest where they had very little chance of being elected. The Women's Municipal party therefore decided on more aggressive tactics and we put up independent candidates to disrupt the party in power by drawing off the female vote. We considered such tactics justified by the need for women councillors who would give special attention to public health measures for the care of child life. The number of women on the London County Council was small and some of the Borough Councils had no women members at all. Unfortunately for me, a vacancy on the London County Council occurred in North Southwark in 1917 and my Committee pointed out the necessity for its President to act up to its policies. I was dismayed, for politics held no attraction for me and my private work absorbed all my energies; nevertheless, *noblesse oblige*, I accepted. Mr. E. A. Strauss was the Liberal M.P. for North Southwark and became a kind friend and a staunch supporter. He was unmarried, and in time, especially during the post-war parliamentary election, I had to speak at all his meetings. Mr. Strauss presided at my first meeting in Southwark and introduced me to the members of the Selection Committee, men on whose approval my election depended, for during the war contested elections had been suspended; by agreement between the parties a vacancy was filled by the party that held the seat. It was therefore only at the end of the war that I fought and won a contested election.

On this first occasion I met some sixty of my would-be constituents and gave a comprehensive speech, for I had been asked to state my views in general. I spoke for an hour, during which my judges lent a kindly and attentive ear. Then Mr. Strauss asked me to wait outside while the Committee took a vote. It seemed to me that it took them as long to decide my fate as it had taken me to state my views, and I was becoming despondent, for, although I had no desire to stand, there was now a question of pride involved in the issue. At last the door opened and Mr. Strauss came in smiling and, grasping my hand, said, "You are unanimously selected as our member for North Southwark."

Relieved, but still doubting, I asked, "But why did you take so long?"

"Because," said Mr. Strauss, "so many had to get up to explain that they could not see how a Duchess could be a Progressive nor how she could understand a working-man's point of view, but since hearing your speech they were convinced of your sincerity and your ability to represent them." I went up to thank them for their confidence and hoped I would not fail them.

The London County Council is the central administering body of the twenty-eight Metropolitan boroughs and of the City of London. It consisted of 124 councillors elected triennially by the ratepayers, and of 20 aldermen elected by the councillors to hold office for six years. The Chairmen have invariably been men distinguished for their public service.

I was impressed by the business-like appearance of the assembly, which at that time still held its sessions in the Old County Council Hall in Westminster. The fine new buildings across the Thames opposite to the Houses of Parliament were then being built. The Council was divided into three parties: the Municipal Reformers, the Conservative party, who were in the majority; the Progressives, or Liberals, to which I belonged; and the Labour members, a small but effective group, with Miss Susan Lawrence, later elected to the House of Commons, as Whip.

The London County Council's sessions differ from the Commons in that debates are rare. The business of administration admittedly does not produce the heated discussions new policies evoke. The real work is done in committees and the reports they issue are models of their kind. In the Council itself questions addressed to the chairmen of the various committees permit short discussions, and there are occasions when a full-dress debate over the allocation of funds becomes heated. Measures for education and public health were interesting, but the provision of houses for the working classes urgent. And the Council had undertaken a tremendous programme involving a huge expenditure. A welcome departure and one which had a permanent influence on all future suburban developments was the planning of garden suburbs.

It was not until March, 1919, four months after the Armistice, that an election of County Councillors for London took place. I stood as a Progressive with the Mayor of North Southwark against two Labour members. At the numerous meetings I held in the various wards of the constituency, I was encouraged by the good attendance at a time when the papers declared that "never has the traditional apathy of the London elector been so marked." On election day I started visiting my committee rooms and polling stations at 9 a.m. and was on my feet until the count, which took place at the Town Hall after the close of the polls at 8 p.m. On my walking tours I was accompanied by groups of children who enlivened my progress by chanting 'Vote Vote Vote for Mrs. Marlborough' to the tune of 'Tramp Tramp Tramp the Boys are Marching'. The London *Daily Telegraph* gave the following account:

> Southwark is again solidly Progressive, the Duchess of Marlborough being at the top of the Poll. Her Grace had a large number of supporters amongst the women, to whom she made a special appeal, and on Wednesday she received a letter of support from Mrs. Lloyd George. Yesterday it was noticeable that she had more motor-cars at her disposal than any other candidate. She was very well received wherever she went.

During the count, at which my sons were present, it looked at one moment as if a split election would result, with myself and a popular preacher who stood as one of my Labour opponents elected, but the final figures showed a good majority for the Progressives. It was to be the Liberal party's last victory; soon after, the Socialists secured and succeeded in holding the seat.

It gives me pleasure to reflect that although my time on the Council was short I was able to obtain a playground for the children of North Southwark, which I put through by first securing a certain measure of financial support and then appealing to the Parks Committee under whose control these playgrounds were laid out and operated.

Work on the London County Council was indeed, as the Lord Mayor had informed me, arduous. It was not the Council meetings but the committees which met every week that required work and the mastering of long reports. With the approach of a General Election I had to speak at all rallies and take as well the women's meetings.

Always interested in housing conditions, I toured the slums of South London and was dismayed by the unsanitary and inadequate houses inhabited by the poor. With the desire to draw attention to Southwark for the housing reforms that were then being advocated, I approached the Prince of Wales and asked him to accompany me on a tour, an invitation he promptly accepted. We drove down in his car, and then proceeded on foot through the worst slums, stopping to look over the most unsanitary habitations. I was amazed by his intimate knowledge of social problems and delighted by the kindly interest he showed. Joined by the Mayor, we soon attracted a large crowd which cheered us on our way. As he drove me home, the Prince sadly commented on the immensity of the task that lay ahead in providing decent and adequate housing, and when we parted, with a boyish twinkle in his eye, he added, "I wish my mother wore hats like yours!" Ever Prince Charming, he was, I knew, complimenting my taste, not criticising a mother to whom he gave a reverential devotion.

At the outbreak of war I had liberated my chauffeur for war work and taken a young girl in his stead, but as the war neared its end she told me she would have to leave me.

"I had three brothers at the front," she said. "One was killed, one badly wounded and now Dad has gone too, so I have applied to the Red Cross to drive a car in France."

And she went, a lovely and gallant person whom I pray life may have blessed. She was succeeded by a shell-shocked soldier. He had little to do, since I hardly ever dined out and driving me to my meetings in the small Renault was child's play. What then was my surprise when during my election campaign my agent, looking very uncomfortable, informed me he had something disagreeable to tell me.

"While you are having meetings," he said, "and speaking on the need for better housing conditions, your chauffeur holds street meetings telling everyone that you yourself own the worst slums in London."

"Well," I said, "put someone in the crowd to ask him to name the slums. Sunderland House is my only possession. Does he complain his hours are too long or has he any grievance against me?"

"None," my agent answered, "but in an election your opponents are ready to give credit to any lie if they can use it against you."

So I had to get rid of the soldier and went to my meetings in the County Council trams, which was no doubt a good electioneering move. One night, as I left the tram and started down the ill-lighted, deserted street on foot, I heard steps behind me and recognised the man who had sat opposite me in the tram. My heart came into my mouth as stories of theft and murder swam in my mind, but he turned out to be a supporter and with relief I saw him later applauding the points of my speech.

Living at Sunderland House was by no means a sinecure. There was no central heating, owing to wartime restrictions, and I lived in a flat on the third floor which the long gallery, being two storeys high, shut off. I worked in a small sitting-room where my meals were served on a tray, and for heat I depended more on the sun which occasionally shone than on the miserable coal fire. Often numb with cold at my desk, I would sit on the floor with my back to the grate, sizzling like a fried chicken—and thus spend the morning alternately grilling and freezing.

Criticism of my occupation of so large a house in wartime had reached me. Of course, those who criticised did not know the discomforts I endured and that I lived there only in order to be able to lend the long gallery to the charities and meetings that bespoke my hospitality as well as my personal services as chairman. Servants were becoming hard to find, for girls preferred working in munition factories, and when the tenth housemaid in two weeks gave notice I asked her to tell me frankly what was wrong.

"Well," she said, "I thought I had come to a private house, but I find it's the Town Hall, and I'm sick of washing that there marble floor after those meetings and refreshments."

I had for some time entertained the same thoughts, and when I heard a lady remark as she tripped down to tea after a meeting, "I have been looking forward to those chocolate éclairs all afternoon; to tell you the truth, it's the only reason why I came," I decided to discontinue the meetings and to place Sunderland House at the disposal of the British Government. Early in 1918 the Government passed it on to the Inter-Ally Council on War Purchases and Finance as their headquarters in London, and my little flat on the third floor was given to the American Advisory Counsel, Mr. Paul D. Cravath. Much later, on June 25, 1919, Mr. Arthur James Balfour sent me the following letter in which he refers to the eventual birth of the League of Nations:

British Delegation
Paris
June 25th, 1919

My dear Duchess,

As the Germans have now told us they mean to sign I presume we are a step nearer the effective establishment of the League of Nations.

I must take this opportunity of thanking you for the help you have given in obtaining the use of Sunderland House for a body on whose successful working so much of the future history of the world will depend! and so far as I have any title to speak on their behalf, I desire to give expression to their gratitude.

Yours very sincerely,
(signed)   Arthur James Balfour

I was now completely immersed in work, and rarely attended social functions. With Ivor, I lived in a little house I had taken near Regent's Park. On leaving Eton, Ivor had failed to pass his medical tests for the Army, and General Sir John Cowans, who was then Quartermaster-General and had his headquarters at the War Office, took him on his staff. In the opening years of World War I there was a particularly odious brand of female who delighted in pinning white feathers on young men in the London streets regardless of the sufferings such indignities inflicted on their innocent and helpless victims. I was glad therefore when Ivor was taken by his cousin Winston Churchill on one of his tours of inspection of the front in France, and, as was invariably the case when accompanying Winston, experienced a first-class bombardment. Winston with his usual thoughtful kindness wrote to me how well Ivor had acquitted himself. Blandford was in France with his regiment, the Life Guards. My brother Harold I saw when he passed through London on his way to join sub-chasers at Queenstown. Both he and my brother William K., Jr., were serving in the United States Navy.

On November 11, 1918, at 11 a.m. sirens announced the Armistice. Cheering crowds poured into every street, commandeering taxis and cars to drive wildly about, singing and waving flags. The tension of four long, and at times disastrous, years had ended. The glory of peace with victory had dawned. My thoughts inevitably went to those brave and gallant Englishmen who had made the great sacrifice. Among them I had lost many friends. Eventually with the signing of peace came the great Victory Parade of the Allied Armies in London. I saw it from the London County Council building as it swung down the Mall. It was a proud moment when the magnificent contingent my country had sent over came into sight leading the

procession. The men were of perfect alignment and height—
they seemed to march as one man. They had, I thought as they
passed, the clear-cut features, the keen eyes and shapely heads
and the athletic build, of the Grecian warriors we see in the
friezes of Phidias. The French contingent was small, with
Marshal Foch in the midst of his generals, the flags of France
in massed array. But as their veteran troops bearing their regimental colours marched by I felt the tears coursing down my
cheeks and the crowds must have felt the same emotion, for their
cheers seemed warmer and softer. Canadians, Australians, New
Zealanders passed with the fine martial precision we had learned
to expect of them. They received a thunderous welcome, but
it was for our own Home Army we had waited, and when the
Tommies and the Tars loomed into sight everyone went mad.
Field-Marshal Earl Haig on his charger, the admirals and the
generals were cheered to the echo.

It was an anti-climax to return to the dull routine of everyday
life. The urge we had felt during the years of war no longer was
there. Nevertheless for those of us who worked in the slums
there was a bitter realisation that much had to be done to make
England "a land fit for heroes to live in"—the promise on which
Lloyd George won his election.

My vitality was running low and I found it an effort to keep
going. I shall always remember my discomfiture when one hot
day in an airless committee room of the London County Council
I fell asleep sitting on a hard chair in the circle around the table,
clutching the numerous reports I had spent hours in reading. Just
as I had reached the delicious but ominous moment when one's
head nods I felt through my unconsciousness a horrible dread
and woke to the fact that every eye was fixed upon me, as the
Chairman with a kindly but somewhat ironic smile said, "I am
afraid we must take that vote again." Automatically I raised my
hand, feeling disgraced and humbled.

Following my doctor's orders I took a few weeks off on the
French Riviera, where I joined my mother. She had bought a
villa with a lovely little garden full of flowers and orange trees
on the shore of the Mediterranean at Eze-sur-Mer. We grew very
close during those last years of her life, each sharing the other's
interests.

Early in 1920 my eldest son's marriage to lovely Mary
Cadogan, the daughter of Viscount Chelsea, was celebrated in

the Church of Saint Margaret's, Westminster, on one of those mid-winter days that have the warmth and promise of spring. A fashionable wedding, it was graced by the royal family's presence. It was also my valediction, for steps had already been taken to secure my divorce.

It was now possible for a woman to divorce her husband for desertion, provided she could also prove that he had spent a night in a hotel with another woman, information that the miscreant at times obligingly supplied. The stain of shame had faded to a gentler hue; society, now less censorious, no longer ostracised a divorcée. The circles from which they were banished were rare. The long vista of lonely years behind me prodded the courage I needed to face the publicity of an English divorce court. But when I consulted my lawyer, he informed me that a legal separation freed a husband from the obligations contracted by marriage and that to secure a divorce I should first have to live under the same roof with Marlborough again. The humiliating process of the law next required that the husband leave his wife and inform her in writing that he refused to return to her. She then had to appear in court and ask the judge for an injunction granting her a 'Restitution of Conjugal Rights'. On the judge's pronouncement the husband would be ordered to comply. On his refusal to do so, the woman could bring action for divorce, provided she had the evidence required to secure it. These were the steps I took to obtain my divorce in the year 1920, having first, in order to comply with existing regulations, spent some days at Crowhurst with Marlborough and his sister Lilian Grenfell, who kindly shared our solitude. The shadow of my first marriage was once again to fall across my life when some years later Marlborough, having joined the Roman Catholic Church and wishing to regularise in that Church his civil marriage to Gladys Deacon, asked me to take steps to have our marriage annulled.

I should like to close this chapter which deals chiefly with my work with the words in which Lord Haldane, in the last pages of his autobiography, sums up his personal philosophy; for his friendship and his counsel had played an important part in critical decisions I had had to make. As a statesman and philosopher, as Minister for War and then Lord Chancellor, as the author of *The Pathway to Reality* and *The Reign of Relativity*, he was supremely fitted to give judgment on the true values of life. He says:

The best that ordinary mortals can hope for is the result which will probably come from sustained work directed by as full reflection as is possible. This result may be affected adversely by circumstances, by illness, by misfortune, or by death. But if we have striven to think and to do work based on thought, then we have at least the sense of having striven with such faculties as we have possessed devoted to the striving. And that is in itself a course of happiness, going beyond the possession of any definite gain.

CHAPTER NINE

A Marriage of Love

THE year 1920 was darkened by my father's ill-health and death. I was with him to the end. Whatever his personal sufferings may have been he made no complaints; not even a gesture of ill-humour troubled the serenity he seemed to emanate. There was a fineness about him that one sensed clearly and it seemed to me that nothing ignoble would ever touch him. In his business and in his life he lived up to the high standard of integrity he had set himself. I remember the tribute the Duc de Gramont, one of France's leading sportsmen, paid him when he came to present his condolences: "I wish to express the grief of the French Jockey Club at your father's death. It is fine and honourable sportsmen such as he, mindful of the best traditions of the turf, we delight in welcoming. His death will be a great loss to the French racing world." From the poor came expressions of affection and esteem and there was sorrow in the clinic he had founded, where I had often assisted my stepmother in her work during my visits to Paris.

We brought him home and laid him to rest in the family vault on Staten Island. The service in our New York house with only the family and close friends present brought poignant memories, as from the gallery, where as children we looked down on festive scenes, came the haunting notes of death's dirges.

There followed a few weeks on Long Island, where my mother had built herself a medieval castle which dominated the Sound. In spite of her suffrage activities her life was a lonely one and she decided to join me in France, where I had determined to live. After years of intensive propaganda, her ambitions were realised with the passage of the Nineteenth Amendment in 1920, giving the vote to women. She had then become president of the National Woman's party and had presented them with their headquarters in Washington near the Capitol, known as Alva

Belmont House. I thought that her decision to live in France might be actuated by more than just the desire to be near me; always an inveterate builder, she welcomed, I knew, the opportunity to build a new home in a new country, being really happy only when thus employed.

On my return to Europe I spent a few weeks in London to pack my belongings, to arrange for the sale of Sunderland House, to transfer a house I had leased in Portman Square to my married son, to give up Crowhurst and to wind up the many activities that had become dear to me. Leaving my work was a wrench and saying farewell to my fellow workers saddened me. Working for others breeds a sense of altruism to which, as time goes on and the habit grows, one unconsciously submits one's decision, weighing the amount of personal happiness one can justly consider one's due. Having voluntarily removed the blinkers self-indulgence creates, I found it became more difficult to hoodwink selfish desires, and fears assailed me about the rightness of my decision. But looking back on the long years of solitude, ranging as they did from my twenty-ninth to my forty-fourth year, I felt I could not give up the promise of happiness that had now come my way, a decision that my eldest son's happy marriage helped me to reach. Moreover, as I ruefully reflected, if I waited for my second son to marry it might be too late for me to follow a similar course. After the war he had gone to Oxford to complete his education; and I felt that with both my sons once more ensconced in the niches prepared for them by tradition I could flee to freer spheres, for niches gave me claustrophobia.

Consequently, after Blandford's marriage I went to live in the lovely house my father had given me in Paris. Though his death had robbed me of the happy companionship I had envisaged, my mother's arrival brought a measure of consolation; and with her sister Jenny Tiffany, who had always been a favourite aunt, we spent many pleasant hours.

Meanwhile, while awaiting my divorce, I leased a villa near the property my mother had acquired at Eze-sur-Mer and as frequently as possible went to England to be with my children.

On July 4, 1921, I was married to Jacques Balsan in the Chapel Royal of the Savoy at nine in the morning. This unusual hour had been chosen to avoid the glare of publicity which had been focused on the marriage of Marlborough and Gladys Deacon earlier that spring in Paris. In order to conform to French law

we also went through a civil ceremony with Colonel George
Harvey, then American Ambassador in London, and my cousin
General Cornelius Vanderbilt as my witnesses. In shedding the
lustre of the coronet it was my hope to avoid publicity. If not
quite successful in that respect, in every other, life with Jacques
Balsan has brought me the profound happiness companionship
with one equally loved and honoured means. It is difficult to
appraise a character so completely in harmony with one's
sympathies, but it can be said that, whether in France, in England
or in my native land, I have rarely met a man or a woman,
certainly never a child, who has not succumbed to the charm of
his personality, to the keenness of his varied interests, to the
subtle intelligence of his understanding, to the wit of his conversation and, above all, to the profound goodness and kindness
of his nature.

It is perhaps not out of place here to give my readers a short
account of his life. He had been an airman in the true sense of
the word, since before aeroplanes were invented he owned a
balloon in which in 1899 he flew from France to Russia. The
following year he won a high-altitude record in France. He has
often told me how, on another occasion, he landed in North
Prussia on the borders of Lake Leta. As his balloon came to
ground he was surrounded by peasants and conducted to the
Castle of the Baron of Bandemer, who received him with the
courtesy one officer accords another, even though they be
traditional enemies. The Baron, an ancient chamberlain of the
Emperor Frederick, and the Baroness entertained him by taking
him for drives through the forests of their vast possessions, and
one day they came to a monument. Reining in his horses, the
Baron proudly said, "I am going to show you something very
interesting. This monument has been raised to celebrate the
defeat of the French armies at Sedan." On returning to the
castle, Jacques Balsan wished his hosts farewell. He had not
realised until his hostess explained it "that no insult was meant,
since the Baron as a Prussian had a *special mentality*."

In 1909—before Blériot made his historic flight across the
Channel—Jacques bought his first aeroplane, and received his
licence as Pilot No. 18. Convinced that aviation would play a
prominent part in future wars, he went to Morocco as a volunteer
airman in the war against the Moors in 1913 and 1914. It was a
brave decision, for the Moors were known to kill their captives

by slow torture and aeroplanes were then monoplanes with a 65-horsepower engine. For exceptional service rendered to the Ministry of War he received the Legion of Honour. His experience in Africa had prepared him for the First World War and in 1914, then a captain in the Air Force, he was appointed by General Maunoury to reconnoitre the first Battle of the Marne. I have often heard him speak of his emotion on seeing the German Army, commanded by Von Kluck, advancing in an effort to destroy the French Army at its point of juncture with the English, a manœuvre that proved to be their undoing.

During the war Jacques commanded a group of Scout planes. In 1915 he, together with my father, who undertook to pay for the transport of any American who wished to fight in the French Air Force, and Dr. Gross of the American Hospital at Neuilly, raised and formed the Escadrille Lafayette, which later was integrated into the American Army. In the last month of the year 1917 he was sent on a special mission to London.

We had met sporadically since my coming-out ball at the Duc de Gramont's in Paris. Balsan had come to Blenheim as our guest on several occasions, and the large toy lion he brought my babies adorned a recess in the great hall for many years. I remember receiving a postcard from him during the war, and when we met again he told me that he had sent it because he had not expected to return from a mission to bombard a certain town and had wished to greet me before his departure.

It seemed almost as if fate had decreed that he should re-enter my life. But even after my civil and religious marriage we were, as I was to find, not considered married by the Catholic Church.

In France divorce is practically non-existent and Catholics who wish to remarry have to apply to the Roman Rota for the dissolution of previous ties. Orthodox Catholics are therefore forbidden to recognise the marriage of a Catholic to a divorced person unless the latter's marriage has been dissolved by the Church. The Balsans, as devout Catholics, could not receive me, and sensing the rift in the family that my marriage to Jacques had made I begged him not to break with them, for I knew the deep affection they bore one another. Coming from England, where Catholics are subjected to religious bias, I found the reverse to be the case in France, and was surprised when in Protestant circles I was acclaimed for refusing to change my religion, as many had done before me.

Looking back on these first years of my second marriage I realised the essentially self-contained life we led. In our close companionship the outer world meant little to us, and if certain families refused to recognise our marriage, we were happily not dependent on the pleasures they could offer.

Sanctified as our marriage had been in an Episcopal church, it was to me completely valid; and I would have been content to ignore the ultra-religious views that prevented the orthodox Catholics from recognising it. But in 1926, when Marlborough decided he wanted his first marriage annulled, the pressure brought by my French family and my desire to see Jacques at peace with them determined my decision to approach the Rota.

On consulting my English lawyer, Sir Charles Russell, a Catholic and a devoted friend, I found that my only valid claim to an annulment was the fact that I had been married against my will. It pained me to approach my mother for her consent, but on learning that the proceedings were entirely private we agreed to take the necessary steps. The evidence once collected, I appeared with other witnesses before an English tribunal of Catholic priests versed in canonical law. My former governess, Miss Harper, gave valuable testimony, since she had personally witnessed the coercion to which I had been subjected. The application was then sent to the Rota, which granted the annulment.

All would have been well had not Marlborough gone to Rome to be received in audience by the Pope. News of the annulment then got about and promptly unloosed a blast of Protestant wrath aimed at the Rota for annulling an Episcopal marriage. Alas, gone were our privacy and peace of mind as once again the Press exposed my story. My mother, with her usual courage, remained undaunted, but I suffered to see her in so unfavourable a light, knowing that she had hoped to ensure my happiness with the marriage she had forced upon me. Religious controversies are apt to be bitter; but there was no truth in the accusation that the Rota had been bribed. Counsels' fees and the cost of collecting evidence were the only disbursements and were much less than the charges of a legal divorce. It was, however, with some bitterness that I reflected that it had required three legal interventions to obtain my freedom, and then a fourth in the form of the Rota, each accompanied by unpleasant and unnecessary publicity.

After the annulment was granted, I was married to Jacques in a Catholic ceremony and joined the family circle. The Balsans lived at Châteauroux in the centre of France. Their cloth factories had been founded by the Prince de Condé at the instigation of the Minister, Colbert, who in the reign of Louis XIV reconstituted the commerce and industries of France. The family lived in the château and its dependencies, which were surrounded by park-like grounds; the factories were near-by.

On this my first visit the doors of the salon opened on a typical family scene. There were at least twenty people assembled in various groups—Jacques' brothers, sisters, cousins, his nephews and nieces. In a *bergère* near the hearth sat a lovely old lady dressed in black with a touch of lace. She was Madame Charles Balsan, Jacques' aunt and head of the family, who with masterful authority ensured the traditional discipline of the Catholic Church. Greeting me with affection, she then called her children by name and presented them, with a word of kindly appraisal for each. That she also had humour and wit I realised as soon as she spoke, and later when she wrote to me I marvelled at her lovely penmanship and the beauty and elegance of her style. When, handing me a golden box—a family heirloom—she welcomed me to the family circle, I sensed her unspoken question: 'Can you appreciate and understand why for so long against our love and personal desires you have been ostracised?' And later when I wrote to her and expressed my understanding, she, in a generous gesture, read my letter to the assembled family. It is in truth a memory of gracious authority I have of her.

The day after my meeting with her, Jacques and I returned to our house in Paris where so many happy years had been spent even before this family reunion. It overlooked the Champs de Mars, that big garden that stretches its green swards from the banks of the Seine to the fine old buildings of the École de Guerre. In the mornings I awoke to the gay gallop of cavalry officers as they rode past our windows on the bridle-path that encircles the gardens. Later, little children came to play there with their buckets and spades. At midday workmen ate their luncheon on the benches that lined the paths, engaging in those heated discussions Latins find so stimulating. Men and women sat reading their papers under the trees. They each had their special chair placed in a favourite spot. In time I came to know the papers they read and the children who answered their call. We used to nod and smile at each other—'*Bonjour Madame*'— as I passed. How lovely were those spring and early summer days. The gay flowers in the parterres, the green velvet of the lawns, the golden rivulets of sand that enclosed them, the scent of lilacs and laburnum, the acacias stretching the stiff bouquets of their blooms to the sky, the birds singing, the swans on the gay little pond and, beyond, the clear grey waters of the Seine lapping against the stone embankments where fishermen fished or read the news. At night the lights from the Eiffel Tower flashed above our roof and the stars seemed to answer from high above. Oh, the heart-breaking beauty of Paris in spring-time!

Our house had been built by Sergent, a French architect, whose chief merit lay in his faithful reproduction of eighteenth-century proportions. We panelled the spacious high-ceilinged rooms with old *boiseries* and found furniture and *bibelots* to complete them. There were exciting days hunting the right thing for the right place. We used to wander up and down the quays and streets with eyes glued to shop windows for a find. Then would follow a strategic approach as with a casual look we would inquire the price of an object. Later, but still casually, we would draw near to our find, and the inevitable bargaining would begin. I will never forget the excitement with which we first came upon Renoir's 'La Baigneuse,' or the pride of possession that pearl-tinted nude gave us when, like a luminous jewel, it adorned our salon. When the war came we greatly feared that it was lost to us, but eventually 'La Baigneuse' came to America with our other possessions. In 1946 we gave it to 'American Aid to France' to provide food for French children. When it was sold for $115,000 I thought of Renoir, who, poor and hungry, had obtained only a few hundred francs for his pictures; and I wished he could have lived to know the sum his masterpiece had brought and how it had provided food for starving French children.

Our house was finally redecorated. *Boiseries* of the eighteenth century gave elegance and charm to the walls and a beautiful Boucher tapestry that my father had owned and which my brothers had kindly given me adorned the dining-room. The collection of furniture, pictures and *bibelots* which it had given us such pleasure to collect was completed. The moment had

come when the result of so much careful research must be submitted to the judgment of others.

The French like meeting foreigners, but seldom invite them.
It seemed appropriate that we should give cosmopolitan parties.
Luncheons centred round a literary or political personality
became our *spécialité*. In a country where general conversation
is brilliant a party of eight or at the most ten is advisable, and
it requires care to secure a successful blend. I found, alas—
perhaps because of their innate politeness—that when foreigners
are present the French rarely wage those controversial discussions
at which they excel. I was struck by the pertinacity of the
Latin mind, by its critical tenacity, by its dislike of vague
verbiage, and by the thoroughness of a knowledge that, if sometimes less extensive, is more often precise. It seemed to me that
the French seldom indulge in the flights of fantasy the English
are prone to. Sentimental journeys are not to their taste, but
realism often holds a deeper sentiment.

Our cosmopolitan parties were gay and the house with its
objects of art provoked interesting discussions, for nearly everyone in France "collects" or has a hobby. How gratifying it proved
to have a guest admire a recent acquisition and how rare it
was to have an iced cocktail glass placed upon a marquetry
table.

Among the parties we preferred were those given at the British
Embassy, the fine house and garden that had once belonged to
Pauline Borghese. French society divided into three quite
separate castes—the *ancien régime,* comprising the great names
of French history under the Kings; the *noblesse d'Empire*
created by Napoleon I and III; and the *Corps Diplomatique* with
the ministers of the Republic. It created a problem for hostesses.
To reconcile these various elements, so jealous of their special
prerogatives, was a thankless task no one would willingly undertake, and only a foreign ambassador could successfully overcome
the problem posed by the etiquette of seating them. At the
Embassy dinners given in honour of the President of the
Republic there appeared to be complete harmony among these
inimical elements; even the Dukes of France and those of the
short-lived Empires, for the time being at least, reconciled their
differences. On the table which seated sixty guests gleamed the
famous gilt service made for Napoleon's beautiful sister. It had
been acquired by the British Government, together with the

house and gardens, for a sum rumour had it the service alone would now fetch. These dinners were invariably agreeable, and were sometimes enlivened by an amusing incident. There was the Ambassador's wife with a reputation for vagueness who, while leading the procession into dinner on the arm of the President of the French Republic, forgot which of the numerous rooms we were dining in, and had to be recalled by an intimidated and harassed butler. Another who was perhaps more addicted to art than to diplomacy would after dinner, quite oblivious of her other guests, retire to her studio with a sitter. And still further back in the annals of time there was one who loved playing poker and dragged unwilling victims to a game. But such eccentrics only added fuel to the fire British idiosyncrasies kept alight, and delighted the French, who are always ready to condone a type! Receptions at the British Embassy, especially during the Marquess of Crewe's time, were done in the grand manner, and yet with the ease and informality perfectly trained English servants make possible. Even though the butler, as I once heard him do, announced the Duchesse de Noailles as the Duchesse d'Uzès and a flustered attaché later presented her as the Duchesse de la Trémouille, what did it matter since she remained a Duchess of France and, who knows, had perhaps risen a rung in the ladder.

Among the parties given by our French acquaintances, I recall a most delightful evening in a beautiful hotel *entre cour et jardin* in the Rue de Varennes. It had been spared from looting during the Revolution and its eighteenth-century *boiseries*, furniture and objects of art remained intact. A ball to be perfect in such a scene needed period dress, and the Duchesse de Doudeauville had bid us come in costumes worn in Louis XV's time. I copied mine from a Nattier portrait—a white taffeta dress with a pink sash slung across one shoulder and in my powdered hair a tuft of roses. When I entered the ballroom a spontaneous burst of applause greeted my appearance, a compliment which for me enhanced an already enchanted evening. The musicians, dressed in eighteenth-century La Rochefoucauld liveries, played soft nostalgic music. The lovely room alight with candles, the assembled company in costumes of an elegant fashion, seemed to reconstitute a past I had at some time lived. The fan I had found in my mother's possessions moved in my hand with a rhythm of its own, and in the mirror a reflection like a ghost of myself brought me the illusion of a glamorous past. It is an evening I love to recall because of its exquisite distinction.

There is still another scene suggestive of past grandeur which I witnessed at the Polish Embassy. Countess Chlapowska had invited their Eminences the Papal Nuncio and the Archbishops of Paris and of Warsaw; and when they swept up the grand stairway in all their pontifical splendour preceded by liveried pages bearing lighted candelabra, as befitted 'Princes of the Church', it was a sight worth remembering. Men bowed and women fell on their knees to kiss the pontifical ring. I was amused by the manœuvres of those who would have deemed the evening lost had they not been spoken to by the guests of honour. How cleverly they managed to edge ever closer and closer until without positive rudeness they could no longer be ignored! I knew that for days after we would hear what their Eminences had told them.

In Paris, an entertainment owed much of its distinction to the beauty of the old houses, arranged with discriminating taste, and to the excellence of the dinner. One had also the impression that the company had been chosen with a view to an exchange of ideas. The long interval, so apt to break the continuity of talk, when after dinner men smoke in the dining-room, does not exist in France; a clever hostess knows how to stimulate general conversation successfully—no one person is permitted to dominate it and at the right moment the proper person is given the sign to intervene. Frenchwomen have this art, but I have never seen it successfully done in any other country.

It was not only aristocratic parties that pleased us. A luncheon in a bourgeois home stands out with equal charm. We had been invited by Monsieur Justin Godart, who then was Minister of Public Health, to a luncheon in honour of the Titular Head of the Knights of Malta, from whom our host was to receive a decoration. President Albert Lebrun, Madame Lebrun, Monsieur Edouard Herriot, and the Dowager Duchess d'Uzès, who at an advanced age still took a prominent part in politics and sport, were fellow guests. As I entered the small apartment on the Quai Voltaire my hostess, a typical French housewife whose practical knowledge embraced every secret of the culinary art, drew me aside to confess anxiety about the ability of her new cook to attain the perfection she desired her luncheon to achieve, and inquired whether I would consider it out of place if she repaired to the kitchen. "On the contrary," I assured her, "it is better to risk the protocol than the excellence of a meal such a chosen company must be looking forward to." When a little later she returned to us, flushed but triumphant, I realised that my advice had been good. Indeed my neighbour, the veteran minister Herriot, who with our hostess claimed Lyons as their birthplace, declared that she had fittingly upheld that city's claim to the best French cooking, and what greater praise could she desire!

I recall still another but very different occasion while Léon Blum was Prime Minister and we had a Socialist government whose sympathies were further to the left than any we had had before. Sinister reports, leaking through the lesser ministerial ranks, were casting depression over the most determined optimist, and at a luncheon at the Yugoslav Embassy I gleaned an inkling of the fears that foreshadowed an earlier Revolution. I had a French deputy as my neighbour, an aristocrat who viewed the trend of politics under the Socialist government with horror and indignation. It was my invariable habit to defend the other side in any argument and I maintained that France would never become Communist.

"Do you not realise," he said, "that Blum has ordered the Préfet de Police to remove every policeman from the streets for the next twenty-four hours and that by tomorrow we may all be strung *à la lanterne?*"

I gasped, "But how dare you, a French deputy, cast fear amongst us when courage and, above all, cool heads are required?"

He did not answer, and I walked home across the Champs de Mars, where workmen were repairing roads, wondering if the paving stones they were amassing would be used as barricades or weapons. Only a few days before, I had seen Blum and his minister Coste sitting on the open back of a taxi driving down the Champs Élysées with extended, up-raised fists, and had barely found safety from a charging crowd in a *porte cochère*, the concierge barricaded behind me.

Communist demonstrations were becoming fairly common occurrences and a feeling of insecurity harried one's dreams with echoes of the tumbrels; and there were nightmares when the Nazi invasion seemed very close and we felt like pawns in a fateful game of chess.

One day my secretary complained that she had been jeered at by a workman as she passed. "We are not cruel like the Russians," he had said, "and we will not kill you, but you are pretty and tomorrow you will be *ma poule*," meaning his girl. I consoled her by saying he was paying her a compliment, and that no threat was implied. For weeks we had been awakened every night by the singing of the 'Internationale' in a neighbouring factory where workmen were on a sit-down strike. They used to pass our house to sun themselves in the Champs de Mars, but they never caused the slightest disturbance, even when our well-dressed guests drove up to attend a charity concert I had organised. For my part, I had complete faith in their good sense, whatever others might say. It is a faith I have never lost.

Throughout all these years, I was blissfully happy in my life with Jacques and with our wide circle of friends; but at first I missed the work I was accustomed to in England. I was therefore glad when in 1926 a group of social workers asked me to help them to build and equip a hospital for the professional classes. The middle classes (so called in France) had no hospital of their own; either they had to take a room in a clinic, often beyond their means, or else resign themselves to beds in a ward.

A beautiful site and garden on the hill of Vincennes dominated by the guns of the old fortress was to be bought. It belonged to Jean Worth, who had been the leading dressmaker of his day. Dr. Du Bouchet of the American Hospital at Neuilly and Mr. Bernard Flurscheim planned a hospital of 360 private rooms together with a home and school for nurses. It was an ambitious scheme for a group of private individuals to undertake, and it was only after numerous conferences with the Minister of Health and a promise from the French government to supplement any funds raised in voluntary donations that we felt justified in buying the premises and starting building operations.

It was estimated that 200,000 francs would endow a room and we made this the basis of our first appeal. I was agreeably surprised by the response, for in those days a dollar was worth from 28 to 35 francs and 200,000 francs represented a generous slice in a French income. Even so it was evident that neither donations nor the sums raised by entertainments could collect the total which, owing to the rising prices which appear to accompany a Socialist administration, reached 45 millions.

In due time we obtained the government's promise to pay the deficit—the necessity for the hospital, the excellence of our plans and the fact that our committee would undertake the administration proving undeniable assets in our favour.

Many entertainments were organised to raise funds, but the most popular and one that became part of 'Grand Prix Day' was the dinner at the Cercle Interallié. It was a gay and charming event, with tables laid out in the garden and the youth and beauty of Paris competing for prizes offered to the best dancers by the leading jewellers and dressmakers. An auction of gifts, including a Fabergé clock I had brought back from Russia and an automobile, brought lively bidding, though I felt sorry for André de Fouquière, who so kindly and ably undertook this *tâche ingrate*.

On one occasion I had invited a prominent American prima donna as my guest and placed her between two entertaining Frenchmen. Inspired to an undue generosity, she offered to sing. for our hospital, but when I asked her to fix her date she answered that she must first be "assured of the Legion of Honour". In spite of the fact that it is an honour more easily accorded to foreigners than to the French, I had not the courage to back so impudent a request. My compatriots, however, were adept in pushing their claims, and on one occasion I was asked to sign a request to a minister which stated that "it would greatly please the American Colony in Paris if Mrs. X were decorated". The lady herself had drawn it up.

As another fund-raising event, an English university rowing eight offered to race against any French eight. It was the first boat race of its kind to be held in Paris. I found arrangements to entertain our English visitors easy, since the best hotels offered rooms and food at nominal cost, and everyone from the Marquis de Polignac, who entertained them at one of his famous champagne luncheons at Rheims, down to the humblest *midinette* co-operated to give them a good time.

It was more difficult to secure the attendance of President Lebrun, who, when asked, announced "If Madame Balsan comes to ask me I may consent." So one morning, dressed in my best, I called at the Élysée and, met by an officer of the President's household, was led through three great rooms. In each were groups of busy officials who rose and bowed as I passed. Eventually we reached the President, in a charming room with long windows opening into the garden. He was sitting at a large table covered with documents to which he was appending his signature. I had met him previously, and realised that as a busy man he would wish me to get quickly to the point, so I at once presented our request. He stated, as if relenting, that he had been told that the President's presence at such entertainments made a difference of many hundred thousands of francs. "So how can you refuse us?" I asked. But he objected that the President of the French Republic was a busy man and that his presence at a boat race might be criticised. "The King and Queen of England honour international sporting events by their presence," I said, "and our object is to build a much needed hospital for *les classes moyennes.*" Then he smilingly accepted, and I retired as I had come.

The race was a great success and the English crew won, though the French—considering the disadvantage of inadequate training—made a better showing than expected. Our English guests promised to return whenever we wanted them. They had thoroughly enjoyed their visit, and one of them, who had spent a night in a French prison owing to an altercation with a policeman, assured us he was glad to have done so, as he wished to sample everything French.

The most touching of all the tributes to Marshal Foch's memory, to whom our hospital was dedicated, was paid by Paderewski. No longer Prime Minister of Poland but still a great pianist, he gave a concert for our benefit in the Théâtre des Champs Élysées. The long programme must have taxed his failing strength; nevertheless, after the public ovation that greeted his finale, he remained to play to a group of students who had gathered round him. Great in his generosity as in his genius, he refused any part of the proceeds, although heavy expenses incurred by his wife's illness were draining his resources.

At a tea given by the Polish Ambassadress after the concert I was amused by the agonised efforts of some of the ladies present to be presented to the Queen of the Belgians, who had come from Brussels to hear Paderewski play. The Queen sat in an armchair; another chair had been placed close by; and grouped round in a circle stood those who considered they should be spoken to by her, and those who equally considered they had a right to be presented to her. Among the former were several Duchesses of France, who after their audience remained in the circle, loath to forgo the malicious pleasure they derived from the frantic efforts of those who wished to be presented. Suddenly a particularly pushing lady succeeded in shoving her way forward. Unbidden, she deposited her vulgar person in the chair next to the Queen. It seemed to me that I would in her place have been frozen by the haughty glitter of Her Majesty's eyes and by the only half-veiled insolence of the phrases that must have reached her from the encircling throng, but, delighted with her successful manœuvre, she remained impervious to any snub.

The day dawned at last on which our hospital was officially opened by the President. French ministers, foreign ambassadors and exalted personages abounded, but our chief satisfaction lay in the opinion expressed by the medical profession that no finer hospital existed anywhere—an opinion confirmed by the Germans in 1940 when they evicted all French patients and took the hospital over for their own use. In 1950 the Fondation Foch du Mont Valerian was rededicated to the *classes moyennes* for whom it had been built. In announcing the good news, Monsieur Justin Godart, to whose unfailing support we owed the successful termination of our work, informed me that I had been named *Présidente d'Honneur,* a mark of appreciation which, after an interval of so many years, deeply touched me.

It was also to his recommendation as Minister of Public Health that I owed my first step in the Legion of Honour which I received in 1931. How well I remember the day he came to our house in Paris to give me the decoration. I had refused the public function he kindly suggested, and nothing could have been more to my liking than the informal ceremony when in the presence of our household he made a little speech and asked my husband to pin the Cross on me, since not being decorated himself he had no power to confer it. He would, however, not be denied the accolade, which he begged my husband's permission to confer. It was all so very French.

CHAPTER TEN

Lou Sueil: Friends and Neighbours

PRECEDING the happy and busy spring months we spent in Paris each year were lovely months of winter sunshine on the Riviera, where our life, though equally social, was more informal. Some years before Jacques and I were married, I had, while recuperating on the Riviera, been attracted by its beauty and its climate. Soon after our marriage we decided to buy a property and to build a house there.

Between the Upper and Lower Corniche—the former built by Napoleon to lead his armies to Italy, the latter following the contours of the coast—there were beautiful slopes where peasants grew vegetables and flowers for the markets below. During World War I these areas were made accessible by the new Moyenne Corniche. We found the property we bought in answer to an advertisement. There were a hundred and fifty acres of land and the negotiations to acquire them would have taxed the patience of any but a Frenchman. There were some fifty peasant owners and it required diplomacy, patience and tact to deal with them. I marvelled at my husband's persistence as he bantered and bartered with them, for they were cunning and cautious, and, although anxious to sell, were loath to part with their land. Just as we thought a bargain had been made we would find one parcel had not been included, and inevitably it was the choicest bit—the piece that rendered all the rest useless— and negotiations would start again. Only when every ruse had been defeated would they finally surrender. Then, seated at their kitchen tables, we sealed the contracts in the strong bitter wines they brewed from their vines. Pouring with lavish hand into polished tumblers, they drank without drawing breath, and rather than offend I sipped the potent vintage and suffered the inevitable headache.

Our house was built in stone and had an inner garden on

which cloisters opened. We chose the Convent of Le Thoronet in Provence as inspiration; it had been built by Cistercian monks in the eleventh century. The fortressed village of Eze, which stood across a ravine from us, had once been a shrine to the moon goddess Isis and ever since a stronghold of those who ruled the Mediterranean. We called our place *Lou Sueil*, which in Provençal means the Hearth, for it was thus identified on local maps.

Our house was built by six brothers who were stone-masons. Every Monday they walked over the mountains from Italy, returning to spend Sundays with their wives. They were accomplished artisans and quick workers, and they built our house within a year. We made our own plans, and Duchêne, who had designed Sunderland House, was again the architect. Only two rooms were finished when we moved in. The others were being panelled as a background for the period furniture we brought from Crowhurst. When it arrived in vans we spent joyous weeks making the rooms comfortable as well as beautiful, for we disliked a house that looked like a museum rather than a home. Deep sofas heaped with cushions abounded, lamps placed near easy chairs made pleasant seats for reading, and there were writing tables in every room. There were *petit point* chairs fit for kings, but one sat in them unmolested; beautiful Ispahan rugs covered the floors, and the house was gay with flowers. The scent of tuberoses, lilac and lilies filled the air. When one entered the cloisters, a succession of flame-coloured azaleas was a lovely sight.

In the garden we planned terraces; for our grounds, like the hanging gardens of Babylon, hung in mid-air and unless terraced on stone walls would have crumbled down the steep mountainside. Under the olive trees the grass was carpeted with hyacinths and bluebells. The spring brought its seasoned order of tulips, peonies and daffodils. Almond trees bloomed first, in pink and white showers; then came the prunus and the Judas trees with their bronze and scarlet foliage. Every month had its particular mimosa cascading in yellow fragrance. Like those Gothic tapestries strewn with flowers, our gardens represented endless toil. In September, after the first rains that softened the soil, we scattered thousands of bulbs; gardeners followed on their knees with trowels. A happy medley of colours was thus achieved, and the effect looked natural. All these bulbs had to be dug up in May and replanted the following autumn, for the drought and heat of summer would have shrunk and killed them.

There were rose bushes as big as hydrangeas. Stone walls were covered with blue kennedya, rose bougainvillaea and purple clematis. Tall cypresses limned their slender blackness against the silver shimmer of olive leaves or grew in narrow avenues encasing a view. Red oil vats filled with flowers stood at protruding corners. This garden, jutting into the Mediterranean on its high promontory, surrounded by an amphitheatre of Alpine peaks, became famous. We opened it to visitors. The money went to charities; one winter we made as much as 100,000 francs.

Across the ravine from us the village of Eze on its pinnacled height was inaccessible but for one steep road through a portcullised arch. Narrow cobbled streets ran between tiers of houses that rose one above the other to where the church stood on a little square. The houses were built of stone, with old tiled roofs, oak doors and arched windows, and on the outer walls looked down a precipice to the blue depths of the sea. Each had a tiny garden from which fig trees spread their gnarled and naked branches to produce most surprisingly their burden of fruit in summer. When we built Lou Sueil only peasants lived at Eze. They were strong and wiry with an endless capacity for work. Even old women carried the produce of their soil down to the markets of Monaco—some ten miles there and back—the heavy baskets balanced on their heads, their hips swaying as they walked. As I passed them in my Rolls-Royce, their fourscore years seemed a challenge to my forty, and one day, accompanied by my husband, I trudged the eleven kilometres to Nice. My silk stockings were in shreds, but I felt less humble.

Two families dominated Eze, the Millos and Assos. They had come there with the Romans in their conquest of Gaul. Aristocrats, they looked with proud contempt on the Romagnan-Birons, another noble family that had come from Spain in the sixteenth century. It was a proud day for us when we were made citizens of Eze. The priest came to bless our home, and with holy water drove out the evil spirits of the mountain.

Gradually the beauty of Eze began to attract strangers. Sam Barlow, the composer, deserted his family home in Gramercy Square to spend his summers there. He bought two or three little houses and fashioned an enchanting home, where he played the piano until the inhabitants complained they could no longer sleep. One New Year's Eve he and his beautiful wife came to dine with us and the Monte Carlo quartet played one of his compositions, which I thought a lovely way of seeing the New Year in. Through it all H.R.H. the Duke of Connaught, ensconced in an easy chair, slept soundly—thus demonstrating to the citizens of Eze that their complaints were unfounded.

The Duke of Connaught was the youngest son of Queen Victoria. On the death of his Duchess and in failing health he was ordered by his physician to spend his winters on the Riviera. Distinguished and good-looking and possessing a genial charm, he was by far the most popular royalty on the Côte. The French more especially appreciated the part he took in the life of the community, for he never failed to be present at a local ceremony.

Indeed, we had more than our share of royalty on the Riviera. The King and Queen of Denmark, both immensely tall, bicycled indefatigably round the countryside, while the King of Sweden played strenuous tennis in spite of his eighty years. We used to meet them at the luncheons the Préfet gave in their honour at the Prefecture in Nice. The Prefecture was an old Grimaldi palace dating from the days when that family reigned over the Kingdom of Savoy and it had the charm, but also the inconvenience, of an old house. Democracy had unfortunately later established the market-place just under its windows and when one arrived for luncheon the water wagons were sluicing the streets of the débris of vegetables, fish and flowers. As one climbed the monumental staircase to the reception rooms the smell of stale fish or, if one was lucky, of faded flowers would drift in on the breeze.

The Prefecture of the Alpes-Maritimes was an envied position and usually accorded to men of distinction, for the reception of important visitors was part of their duties. The Préfets I knew during the score of years we spent on the Riviera were able, polished men who entertained with ease in a democratic and yet essentially courtly manner.

The most eccentric royal person we entertained was a young brother of the Emperor of Japan. He had been sent to England to be educated, and was brought to us by an old friend of mine who had been appointed his cicerone. An Englishwoman, well over six feet tall and equally majestic in appearance, she towered over the unfortunate Prince and his suite. I spent a miserable luncheon trying to make conversation in a mixture of French and English, neither of which he appeared either to speak or to understand. As he prepared to leave I asked him to sign the visitors' book, little dreaming that the mere inscription of his name in vertical classical characters would take at least ten minutes while we all stood round in embarrassed silence.

Our life at Eze was very social. Owning a beautiful place has its evident drawbacks. Luncheon-parties were as a rule limited to twenty, at two tables of ten. On certain occasions I counted seven nationalities present—English, American, French, Austrian, Polish, Belgian and Italian. French was the prevalent language. After luncheon we took our guests round the garden; a short and easy round for the old, with a more extended tour for the hale and hearty. My husband never tired of running up and down our mountain, but sometimes I could see the demoralising effect of these climbs on men and women who considered themselves athletes and in the pink of condition. On one occasion a fat English banker, collapsing on a seat beside me, faintly asked for a glass of water—but later found a certain satisfaction in thinking he must have lost at least three pounds in the climbs my husband had imposed.

Entertaining brought its contretemps. When they happened, they were annoying, but in retrospect they are amusing. There was the occasion when one of our guests telephoned that he would walk up from Monte Carlo to lunch with us. The distance being about five miles and uphill, I warned him to start in good time; but cocktails had been served and still there was no sign of him. The person in question being a British M.P. of ministerial rank, I thought it politer to wait a little longer although a score of guests had already assembled. Then, as our minister still did not appear, we began luncheon. Half-way through the meal our butler whispered to me, "A gentleman has arrived and wants a bath." "A bath!" I said. "Yes, a bath," he repeated. "He got so hot walking up he must have a bath." Some time later our butler again appeared looking worried. "I don't know what is the matter with the gentleman but he is throwing all his clothes out of the window to the gardeners and telling them to keep them!" 'Good heavens,' I thought; 'I hope he does not mean to come in naked,' for not knowing the man I had some apprehension he might be another 'Milord Anglais fou'. At last our M.P. entered (thank goodness, properly clothed), not at all abashed at being forty-five minutes late. "I like walk-ing," he said airily, "and always take a change in case I get hot. Hope you did not mind my throwing my underclothes to your gardeners, it avoids the trouble of carrying them down." "Oh, not at all, I only hope they were properly grateful," I answered. After a hasty meal, without a word to the numerous company or even a look at the view we were so proud of, he departed to walk down to Nice, and I no longer wondered why the English some-times are considered eccentric!

Still another time I had an American next to me at luncheon who refused every dish with such increasing haughtiness that it amounted to rudeness. At last, stung by his behaviour, I expostulated, "I am sorry you do not like our food, but is there anything else I can order you?"

"Considering," he answered, "that I wrote you exactly what I could eat and even sent you a menu of the dishes I wished provided, I am surprised you should ask me such a question!"

"But I never got your letter," I said, horrified. And sure enough, as we came out of the dining-room he saw his letter lying on the table in the cloisters where our mails were placed, and pounced upon it; it had been delayed because he had mis-directed it. Since then he has always telegraphed us about the food he can eat, which makes relations more amicable.

It is pleasanter to recall a more fortunate occasion when, mindful that Hindus could not eat beef, I ordered lobster and chicken for the Maharajah of Kapurthala. He thanked me warmly, saying his aide-de-camp had forgotten to let me know that he could not touch beef, and added ruefully, "I am so often given nothing else, and once as an alternative tongue was served, my hostess not seeming to realise that tongue came from the cow." The Maharajah was a handsome prince. He spoke English and French fluently and was an accomplished diplomat and sportsman. As a young man he had seen me at Marble House in Newport. I was then a girl of sixteen and he had told my mother that he wished to marry me, a wish he was apt to recall on occasions. Ever since, he had brought me mangoes from his Indian gardens with a gentle deference the years had not changed.

In 1938 the Polish Ambassador, Count Chlapowski, was our guest. While discussing Hitler and the possibilities of a war—which was then, and alas is again, an engrossing topic—he told me a revealing anecdote about Göring, whom he had met at a reception. Apparently Göring was boasting of his famous shoots. "Alas," commented Count Chlapowski, "in Poland we have so many poachers our preserves of game are sadly diminished." "Poachers!" snorted Göring. "Take it from me, Excellency, you have only to shoot two or three as I have done and you will have no more trouble!" Only one year later, during the invasion of Poland, Count and Countess Chlapowski were dragged away from their castle by Nazi officers and imprisoned. The Countess's description of the scene when I met her again in 1940 is worth recording. She said that the servants had been herded together at the castle's entrance, where cars were waiting to take the owners away to imprisonment in Warsaw. In the confusion and terror of the moment an old servant got into a car by mistake. The Countess said that she can never forget how, at the commanding officer's order, the Nazi guard fell on him and, dragging him out, beat him unmercifully until he was unable to stand. "It may have been done to intimidate us," she said, "but it was inhuman!" While in prison the Count succumbed to illness and ill treatment; the Countess, after many months of solitary confinement in a cold, unlighted cell, was liberated owing to the intervention of the Pope and President Roosevelt. At liberty in Warsaw, she managed through the underground to find her way across the frontier. Reaching Italy, she was again obliged to flee when that country became Germany's ally. Eventually she reached Lisbon, where we met, both of us refugees, happily anticipating the hospitable freedom of my generous native land. Countess Chlapowska told me later, when she came as our guest to Florida, that while she was imprisoned by the Gestapo she was not allowed to see her husband. The guard who brought her food daily taunted her, saying, "Your husband is ill and will soon die, but you will not be allowed to see him." Just before the end she was, however, allowed a short interview, when the sight of her tortured husband almost destroyed the magnificent fortitude that had caused the Gestapo to comment, "How can we break down this damned woman?" It was faith and prayer that gave her the strength to withstand and survive all her trials, though she told me that the long hours of darkness of those winter nights were almost unbearable. Her son, like so many Poles, served in the British Air Force during the war, and I am sure lived up to Winston Churchill's encomium when he observed to me, "When we want to be particularly ruthless we send the Poles."

Among the many interesting guests we had the pleasure of receiving at Eze, no one contributed more to the diversion of a party than Serge Voronoff, Russian surgeon and physiologist, who was widely known for his experiments in gland grafting. He had been educated in Paris and had risen to the important post of Director of the Biological Laboratory at the École des Hautes Études and later to the directorship of Experimental Surgery of the Station Physiologique du Collège de France. He had bought a château in Grimaldi on the frontier of Italy and France. His gates were just opposite the Customs and the gardens looked out on the sea. Here in the rocks and grottoes he had built large cages for the monkeys he had brought from Africa for his operations. He was a brilliant raconteur, and knew how to tell a *risqué* story without undue stress. His descriptions of some of his experiments in gland grafting and their results, as well as of the astonishing "types" who came to be operated on, were extremely amusing, but only Voronoff or my husband are capable of doing them justice.

A delightful and hououred guest was Lord Curzon, who came to spend a fortnight with us in 1925, a few weeks before his death. He had written that he was in much need of a rest, and added that he would prefer to be alone with us, since he would be busy editing three books he had just completed. In the interval that preceded his arrival we suffered the qualms every host experiences, for our guest was not only a man of distinction and taste—he was also sensitive and high-strung, and his infirmity necessitated the observance of more than ordinary hospitality. I knew, for instance, that he could not sleep if a crack of daylight entered his room, so a black-out material had to double-line his curtains. I knew that he spent his nights writing, and provided an assortment of Chippendale tables whereon to lay his literary paraphernalia and the more prosaic food of physical sustenance. I attempted to provide every material comfort, leaving to Jacques the more difficult task of conversation, and when the time came he proved equal to it, producing a fund of anecdotes every whit as good in French as Lord Curzon's were in English.

During the two weeks he was with us he wore himself out editing his books. With the meticulous attention to detail so characteristic of him, he insisted on making in his own hand all the tiresome corrections and notations editing entails; and when I remonstrated, "Why not have a secretary?" he replied, "Do you think anyone but myself could master the intricacies of my Indian administration or the spelling of those Indian names?" He did that work at night and it must have meant toil, sweat and tears, and agonising pain, yet in the morning he would appear gay, debonair and smiling, delighting us with amusing stories of his Viceroyalty which he told with inimitable humour and rollicking laughter.

A characteristic that I found most endearing was his love of beauty, especially of an architectural nature. "A house," he recorded but a few days before his death, "has to my mind a history as enthralling as that of an individual."* He had restored Tattershall and given it to the nation; Bodiam was to follow. On his death, Harold Nicolson further recalls, "Six vast kit-bags were discovered packed to overflowing with the material, the notes and many complete chapters of six separate monographs dealing with Kedleston, Hackwood, Montacute, Walmer Castle, Tattershall and Bodiam."

To those who loved him it is comforting to realise that in such lasting monuments he found consolation for the bitter disappointments he suffered, first in 1923 when Baldwin was chosen Prime Minister over him, and again in the following year when Baldwin formed his second Cabinet and passed over Lord Curzon's claim to return to the Foreign Office in favour of Austen Chamberlain. He had, I thought, never quite recovered from these griefs, although he loyally continued to serve as Lord President of the Council and Leader in the House of Lords.

There were times when, overwrought with political responsibilities and physical pain, he succumbed to the weakness of tears. I remember finding him thus one day in his house in Carlton House Terrace. It was in the summer of 1916 when he was a member of Asquith's Coalition Cabinet. He had expressed the wish to see me and, arriving early, I waited until the departure of Lord Lansdowne, who was with him at the time. Going up to his room, I found him in bed against a mound of pillows looking like a recumbent proconsul. He had evidently had a trying interview and seemed worried and weary. Nevertheless, during the short space of my visit the telephone on his bed rang incessantly.

* Harold Nicolson, *Curzon* (Harcourt, Brace & Company, 1939).

First it was an inquiry from the chef—next a message from the chauffeur—then one from the butler—all of which could have been easily dealt with by a secretary. There was something rather ridiculous and altogether pathetic in the manner in which, interrupting his talk, he would answer the most trivial questions in grandiloquent language and a strong North Country accent, while all the while large tears were rolling down his cheeks. He was, I remember, discussing certain difficulties that loomed in the way of his second marriage.

I shall always recall that last visit to us at Eze, so perilously near his end, with feelings of emotion, and I well remember the day of his arrival and his request to view the house and grounds. Leaning on his stick, encased in his steel corset, he insisted upon walking down and then up our mountain. No one could have been more appreciative, and when finally we rested, looking down on the glorious view that from Toulon to Italy spread before us, he turned round to me and said, "Then it has been worth the sacrifice?"

"Sacrifice?" I inquired, somewhat startled.

"Yes—to give up being the beautiful Duchess of Marlborough and all it meant?"

I could not help smiling. "But of course, George, I willingly gave up and have never regretted no longer being a Duchess—but if, as you so kindly suggest, I should have had to give up whatever beauty I may possess—that would have been another problem!" He looked at me wonderingly.

Lord Curzon's detractors have stressed his pompous manner and innate snobbishness. That he was so evidently pleased with his rank and privilege amused me. It added a comic touch to a personality that without it might have been priggish. Every afternoon I took him motoring through the lovely country, and on one of these expeditions we came across an ancient château that looked deserted. Ever interested in historical research, he wished to visit it; so we rang the bell, which, after a long wait, was answered by an elderly woman, shabbily dressed but with a dignity of bearing that made me surmise she was the owner. Lord Curzon, taking her for the housekeeper, handed her his card, and as he passed it to her he remarked to me, "It looks very grand, does it not?" He was just like a child showing a new toy, for he had by then become Marquess Curzon of Kedleston. During our visit it gradually became obvious that the lady was a

White Russian of noble birth and as we thanked her for her
courtesy, Lord Curzon, with magnificent condescension, introduced me, adding, "She used to be Duchess of Marlborough in
England—that is how I knew her." On our way home he
expressed surprise that a Russian Princess should have answered
her own door-bell. Alas, had he lived, he would have had many
worse shocks. During that drive he spoke to me of the hereafter,
and with a touching faith, perhaps inspired by that of his father,
Lord Scarsdale, who had been a clergyman, said, "I know that
Mary will be the first to greet me in Heaven." A few weeks later
he went to join her.

Our only social venture during his visit, and one I deeply
regretted, was a dinner at the Palace of Monaco. The Prince of
Monaco was a simple man who delighted in recalling his years
spent in the French Army, but Monaco was an ancient
principality, and boasted one of the oldest reigning families in
Europe. My evening was rendered anxious by Lord Curzon's
discomfort; for he was evidently suffering intense pain as we
stood about waiting on the pompous protocol the Court insisted
upon maintaining. Our quiet evenings at Lou Sueil lightened
by reminiscences of his Viceregal career were evidently more to
his taste and I was glad afterwards to remember that we never
imposed another party.

The nearest approach to Lord Curzon in French politics it
was my good fortune to meet was André Tardieu. His attach-
ment to the policy of Clemenceau, with whom he was closely
associated, caused him three times between 1919 and 1924 to
refuse to enter the French government. His career marked him
as a man of brilliant intellect, and trenchant and cutting it
certainly could be, to the terror of enemies and friends alike.

He had bought a villa on a hill behind Menton, where we
went one day to lunch with him. Opposition to existing regimes
had no doubt engendered an acerbity which his ill-health
accentuated. Having heard echoes of his *bon mots*, which were
anything but "bon" to the recipient, I was surprised by the
urbanity of his greeting, though this could, I knew, in a measure
be accounted for by his friendship with my husband and his
sympathy with Americans and admiration for my country,
which dated from 1917, when he acted as Special Commissioner
in the United States. We were a small party of eight or ten and
luncheon progressed happily, enlivened by anecdotes our host

and my husband handled with equal skill. A delicious *pâté de lapin*, a speciality of his Cordon Bleu, had just been served when Tardieu, perhaps inflamed by the excellence of a Château Margaux, suddenly fixed an ironic eye on Madame P., a lovely Russian, and lifting his glass gallantly said, *"A Madame P. toujours aussi belle et toujours aussi bête."** There was a moment's deathly silence and I wondered if Mr. P., the husband of the injured beauty, would protest; but with unexpected presence of mind she smiled and conversation was resumed. Then Tardieu, turning to my husband, remarked that he himself had often helped friends in need, but that when he needed funds for an election the only man who had answered his appeal was "my friend Jacques Balsan, who sent me 50,000 francs." He was proud of that small domain recessed in the Alps where he grew vegetables, fruit and wine, and I thought of the politicians who since Cincinnatus had found redress from man's ingratitude in nature's gifts.

Gallic wit was more tolerantly exemplified in another neighbour, Sacha Guitry. Guitry was still madly in love with his wife, Yvonne Printemps, but she was beginning to tire of his selfishness and, like all women, longed to play first fiddle. On their visit to us it struck me that Guitry was jealous of his wife's success not only as a singer but also as a wit. He firmly dominated the conversation, but with feminine ingenuity and an ingénue smile she invariably capped his brightest sayings! How lovely she was and how inimitable the savour and warmth of her flexible voice. I remember hearing Printemps in one of her operettas. Dame Nellie Melba was sitting near, and turning to me she exclaimed, "That to me is the most irresistible voice in the world." I felt equally moved by a special nostalgic sadness which only the tenor Tauber and the bass Ezio Pinza have been able to create in an equal degree..

Charlie Chaplin was, I think, the only famous cinema star to be our guest. I found him interesting to talk to, and noted his strong socialist tendencies. There was a melancholy undertone to his humour which reminded me of the traditional sadness that underlies all clowning. After luncheon, surrounded by our guests, he gave an excruciatingly funny description of a hunt he had had with the Duke of Westminster's hounds in Normandy only a few weeks before. Describing his unwillingness to

* "To Madame P., still as beautiful and still as stupid."

take part in the hunt, averring that horses frightened him, he told us how all his objections were firmly discounted by his host, who, as is customary with hosts, wished his guests to enjoy the diversions he had to offer regardless of their personal predilections. Mr. Chaplin, having no riding-breeches or coat, was dressed in some of the Duke's, which, as his host was well over six feet, naturally were far too big for Mr. Charlie Chaplin. Nevertheless, with a coat that reached well below his knees and a cap that covered his eyes he was hoisted on to an enormous horse. Terrified, he clung to the reins, now and again diving dangerously down to his pocket, which was somewhere near his ankles, for a handkerchief to wipe the perspiration his ride and emotions were causing. With all the vim and humour of his early films he illustrated that ride, and it still stands out as one of the funniest and most spontaneous descriptions I have ever heard. Sir Philip Sassoon, who was a friend of his, and Elsa Maxwell, who was our guest, egged him on to what would certainly have been a priceless entertainment on any stage.

Edith Wharton came often to Eze and we delighted in visiting her at Hyères on the Riviera or at the Pavillon Colombe near Paris, where she had created lovely gardens. She liked to show them, being proud both of her taste and of her horticultural knowledge, for she had the faculty of remembering the name of every plant, however rare. A tour of gardens with an amateur is apt to be tiring because of the maddening habit they have of loitering over unique specimens, explaining their characteristics in detail. It is tedious to listen to long dissertations on the habitat of rock plants, often buried under stones which have to be removed to permit one to view their diminutive blooms. But Edith Wharton was a passionate lover of flowers and would dissect their mutations with the same ruthless precision she practised in analysing the characters she portrayed.

I used to wonder whether the warmth of her nature had found its only blossoming in her garden, for to me her novels lacked the glow of humanity, and the hard, ambitious types of American womanhood she depicted were particularly unpleasant. She gave the impression of intellectually controlling her emotional contacts and lacked the spontaneity which to me is the keynote of friendship. In appearance she had the precise primness of an old maid—there was something puritanical about her in spite of the cosmopolitan, rather bohemian, life she affected. Her features were neat, her chin determined, and a rare smile showed good teeth. She took infinite pains with her dress, and what is now called a tailored woman would be an apt description of her. In the country she wore a suit, a small hat and neat workmanlike shoes with square heels. A veil kept every hair in place.

She seemed terribly disillusioned and her successful and useful life (for she was always helping a good cause) had evidently not erased some secret sorrow. It was to Walter Berry, her cousin, that those who knew her best attributed this sorrow. Her brilliant intellect no doubt found unending inspiration in his no less accomplished companionship, but he was a cruel master who, as was said, delighted in perverting the minds of young and pretty women. "What a pity he does not leave them in an interesting condition," Frank Crowninshield once retorted.

Edith Wharton, neither young nor pretty, may have been too self-centred to waste pity or time in unprofitable thoughts; nevertheless, she may have suffered more intensely than her reserved and frigid character gave one reason to suppose. She was invariably accompanied by a male friend, and gave the impression of disliking, if not actually despising, women, although to me she was always kind.

My mother had been to school with Edith Jones, as she then was, and I gathered they had disliked each other. Indeed, whether from intellectual arrogance or because of her cold disdain, Edith Wharton repelled rather than attracted sympathy. Since reading her memoirs I realise that it was perhaps shyness that made her so inaccessible.

The first time I saw her she was still a young woman and was accompanied by her husband, who somehow, when in England, seemed more of an equerry than an equal, walking behind her and carrying whatever paraphernalia she happened to discard. She wore an ostrich boa she had a habit of dropping. Indeed, Edward Wharton could not hope to do more than fetch and carry for a personality so far removed from his orbit.

We met in an English country house where I had arrived rather late. My hostess, the beautiful Daisy White, first wife of Harry White, then attached to the American Embassy, took me to the window and, pointing to two distant figures walking on the lawn, said, "Do you know those famous compatriots of ours?" They were Edith Wharton and Henry James in deep conversation.

This was, I think, the only time I met Henry James, and I have but a vague memory of his dominating personality. I believe I was more impressed by the reverence with which my fellow guests treated him than by anything he himself said. Meeting Americans in England in the gay 'nineties—I am referring to men, and more especially to those who considered themselves important—always caused me a slight embarrassment as I became conscious of their slow and weighty phrases. It seemed to me that even when discussing the weather, that prevalent subject for conversation, they indulged in superfluous ponderous preambles, and when recounting a story took hours to reach the point—a point that, alas, was so often lost on English listeners! It was easy to acquire a British sense of humour, but I always found it difficult to make my English friends appreciate our American jests. Fortunately for the Atlantic Pact, a wider and more sympathetic understanding has since succeeded in eliminating such minor irritations and in emphasising our points of contact.

Winston Churchill and his beautiful wife were among our favourite guests during the seventeen winters we spent at Lou Sueil. Although I had known him some thirty years he always seemed as young to me as he had ever been. Even in his sixtieth year he was playing polo, and his interests instead of waning were growing. He used to spend his mornings dictating to his secretary and his afternoons painting either in our garden or in some other site that pleased him. His departure on these expeditions was invariably accompanied by a general upheaval of the household. The painting paraphernalia with its easel, parasol and stool had to be assembled; the brushes, freshly cleaned, to be found; the canvases chosen, the right hat sorted out, the cigar box replenished. At last, driven by our chauffeur, accompanied by a detective the British Government insisted upon providing, he would depart with the genial wave and rubicund smile we have learned to associate with his robust optimism. On his return he would amuse us by repeating the comments of those self-sufficient critics who congregate round easels. An old Frenchman one day told him, "With a few more lessons you will become quite good!"—a verdict connoisseurs have already endorsed.

Our chef and staff must have been highly taxed by the almost daily luncheon-parties it required to entertain our numerous acquaintances who ranged from Cannes to Menton. There were, also, certain people, among whom were the Préfet, the Prince of Monaco and admirals of visiting fleets, that it was more or less a duty to entertain.

Our house guests provided another problem. In my invitations I invariably stated the date of departure as well as of arrival, since we had a limited number of rooms and visitors had to come and go in an ordered succession. But sometimes a departing guest would be seized by some nameless disease which prevented his leaving. Strong measures were required with such delinquents, who had no thought for the convenience of others. Arrivals from England could not be turned out because of the desire of others to outstay their welcome.

There were still others who rendered one uncomfortably aware of one's lack of hospitality. There was Margot Asquith, for instance. Shortly after Lord Oxford's death, she telegraphed: "Will you have me and a charming secretary for a stay greatly in need of a rest." A few days later she arrived. We had put off other guests, thinking that after so recent a loss she would prefer seclusion. With her first words we realised our error. "Darling, are you alone? Don't put off guests on my account; I love seeing people!"

It was Margot's habit to send notes scribbled in pencil which were brought to me on my breakfast-tray. The next morning, the first read, "Darling, I have nothing to wear. I must order a little black dress." The following day we had a luncheon-party of her friends. Margot came down in the little black dress, but to my dismay she had added a red scarf. "Darling—I put on this little red scarf because the dress looked so dreary." "But, Margot," I said, "French people are very conventional; you cannot wear a red scarf so soon." Very reluctantly she removed the scarf and went out into the garden, returning with a bunch of red anemones pinned to her shoulder. "They can't be silly enough to object to flowers!" she said, but I saw by their expressions that they were. Later she complained, "French people are so unsympathetic—they never even mentioned Henry's death to me." On yet another occasion we invited a few English friends to dine. Margot asked Jacques to turn on some dance music, and just as our guests arrived she accomplished a high kick over my husband's head. All prepared as they were with expressions of condolence they speechlessly shook hands with her and I wondered whether another sweeping indictment on their lack of sympathy would be forthcoming. To a personality so original and intolerant, conventions as such meant nothing. With admirable courage she fought the sharpness of her sorrow, delighting us with the spontaneous and irrepressible gaiety that was her greatest charm.

My brother Willie and his lovely Rose were favourite guests. Willie had inherited a large share of my father's charm. He had the same joyousness and overwhelming spirits, and he possessed a sense of humour which a vivid imagination enhanced. He was very human, very lovable and very popular. I have never known a better host. When one crossed the threshold of his home or boarded his yacht the genial friendliness of his welcome immediately awakened a sense of well-being. He seemed so happy to see one and so anxious to give one a good time. And, generous by nature, he gave of himself as well as of the wealth with which he was endowed. At the outbreak of World War II he parted quite definitely with the thing he loved best when he gave his yacht the *Alva* to the Government of the United States. I believe that in his heart he knew that never again would he go on those long voyages in search of marine specimens for his museum, or stand on the bridge in a storm navigating his ship. From his earliest years he indulged in speed, and brought the first racing automobile, 'The White Ghost', to America. As a master mariner he took his yachts *Ara* and *Alva* round the world and, towards the end of his life, in his seaplane he flew round South America. When he died at sixty-four the tributes from comrades in the Navy, in which he had served in World War I, and from friends in every walk of life were sincere and touching. There had been something fundamentally so good and kind in him; few failed to recognise it.

We found our life on the Riviera, which combined the pleasures of the country with the more intellectual attractions a city offers, very pleasant. At the opera at Nice and in the Prince of Monaco's little theatre new operas were given and one heard the best artists. It was there I witnessed Horowitz's triumph when as a young and unknown artist he emerged from Russia. Toscanini was living near-by and the engagement and marriage

H*

of his daughter to Horowitz later became the romance of our neighbourhood. Diaghileff and his Ballet spent winters at Monte Carlo, where many new ballets had their first nights. He brought his dancers to a garden-party we gave, but the ballerinas were less beautiful in the vast amphitheatre of our mountains than in the perfect lighting of a stage setting. Only Karsavina with her poetic distinction held her own.

Among the works of young composers which the Principality so lavishly produced, I remember the ballet *Britannia* which Lord Berners came from England to launch. With patriotic fervour our large English colony turned out to applaud. Lord Berners came to lunch with us at Lou Sueil, and I had occasion to examine his car. There was in front of his seat a small harmonium on which it was his habit to note motifs inspired by the countryside. The lining at the back of the car had butterflies stilettoed against it. A few days later, in one of our drives, we passed a drawn-up car from which came the sound of music, and saw him sitting at his harmonium with butterflies as a halo round his head, an ironic smile on his lips and a monocle in his eye. We realised how easily French passers-by might observe, *"Un autre de ces milords Anglais fous!"*

Driving to Monaco, I used to think what a pity it was that a greater vision had not been granted to a Prince who, to his royal prerogatives, added the privilege of a kingdom where a casino paid the charges and citizens were untaxed. What other country could have offered such opportunities? Where but here could one have created a Court like that of the Medici or Valois where men of genius were honoured and artists encouraged? The Palace which now only achieved garishness might have been beautiful. Evenings of boredom might have held eclectic pleasures. One came away intolerant of such wasted opportunities.

But if the little city lacked the beauties men can achieve, its setting was incomparable. Motoring over those beautiful mountains into some hidden valley, picnicking near a torrent still icy from the snows above, then climbing again to the peaks in search of Alpine flowers—these were delights we often enjoyed. We used to go, a cavalcade of cars, with our spades and trowels, to dig up the wild flowers of the Alps, to transplant them to our gardens. There were so many species, they were so delicate and fragile, one wondered how they could have grown in the arid soil and the snows.

In our little group there was Henry May, a dear friend, whose knowledge of art enhanced the pleasure of finding the primitives we often discovered in some old Romanesque church in a fortressed village perilously clinging to the mountain-side. There was Johnny Johnson, an American, whose love of flowers led him to create two of the most beautiful gardens I have ever seen—one in the heart of England and one at Menton, in whose favoured climate he grows shrubs and flowers he scours the earth to find. A flight to China in search of a new azalea, a hop to Corsica for wild flowers, a voyage to Australia for a rare acacia, were nothing to him. In his garden all newcomers seemed to thrive, and with unfailing generosity he gave us the fruits of his labours. There was Lady Katherine Lambton, whose beauty and charm made me think of her royal Stuart ancestor, and Norah Lindsay (Mrs. Harry Lindsay), whose Irish beauty recalled Sir Joshua Reynolds's children, those puckish faces with elfin eyes. She was an accomplished pianist, a tireless reader and possessed the Irish gift for an amusing tale. She often helped us plan our flower borders and laughed with us over the French gardener's dismay at the riotous disorder of an English herbaceous garden. One day in trying to explain why the phloxes had not kept true to colour, waving despairing hands, he cried, "But, Madame, I cannot prevent the butterflies from playing with the flowers!"—a lovely description of nature's propagating act.

With these friends we explored the towns and ruins of Provence, often lunching alfresco. We each brought a dish— cold curried chicken—potato salad—the little artichokes that are so tender and flavourful—cheese and light pastries with the purple figs—or cherries just picked from our trees. A *vin du pays* and steaming coffee ended a perfect meal. The dogs that accompanied us had their specially prepared bowls.

Sometimes instead of picnicking we went to an inn renowned for mountain trout or the Mediterranean *loup*—a fish that when grilled on the cinders of aromatic herbs is no longer a fish, but a dish fit for gods. We grew to know *toutes les spécialités de la maison*, from the *bouillabaisse* with its saffron flavour to the meringues with a pastry light as thistledown and a cream whipped to a bubble. The *vin du pays—bellet*, iced to a rosy glow—added the headiness which in America is supplied by the cocktail; but it was a headiness founded on a perfectly cooked meal, not on the yearnings of an empty stomach, a headiness, moreover, whose ebullience is flavoured by wit and gaiety, like the warm sparkle of the sun.

Driving home in open cars with the sun gliding into the sea, its pink glow cast upwards on to the snow-capped Alps, one held one's breath as round each bend a new beauty came to view— low olive trees with their silvery foliage, straight sombre cypresses, stunted oaks clinging to steep planes where sheep grazed on meadows that smelled of rosemary and thyme. Cascading brooks leaped down the mountain-side and from far above we heard the bugle calling the *chasseurs des Alpes* to their rest. Sometimes we met them on the mountain roads— long convoys of mules and men hurrying with their short, quick step on some route-march, for the frontier was near and Musso-lini unaccountable. Sometimes we crossed into Italy, where the mountains were steeper, less welcoming, and there were no little inns with their tables and chairs under red-and-yellow awnings, no culinary appeal to tempt our appetite. I was always glad to come back to France, where the peasant said "good day" as you passed and made life friendly with his courteous greeting.

Very different from such lovely days were those we spent at Monte Carlo watching international tennis championships, in which such players as Tilden, Von Cramm, Cochet, Borotra, Miss Ryan, Mlle. d'Alvarez and Suzanne Lenglen came to compete. The practical short white linen dress had just been introduced by Lenglen. Suzanne had an ugly face but an athletic body which she used with grace, the precision of her footwork having been taught her by her father on a tennis court marked in squares like a chess-board. On one of Lord Balfour's visits to us she partnered him at tennis on our court, and with her quick mind her repartees were sometimes as good as her volleys.

Sometimes we went to the horse races on the pretty little track at Nice. There appeared to be races of sorts every week— bicycle races and foot races over the mountains, and an auto race in which cars circled the Principality a hundred times, emitting the most horrible noise. I remember a nightmare of such rush-ing, roaring speed which I witnessed from Mr. McComber's yacht in the harbour of Monaco. We had a splendid view of the competitors as they climbed the narrow streets, streaked

dangerously round corners, and came rocketing down the outer
boulevard. Strangely enough there were few accidents, no doubt
because of the precautions taken and the sandbags that banked
the turns. But I was always glad to leave that inferno of rushing
noise below and to climb back to my mountain, though even
there distant echoes reached us.

With the coming of spring in the North we longed for the
fresh green of budding leaves and, turning our backs on the
azure sea, we would motor back by way of Aix and Avignon
or else across the Alps to Grenoble and the eastern provinces and
so on to Paris, following the road taken by Napoleon on his
fateful return from the island of Elba.

CHAPTER ELEVEN

Saint Georges-Motel: Peaceful Summers

As THE years had passed we had found our house in Paris beginning to demand a special life of its own, as houses are apt to do. This was not to our taste, since we both preferred the simpler pleasures of the country. So about 1926 we began to look for a small place near Paris, and happily at Saint Georges-Motel came upon the little château where thereafter we spent our summers.

It was love at first sight—a love we have remained faithful to, for of all lovely places I have seen it has the most charm. Situated on the border of Normandy near the forest of Dreux, it stood in a glade of high trees; one saw it only as entering the gates one came down from the village through a wide avenue of great lindens and chestnuts. It was a tall and elegant house built of pink bricks and was capped by a high roof of blue slates. In its narrow centre were evenly spaced windows through which one saw running water and green parterres beyond. At the two ends were towers bathed in a wide moat whose waters were deep and clear. These waters also enclosed the forecourt, which one entered across a bridge through an iron grille that bore the stamp of Louis XIII. The château itself was some years older; in one of its rooms, it was said, Henry IV had slept the night before the Battle of Ivry which gave him Paris. It was the rapt seclusion of the place that charmed us. Immense trees attested to the dignity of pleasances planted for pleasure in days when life had an unhurried ease. In a wood close by, one saw down an alley a stone boar on its pedestal, recalling scenes of past hunts, and on occasions a stag from the forest beyond would be driven to bay in our river.

The château and grounds had long been neglected, since the owner lived with his thirteen children in another house better

suited to so large a family. It was rumoured that a descendant
of the first chatelain—a count of the old regime—had with his
wife been victims of the Revolution. He must have been a man
of taste to have respected the house built by his ancestors. It
was only later that pavilions had been added. We removed these
modern structures, which left the château intact in its rose-
coloured beauty. We restored the gardens and laid out parterres
where fountains played amid boxwood traceries. My favourite
garden was away in an apple orchard. Enclosed in high walls
on which grew roses and honeysuckle, it held a pool and borders
of sweet-smelling flowers. There were also water gardens with
weeping willows, hydrangeas, iris, day lilies, lupins and
anemones. Meadows beyond skirted the River Avre, and where
it joined the bigger River Eure an old mill stood. This mill in
time became an enchanting place which we lent to friends, and
in the summers of 1938 and 1939, when it was full of children,
Motel was gay with laughter and sound. There were children
riding in the forest or jumping their ponies over hurdles in the
fields, children playing tennis and swimming in the pool,
children fishing for trout in the rivers or canoeing on canals,
children playing golf or bicycling in the gardens—it is with a
pang that I recall the sweet careless gaiety of those last pre-
war summers.

The villagers loved their château. They watched the changes
we made with critical eyes. In September we used to give a
fête champêtre for our neighbours. It was a gay garden-party
to which chatelains from properties near-by brought their house-
holds, and peasants came in all their finery. The village priest
and the lady of light virtue were equally welcome; everyone
was asked without distinction. The invitations stated from four
to seven, and punctually at four I would see from the hall where
we awaited them a long procession coming up the avenue and
crossing the Cour d'Honneur. As we greeted them I had a
present ready for every child. There was a platform for dancing
on the lawn beyond and on either side stood a pavilion topped
by flags where champagne, cider, brioches and every kind of
cake were served. Under the trees the children ate at long laden
tables. A band played and there were conjurers and clowns. I
remember one year when the children from our vacation school
danced a minuet for our gratification. As they emerged from
the château they looked like little ghosts from an elegant past,

the boys in breeches and wigs, the girls in hooped skirts with powdered curls.

Towards the end of the evening the dances would become gayer, and men grown garrulous with champagne would argue with their wives who wished to take them home. But good manners invariably prevailed, and we never had a disagreeable incident; for everyone looked forward to "Madame Balsan's fête".

During the summer holidays we opened a recreation school for the village children, for I was dismayed to find how little French children played. There was a stream where they swam and a playground for games, and the girls were taught to sew, while the boys engaged in carpentry. At the end of the holidays the children put on an entertainment in our honour, and a grand finale with 'The Star-Spangled Banner' sung in English and the 'Marseillaise' in French invariably ended a delightful performance which actors and audience equally enjoyed. Remembering how shy the children had been at the school treats I had given at Blenheim, it struck me as typical of democracy that these French children wished in some measure to repay the good times we had given them; and that they succeeded was somehow part of the French genius.

Here at Saint Georges-Motel we were privileged to become hosts to a number of friends to whom we lent small houses on the estate. This group of artists, musicians and writers centred round Paul Maze, himself a Norman, who on his marriage to a Scottish widow had perforce adopted her nationality. Paul is an artist not only in oils and pastels, but also in his truly bohemian mode of life. I often heard him describe, in a bilingual flow of French and English, an incident during World War I, when he joined the British Army as a volunteer. In the retreat from Mons he became separated from his unit, and when eventually he was found by an English company, his loss of his identification papers together with his French accent and English uniform caused him to be arrested as a spy. There was short shrift for spies in that disastrous retreat, but as luck would have it an English officer who knew him happened to ride by and shouted, "Hello, Paul, what are you doing there?" To which Paul answered, "I am about to be shot!"

He faced life with the same equanimity and lived gaily with his Scottish wife, who added two Maze children to the five already born to her. They lived at the Moulin during the summers, and around them gathered painters such as Dunoyer de Segonzac, Simon Lévy, and lovely Odette des Garèt. There were also writers who came from Paris and friends from England; and during the last pre-war summer Yvonne Lefèbure, the noted pianist, lived in one of our cottages.

One week-end when Winston Churchill and his beautiful wife were our guests, a unique picture was made. Its distinction was that it was signed by five artists. It came about in this fashion: Winston was painting on the lawn in front of the house. A view of the long canal shaded by overhanging trees stretched before him. I had invited Paul Maze and three fellow artists to luncheon. They approached Winston, standing in his white coat in front of the easel, and crowded round him. Undaunted by such critical observers, he drew four brushes from his stock and handing them round said, "You, Paul, shall paint the trees—you, Segonzac, the sky—you, Simon Lévy, the water and you, Marchand, the foreground, and I shall supervise." Thus I later found them busily engaged. Winston, smoking a big cigar, a critical eye on the progress of his picture, now and then intervened—"a little more blue here in your sky, Segonzac —your water more shadowed, Lévy—and, Paul, your foliage a deeper green just there." It was all I could do to drag them away to luncheon.

That was the week-end Winston decided he wanted to paint our moat. After careful thought he made up his mind that he preferred the water rough to smooth. Sending to Dreux for a photographer, he placed two gardeners in a boat and told them to create ripples with their oars. I can still see the scene with Winston personally directing the manœuvre—the photographer running around to do snapshots—the gardeners clumsily belabouring the water. With characteristic thoroughness Winston persisted until all possibilities had been exhausted and the photographer, hot and worried, could be heard muttering, "Mais ces Anglais sont donc tous maniac."

Sometimes we went to Paris to dine in one of the small restaurants frequented by artists. The evening would be enlivened by Segonzac and Paul, who would act comic scenes, inventing them as they went, eventually to be joined by the waiter and the proprietor, who thoroughly enjoyed the fun.

One evening we had a fancy dress ball at the Moulin for my grandchildren and their friends. The best part of the fun, as is

invariably the case, was making one's own costume. We danced
to a gramophone and the children did imitations in the manner
of Paul. But even then the cloud of approaching war over-
shadowed us and I thought with apprehension of the future
awaiting those young boys and girls. Only a few years later two
of the most brilliant were sacrificed.

Our happy life at Saint Georges-Motel had earlier inspired my
mother to acquire a château near-by. Not far from Fontainebleau, it was built of stone and was of the Renaissance period.
What immediately appealed to her was the legend that the
great financier and builder, Jacques Cœur, had given it to his
daughter; from this she derived the vicarious pleasure any
tribute to the female hierarchy gave her. Once settled, she proceeded to let her fancy roam, creating improvements so steadily
that in spite of failing health her last years were happily
employed. She was for ever critically surveying her demesne.
Walking in the garden with Jacques and me, she would
suddenly stop us and, pointing to the river which flowed past
the house, would say, "This river is not wide enough; it should
be twice as large"; and when next we came an army of workmen
would have enlarged it. A great forecourt separated the village
from the house. It was sanded instead of being paved. "This
is all wrong, it should be paved," my mother commented
severely; and the year of her death old paving stones brought
from Versailles covered the court. Her intellectual activity, by
no means abated, found vent in an International Council to
secure equal rights for women the world over. The Council had
its headquarters in Geneva, and my mother, with Miss Alice
Paul, directed its work nearer home. She also furnished and
maintained a recreation hostel for the use of nurses from the
American Hospital in Paris, and took a friendly and helpful
interest in the lives of the people among whom she lived.

Augerville-la-Rivière possessed, as do most French villages, an
old stone church not devoid of architectural beauty, but for my
mother it lacked an essential—a statue of Joan of Arc; it irked
her that the Saint who to her represented Militant Womanhood
should not be honoured in the church of what had now become
her village. Being a Protestant, she could not herself donate the
statue, but her ingenuity found a solution in persuading Mrs.
Harry Lehr, an old friend and a Catholic, to present it. Fully
aware of Mrs. Lehr's parsimonious habits, my mother did not

entrust her with the choice of the statue, but herself selected a
fine life-sized example. A neighbouring Bishop having agreed
to induct the Saint in a fitting ceremony, a chosen company
repaired to the château for the occasion. With Saint Joan
held aloft on a daïs, the Bishop surrounded by acolytes and
priests, we marched in procession to the church, passing through
a throng of kneeling villagers. Mrs. Lehr, as donor of the statue,
had a prominent position behind the Saint, and her chatter,
which she was unable to restrain, desecrated the solemn silence.
My mother, who could always be relied upon to dominate a
situation, furiously and loudly observed, "Bessie, will you shut
up!" Thankfully I observed that, obedient as we all were to
such admonishments, Mrs. Lehr thereafter maintained the dignified deportment the occasion decreed.

Saint Joan having been devoutly ensconced in her niche
embellished with votive candles and flowers, and a Mass
celebrated in her honour, we returned to the château for
luncheon. Noting that our French friends were surprised by
this, to them, incomprehensible ceremony—for how could an
American Protestant wish to exalt a French and Catholic Saint?
—I explained, to their amusement, that it was Joan as a militant
rather than Joan as a Saint that appealed to my mother.

On my next visit to her it saddened me to see my mother in a
bath-chair. It was one Queen Victoria had used during her
visits to Cimiez, which had been made by a famous French
carriage builder. Its beautiful lines had captivated my mother,
who had ordered a donkey, complete with its harness, to be sent
all the way from Sicily to draw her. Now the chair stands with
other elegant vehicles of the past in the museum of Compiègne,
to which we gave it.

Gradually my mother weakened, and we took her to her little
house in Paris, where, in the winter of 1933, she died. Leaving
the old world, with its marked respect for the departed, where
men have time to doff their hats and women to cross themselves
in greeting, I found it strange to be met in New York by policemen on motor-bicycles who preceded the hearse while we raced
to St. Thomas Church. But the service there was triumphantly
symbolic, with suffrage societies flying their banners as they
came up the aisle wave upon wave. A hymn my mother had
herself composed was sung—it naturally concerned a woman. It
was only fitting that such tribute should be paid to the courage

she had shown in braving popular prejudice and established custom to secure better conditions for women the world over.

We spent a few weeks in Florida with my brothers. Having married so young and lived in Europe so constantly, it was a joy to me to see them and to recall events of a youth that seemed long past. From a childhood memory Harold now became a very dear brother, whose sensitive nature I learned to appreciate, and I was glad to have the pleasure of meeting the cultured and charming lady who shortly became his wife.

On our return to France, I plunged again into my work in Paris and with the children at Saint Georges-Motel. In time my chief interest there became a sanatorium or, as it is called in France, a preventorium, where there were some eighty young children who were recuperating from operations or in need of preventive care. Later the Ministry of Health stressed the needs of children in the early stages of tuberculosis and we added fifty beds in open-air shelters in the woods near-by.

So many children aged from one to five required a large staff, so to our hospital nurses we added some thirty young students and trained them as children's nurses. We were encouraged in our work by the Minister of Health and the Académie de Médecine, which gave us their Médaille de Vermeil and their Médaille d'Or. The visits of foreign pædiatricians and nurses who attended the international congresses held in Paris were even more flattering. I remember that on one occasion at the time fixed for departure the German pædiatricians could nowhere be found and the motor-buses had to return to Paris without them. An hour later we discovered them busily writing in notebooks; they explained that Hitler himself had given strict orders that in every institution visited any new departure must be carefully described. We were deeply impressed that these elderly men should observe his dictates with the punctiliousness usually attributed to students.

During the American advance in Normandy our hospital was slightly damaged by gunfire, and later we gave the buildings to the Department of the Eure, whose own preventorium the war completely destroyed.

I have always loved children; but like the old lady who lived in a shoe, what with my preventorium and recreation school and, in 1939 and '40, a few hundred refugee children from Paris, I had so many I very nearly did not know what to do. But at least it meant that we never experienced the tedium of country life.

My day began early, for there was always much to be done. I used to walk to the three separate establishments where our refugee children were housed. There were also the sanatorium buildings on the hill just beyond the village to visit. Walking quickly I could do it in the three hours before lunch, unless delayed by too lengthy reports. I used to think how fortunate it was that the nurses in charge were too busy to spend time in unnecessary conversation; otherwise I should never have completed my task. There was also the temptation to play with the babies in the *communs*—there were sixty of them and all so sweet—which had to be resisted. There was just time to note their needs on the pad I always took with me.

The sanatorium with its eighty small children came second in the daily round. I took time to visit the various departments, the wards, the playrooms, the nurses' quarters, the kitchen, the outdoor playgrounds and the reception pavilion where newcomers had to be isolated to prevent the introduction of possible infections. Each child had its own cubicle enclosed in glass. There was a crib and a bath in each, as well as a table and chair and special toys, and in front of every room were individual outdoor runs separated by glass. The building faced south and was gay with sunshine; and the children, seeing each other and doing whatever they pleased, did not appear to suffer from their isolation.

From the isolation quarters I would go to the shelters in the pine wood where children in the early stages of tuberculosis lived. There were some thirty of them sleeping and eating out of doors. But there were two heated rooms where they were bathed and dressed. It did one good to watch the roses coming back to their cheeks. My only complaint was that they grew too fat. One had for ever to buy new clothes for them. Dr. Du Bouchet, our pædiatrician, directed this little colony and also supervised the refugee children in the other buildings. She would sometimes accompany me down the hill to the "Little Mill" in the village.

We had originally bought this building for our vacation school and had since added to it, so that now some twenty children lived there, refugees sent to us from the Red Zone of Paris. Ardent little Communists, they sang the 'Internationale' instead

of the 'Marseillaise', and when told to salute the French flag
balled their little fists and shouted, "Heil Hitler, who comes to
deliver us." It was these boys and girls, not yet in their teens,
who gave us the most trouble. I had three different super-
intendents before I found a young woman able to cope with
them, for they were both undisciplined and untrained, and
displayed a marvellous ingenuity in destruction. On every visit
I had to register a new complaint. Throwing things down the
water closets was one of their chief amusements. It was often
impossible to get a plumber, since most of them had been
mobilised, so that one of our old gardeners had to do a job which
for him was complicated and difficult.

The successful superintendent was a pretty young woman, the
daughter of a distinguished career officer in the French cavalry.
She was trained in child education, having with her diploma
achieved the distinction of securing the best marks ever given
to a graduate. Under her direction the children changed
astonishingly—they even ceased balling their fists and singing
"Heil Hitler". It was soon apparent that this charming little
person possessed an astonishing degree of courage, energy and
decision. The authorities responsible for evacuated children
informed us that we were not authorised to move them and that
in case of need Army lorries would be sent for them. So when
we moved our sanatorium children, the others had to be left
behind, awaiting the promised lorries. Even had we been permitted to move them there were not sufficient cars for over one
hundred children and a numerous staff. When later French
Army lorries came and forcibly took these children away,
precariously leaving them in zones just removed from the fighting, this young girl struggled continuously to find food, lodging
and safety for 120 children, two of whom had been wounded
and for whom she cared. Contending against many difficulties
and hardships she finally worked her way back from the
Vendôme area and three weeks later, after the armistice had
been signed, brought her charges safely to Saint Georges-Motel.
Demanding an interview with the German general who had
taken possession of our château, she informed him that it was
his business now to house and feed the children until she could
return them to their parents. Which he did.

From the Little Mill my way lay along the River Avre, a
lovely clear stream where trout abounded. It led past gardens

and through fields and even in winter it was peaceful and beautiful. As I approached the Big Mill I could hear Pauline Maze practising her piano. Paul's daughter was specially gifted and Mlle. Lefèbure, who herself had been Cortot's favourite pupil, was training her. A Bechstein baby grand brought from our house in Paris filled the sitting-room of the house we had lent the Mazes. Pauline practised at least eight hours a day, and Paul, who was suffering from a period of non-production which in itself causes artists to become neurasthenic, threatened to go mad if he heard another scale. But, with the utter insensibility one genius shows another, Pauline persisted, and Paul, with cotton-wool protruding from his ears, worked in his garden. I often found him surrounded by the children who lived at the Big Mill.

These were the oldest we had, and ranged up to fifteen. The lady superintendent was a widow of World War I and her daughter was a ballerina from the Paris Opera. The ballerina, alas, could not practise her *entrechats* as did Pauline her scales. Jealousy therefore marred what might have become a friendship. In the frustrated idleness of an enforced seclusion the children had got on the ballerina's nerves. Paul's nerves were also taut, and there were sharp encounters in which Mme. la Directrice's authority suffered, greatly to the children's joy. I used to wonder as I reached the scene what new conflict would engage my attention or what problem would have to be solved, for those older children were difficult to handle. We had no authority for any but inadequate punishments, and yet the parents expected us to train and educate them. I remember an impossible youth of fifteen who spent his energies bullying the younger ones and leading them astray, so that we finally asked his parents to remove him. When the day dawned I found the Directrice and nurses in tears, humiliated by their failure to handle him; while the parents, reluctant to remove him, were surrounded by groups of overawed and distressed children. He left a general feeling of failure in his wake such as I imagine is felt in prisons when a hardened criminal goes back into the world.

Aware of increasing restrictions, we nevertheless lacked neither food nor fuel for the children. Our coal came in sacks on a hearse-like dray drawn by black horses with funeral trappings. The driver perched on a high seat, with a hat somewhat like a

sombrero, looked like an elderly Don Quixote. Since he emptied
the coal sacks, he was as black as his horses; nevertheless, he had
a wonderfully grand manner as he swept his hat to the ground—
he might have been a Spanish grandee expiating the sins of a
former existence.

In spite of many anxieties and difficulties, it was a happy
little world we lived in, for everyone was busy and the children
were invariably gay. The nicest tribute we had came from the
inspector of the National Health Insurance in Paris, who remarked, "When I have the *caffard* I come to Saint Georges-
Motel and the children invariably cure me of my troubles."

During the last summer before the war, the Queen of Spain,
who as Princess Ena of Battenberg had come to Blenheim so
many years before, motored over from Fontainebleau with one
of the Infantas and her son-in-law, Prince Torlonia, to lunch
with us. We were alone and talked of old times in England, and
I asked the Queen, who was then a fugitive in France, why she
did not return to her native land instead of living in Fontainebleau. After intimating her dislike of being a refugee, she
admitted that she had decided to return home, because recently
she had seen the very same gypsies and hawkers touring France
as had heralded the revolution in Spain and she was convinced that they were Fifth Columnists.

That summer we went to Blenheim for the coming-out ball of
my eldest granddaughter, Sarah, who is now married to an
American. My son had succeeded his father as tenth Duke in
1934. The ever-growing burden of taxation was rendering the
upkeep of so great a monument difficult, and the flame of socialism which Lloyd George's legislation had fanned had increased
the tension. Nevertheless between the Palace and Woodstock
the most friendly relations prevailed; my son had been elected
Mayor and Mary his wife was to succeed him in this office. It
may be invidious to praise one's own, but to withhold what is
due would be churlish. In the tradition that has kept for England her aristocratic heritage my son determined to maintain
and to hand down the gift a grateful nation had bestowed on his
family in perpetuity; so when the Ministry that occupied the
house during the war returned to its permanent quarters, he
prepared to open Blenheim to tourist traffic on a hitherto unprecedented scale. For in such a way alone could taxation be met
and the upkeep of so large a house assured. His efforts have

been crowned with success. Well over 100,000 tourists, with a price for adults of two shillings and sixpence, visited Blenheim during the opening year, a record since surpassed and maintained.

During the war the family lived in the east wing, where their suite of rooms contained a small library and dining-room in addition to the Duke's and Duchess's private apartment. There were rooms upstairs for the children and for a few guests. Many of my countrymen came to know Blenheim under these conditions. My son was Military Liaison Officer to the regular commander of the Southern Region and Lieutenant-Colonel Liaison Officer, United States Forces, from 1942 to 1945. My daughter-in-law's gift for organisation and her admirable devotion to public service found expression as Chief Commandant in the Auxiliary Territorial Services, and later in the British Red Cross.

My readers will, I trust, forgive this digression, remembering family feelings they no doubt themselves indulge; and since these memoirs have, against my wishes, become a personal record, rather than simply the picture of a period I had at first envisioned, something must be said of those dear to me.

In 1939 I went to Blenheim with anxious forebodings, for the international horizon was dark. At dinner, sitting next to Monsieur Corbin, the popular French Ambassador, I found it difficult to share the diplomatic detachment his conversation maintained. Yet at that same dinner, at my granddaughter's table, was the eldest son of the German Crown Prince, whom, I was told, Winston had suggested using as a counterfoil to Nazism under Hitler. Monsieur Corbin, the perfect diplomat, avoided such issues, preferring a personal topic, and I listened with growing pleasure to his praise of my son Ivor's accomplishments. Possessor of some fine pictures which ranged from Cézanne to Matisse, Ivor had acquired both knowledge and taste. His controversies with Roger Fry in art journals may have been incomprehensible to all but the initiated, but the exhibitions of French contemporary art he arranged had won him a consensus of praise, and later his work for General de Gaulle brought him the Legion of Honour.

Nevertheless, in spite of these, to me, flattering considerations, I suffered the same unease that had afflicted me once in Russia when, surrounded by the glittering splendour of the Czar's

Court, I sensed impending disaster. For again, in this brilliant scene at Blenheim, I sensed the end of an era. Only a few months later these rooms were dismantled and the ugly paraphernalia of officialdom installed for the duration of a tragic war. But on that evening the scene was still gay, and my pleasure great in meeting so many old friends. I supped with Winston and Anthony Eden and wandered out to the lovely terraces Marlborough had built before his death. These, together with the reconstructed forecourt, were the work of Duchêne. With their formal lines and classic ornaments, they were the right setting for so imposing a monument as Blenheim Palace. Indeed, Vanbrugh had contemplated the forecourt Duchêne designed, as we discovered when breaking through foundations.

How rewarding are my memories of Blenheim in my son's time when his life, with Mary and his children, was all that I wished mine could have been.

We returned to Paris in time to witness the great military review held there on July 14, the national holiday. Winston Churchill, a guest of honour in the reviewing stand, said to me afterwards when I commented on the large tanks that had shaken the Champs Élysées in their progress, "The Government had to show the French that their economies had been transferred from the idleness of the stocking to the safety of the tank."

But I was horrified to hear that the parade had held all our tanks, for their small number did not suggest safety. During the procession the chief applause went to the magnificent Foreign Legion, which, martial and workmanlike, marched, I thought, as well as if not better than the British Guards.

When I next saw Winston in France it was midsummer. He came to Saint Georges-Motel on his return from an inspection of the Maginot Line which he had made in the company of General Gamelin and General George. He seemed to share the admiration these fortifications usually evoked; but when I inquired about the state of our defences from the end of the Maginot Line to the sea, all I could gather was that they depended on pillboxes and wire—which did not reassure me.

It was all rather worrying, with a new war in the offing and Hitler and Mussolini playing up to each other, and America, so it seemed to us, living in a halcyon world where even the shadow of war never cast its gloom. In 1939, just before Munich, I went with my husband to see a minister in the French Government to offer him the Fondation Foch Hospital in case of war. Turning to Jacques he whispered, *"Nous sommes fichus"*; but I heard the ominous words, which ever after haunted me, for I knew the French to be realists.

CHAPTER TWELVE

A Corner of France, 1940

SOMEWHERE IN the hinterland of my consciousness lies the sadness, the haunting anxiety of that cold and desolate winter. We were icebound in our little château. Spirals of fleecy mists wound upwards from the frozen ground. The fountains stood silent in mid-air like gleaming silver plumes. The trees covered with hoarfrost had their branches etched in black and white against the sky. In that snow-covered garden nothing moved, everything seemed tense—*waiting*. And so one woke to another day. My maid brought my breakfast with the terse news, "*Rien de spécial à signaler*"—"There is nothing new to report," with which the official radio stilled our apprehensions. The papers would come later with their sparse news. We were not fed by commentators.

With the advent of refugees from the eastern provinces, the Préfet of the Eure asked me to visit the lodgings allotted to them and to report on the conditions in which they lived. The Eure is not a big department; nevertheless it ranged from our village, which lay at its southern extremity, right up to Pont de l'Arche in the north and to Broglie in the west, with Evreux as its capital. The refugees were distributed among the chief towns. These old Normandy towns were picturesque, with half-timbered houses with gabled roofs. The churches, too, were fine, with fretted stonework, and there were old inns with good food and wine, but there was little accommodation for refugees. It was indeed regrettable that no better provision could be made for them, but with humble philosophy they accepted the makeshift lodgings that were all one could give them. It was surprising, considering the influx of so many strangers, that we had no serious epidemic; but we made a point of securing better care for the children, for whom we provided serums and certified milk. The adults were, as a rule, well fed in some central hall, and we found in nearly every case that the Mayor had done his best to carry out the Préfet's instructions.

On these visits of inspection, accompanied by Dr. Du Bouchet, we used to leave the château at 9 a.m. provided with a hot dish of food and a thermos of coffee, and often returned only after dark. It was so cold that winter that even with hot-water bags at our feet we used to freeze as we stopped to eat our meal. One night as we were returning home, the chauffeur suddenly pulled up in the dark and I found myself looking down the long barrel of a field-gun, while English voices shouted to us to stop. It was an English regiment on its way to Evreux— one of their headquarters.

Personal reports sometimes reached us from the front. Our agent, during the few days' leave he spent with his wife, told us of the thousands of mines the enemy had laid in the abandoned villages in no-man's-land. They were hidden with such in-genuity that a false step or a curious impulse could result in ignominious death or maiming or blinding, and the men had in some cases become demoralised, refusing to deal with so tricky and deadly a menace. He explained that in order to encourage the men, an officer would lie on the ground and with his left hand grope for the mines; then with his face hidden and his right hand safely by his side, he would undo the detonator. We were spared the recital of how many had lost their lives or been maimed in the process.

The French Government, perhaps thinking that we in the safety of our homes did not realise what this so-called phony war meant to the men in the front line, one night turned the radio on to a French outpost and for a few short minutes we lived with those men. At first we heard them talking in low tones. Then came a sentry with the news that a German patrol was approach-ing. In the pregnant silence we were conscious that the men were taking their arms and positions. Then with the crack of hand grenades we knew they were fighting. I could not bear the words "phony war" after that evening. They seemed to me an insult to brave men whose nerves were as sensitive as ours, and on whose endurance our safety depended; but it was not often that we had such direct evidence of men in action. At best there was little news of a trustworthy character, so that rumours and hearsay appeared all the more ominous. As the winter neared its end, every day brought fears that the invasion of Holland and

Belgium had begun. The German radio gave much more news than the French and inevitably one listened to its terrifying propaganda. Dressed in fur coats to keep warm, we used to huddle round the fire those long winter evenings, my husband and Paul and a White Russian, a friend who replaced our agent and helped us manage our property. Sometimes Paul and Basil Davidoff and I played Towie; it was better than talking, which somehow increased one's anxieties. Jacques had rejoined the French Army and was often away on various missions.

On Friday, May 10, my maid woke me with the news that the Germans had invaded Holland, Belgium and Luxembourg, and were marching south and west. We knew then that the inevitable had begun and would soon be upon us. I told her to pack a valise and to put it under my bed.

There was not much done that day. Everywhere people were gathered in groups discussing the news. The last few men of military age or those on leave had gone to join their regiments. The radio informed us that bombs had been dropped on Lyons, Lille, Nancy and Pontoise. German planes were evidently numerous enough to visit every corner of France, besides carrying on a great offensive.

At the sanatorium I found my matron worrying about what advice she should give our pupil nurses. Some of the parents were telephoning their daughters to return home. Most of the girls wished to remain at their posts; others felt they should be with their mothers who had been left alone. It was difficult to find an answer to the plea that at a time like this families should be united, but there was work to be done in the sanatorium and most of them stayed at their posts. Parents were coming from Paris to ask if we would keep their children with us. I reassured them that we were not closing the sanatorium.

The village of Saint Georges-Motel had three hundred and fifty inhabitants, and on the assumption that such a small community would not be considered worth bombing no shelters had been provided. We relied upon the forest of Dreux, only a kilometre across the river, for safety.

Returning home from the sanatorium I found Paul Maze, his daughter Pauline, my husband and Davidoff listening to the latest news. The cold impersonal voice of the speaker as hour by hour in measured tones he announced the German advance in all its incredible swiftness was somehow shocking. We studied our maps in sickening apprehension. Every one of us knew in our hearts that there was no hope, but our lips were sealed. My husband was the only exception; he kept us all cheerful, his trust in the French Army remained firm and in spite of every new disaster he refused to be shaken.

With the invasion of the Lowlands came an ever growing influx of refugees. Hurrying south, they flowed even into our little backwater of a village. First came the automobiles of the rich. They did not stop at Saint Georges but I met their owners at Dreux in the Bank of France, exchanging their worthless money for French currency which still had its quoted value. Then followed a sad procession. Once again the great farm wagons drawn by four splendid Percherons were trekking south leaving their crops, their cattle, their homes to the mercy of the invader. How typically French they were, those farm wagons, filled with hay and household goods, accompanied by a boy who cracked his whip as he walked beside his horses. Perched on the top of one of these I saw a little old lady in an armchair. She was surrounded by her grandchildren, and was dressed in her best black gown with a shawl crossed over her chest, on her head one of those lacy high bonnets French peasants still wear. When I spoke to her she said sadly, "This is the third time *les Boches* have driven us from our home—once before the Battle of the Marne—a second time in the late German drive just before the end of the last war—and now again." I knew then that the enemy was in France; of late the radio had been strangely vague. Bicyclists were now passing through in droves. One day I saw an old man slowly pushing his machine along while holding his wife on the seat. They were exhausted, for they had been on the road two weeks, and we made them rest with us until they had sufficiently recovered to proceed. We had opened a canteen in the main street and laid mattresses wherever there was room.

On May 11 the bell clanged from the church tower and the priest summoned us to a service of intercession. Dressed in black, the women walked through the village streets with bowed heads and clasped hands as if in prayer. From all sides processions of children joined me as I hurried to the church; even the babies came, solemn and wide-eyed. They had been told to pray for their fathers. In the church I saw women who had been widowed in the last war now interceding for their sons, and orphans were praying for their brothers. Many candles had been lit—it seemed strangely still and sad. On my way home I met one of our gardeners. He was an old man and when I spoke to him he seemed obsessed. *"Cette fois ils nous auront"*—"This time they'll get us," he kept repeating. I tried to reassure him and I remember saying, "The Americans will surely liberate you," but he shook his head. *"Trop tard,"* he said. And for him it was too late, for as the Germans moved in he shot himself.

The evacuation of our sanatorium and of the refugee children presented a difficult problem. It gave me much anxious thought and was complicated by the attitude of the Ministry of Health, which refused to give me definite instructions. After numerous telephonic communications of a fairly acrid and dictatorial nature—in which I had been told to observe the decrees of the military authorities, which forbade the evacuation of refugee children, whom the authorities themselves would evacuate should the necessity arise—the right to move the sanatorium was finally conceded, since it was a private, and not a public institution. The Minister, however, stressed the need for discretion, explaining that the children must be moved in small groups, so as not to create panic in the village. I was advised to look for a house in the south which could be used as a temporary sanatorium. All the while the Germans were nearing the Seine, which was only thirty kilometres away, and I heard of a sanatorium near Roubaix which had not been evacuated in time. Engulfed in an awful silence, its occupants had become lost to their world. In my telephonic conversation with the Ministry I brought this up as an example of what might happen to us. *"Ah oui, Mme. L. a été bien légère—mais elle est intelligente—elle se débrouillera,"* was the laconic answer. Having no wish to be considered 'careless' by parents who had expressed confidence in my judgment, convinced that I would never settle matters satisfactorily with the Germans, I became obsessed with the desire to evacuate these children in time. Plans were made to remove them in the various trucks, ambulances and cars we had. We tied clothes in linen bags to each car—we stowed foodstuffs under the seats—we piled mattresses on to the floors and roofs. Then we had a rehearsal so that everyone should know exactly what to do in case of emergency, for contact with the refugees had shown me that one rarely thinks clearly under the stress of fear. Indeed, I had been appalled by the useless things many had carried away in the haste of departure. One old man in particular had impressed me. He carried a basket with great care. I hoped he had saved something of value, but when he opened it ten little ducklings walked out and he asked my permission to put them on our pond. "Is that all you have brought?" I asked him. "Yes, madame," he answered. "We were told the German Bicyclist Corps were only five kilometres away, and—*comment voulez-vous?*—I could not leave these ducks for them."

A few days later, as I was writing to a friend in America, a servant rushed in looking for Monsieur. It appeared he had seen a German plane drop a parachute in the forest of Dreux a few hundred yards across our river. Monsieur was shortly found, and, armed with a shotgun and accompanied by Louis, who had spotted the parachutist, went off in a small car to hunt for him. Meanwhile, running to the Big Mill, I alerted Paul and sent him, with his antiquated pistol, to join in the chase. But the forest of Dreux is large, and this Fifth Columnist was never found. Disguised as a French priest, a gendarme or a commercial traveller he was without doubt already engaged in some nefarious plan for our destruction. Parachutists were now becoming numerous, and during the night one heard enemy planes overhead. Something had to be done about it, and the Mayor of our village called a public meeting. Plans for our safety were to be discussed. The *garde chasse* announced these meetings, beating a drum as he walked through the village streets, but since he was very old and his voice very weak he was accompanied by a child who in shrill tones shouted the hour and place of assembly. Jacques and Paul attended the meeting. It was a scene such as Balzac could have written and Coquelin or Raimu have excelled in acting. What comedy and tragedy it contained—that group of elderly villagers summoned to stem and outwit a corps of Hitler's Fifth Columnists! For such was their assignment. It is truly remarkable that any parachutists were taken, but there were at least ten alarms for every genuine one. All through that week the villagers retailed reports of doubtful characters they had seen, and we would comb the countryside in fruitless searches. Questioning them was confusing, for no two witnesses agreed. There were long and circumstantial descriptions of strangers seen or conversations overheard, which led nowhere, for often with surprising levity the

I

witness would suddenly discredit the whole tale and with the peasant's dislike for being cornered reply, *"Eh, que voulez-vous —j'ai peut-être pas bien vu"*—"What would you, perhaps I did not see aright."

On May 17 the Préfet summoned me to Evreux, a town some twenty kilometres distant. He asked us to prepare food and quarters for 45,000 refugees who were due in trains from the north. It was an emergency order. The following day they would be sorted and sent to towns in the south indicated in the evacuation plan. No sooner had we begun than another order came to prepare hospital accommodation for wounded civilians for whom no provision had as yet been made. There was a Boys Vocational Training School which we immediately evacuated, returning the boys to their parents. We put clean sheets on the four hundred beds and installed a first-aid clinic; a cook prepared a good meal, the matron and several nurses from our sanatorium were put in charge, and at sunset we were ready to receive them. All night they waited—the wounded did not arrive until next day. Their train had been bombed and disabled, and they had taken refuge in ditches, and were finally brought to Evreux in motor-cars. Many had been obliged to walk, and on the road they had been raked by machine-guns from low-flying planes. A distraught woman told me that her two children had been killed walking a few yards in front of her. "I saw the aviator's eyes as he aimed at them," she kept repeating in her frenzied grief. They were all in desperate straits, their garments caked with blood, their shoes in shreds. My husband and I went out to buy clothes for them. I shall always remember a young woman's joy when we spread a pretty little dress on her bed: *"C'est pour moi? Oh, Madame, comme vous êtes bonne!"* —"It is for me? Oh, Madame, you are very kind," and for a moment she forgot the bullet in her breast and the loss of all she had. The magnitude of the disaster appalled me. What could one do with these thousands of human beings, lost as they were in a whirlpool of terror and misery? They had but one thought—to escape from the tanks and bombing planes of a ruthless enemy.

In the wards doctors and nurses were removing bandages and we saw the serious wounds bombs and bullets had made. In some cases gangrene had already set in, necessitating amputations. The patients were brave and composed. One woman kept telling

me that a doctor who had given her first-aid had recommended
an X-ray examination. It was hard to explain that this little
impromptu hospital had no X-ray available. The military
authorities had announced that only the graver cases could
remain in Evreux; all those who could be moved were
immediately to be evacuated to safer zones.

German planes had been overhead and German mechanised
forces were drawing closer. The women, shaken by the bombing
and machine-gunning they had suffered on the roads, were
apprehensive of raids. We reassured them as best we could. They
wished to get in touch with lost relatives. One begged me to
telephone to Amiens to her husband who, she said, was in the
hospital there. It seemed cruel to tell her that Amiens had
fallen to the Germans. A woman dragging herself up the stairs
next attracted my attention. She was surrounded by her seven
children. The eldest boy, who appeared to be nine, was carrying
the youngest in his arms. She told me that they had walked for a
week along the roads and had sometimes been lucky enough to
get a lift in a wagon. Before leaving her home the mother had
carefully dressed the children in their best, but their boots were
worn now and their clothes tattered and soiled. She was expecting her eighth child and confessed that her hour had come.
Luckily our car was waiting and my husband drove her to the
Maternity Hospital, where she gave birth to a boy. I wondered
how we could feed this increasing flood of destitute humanity.
It seemed to me as if the little town of Evreux had suddenly
become the hub of the universe. Hundreds of trucks and cars
were crowding the street. English troops moving north crossed
refugees moving south. In spite of the incredible crowds I never
saw troops held up or a traffic jam. Small boy scouts directed
cars down appointed streets. The people were disciplined and
orderly. Canteens had been organised and centres of information where refugees were told which towns would receive them.

Driving home I saw a lovely sight—a string of beautiful
dapper ambulances. They were so new and spick-and-span in
that drab crowd. Their women drivers and stretcher-bearers
looked so pretty in smart blue uniforms. Every ambulance had
an inscription: 'Given by the women of the Argentine'. I
wondered where they were going!

When we reached Motel we found one hundred and fifty
French soldiers with three officers and a *mitrailleuse* there. They

had become detached from their unit, for which they blamed the hordes of refugees. It seemed to me that we had done enough for one day, but we found rooms for the officers in the house and laid straw in the orangery for the men. We killed a sheep, and their field kitchen soon prepared a good meal. They told us that in some of the villages they had been shot at by Germans disguised as Frenchmen. We found it difficult to credit their tale, but in time we learned that the Fifth Columnists employed such methods in order to create havoc and demoralisation.

The increasing number of refugees passing through the village was, I noticed, imposing a strain on our people. Even Dr. Du Bouchet, who had infinite kindness, was inclined to rebel when on returning from a hard day she found refugees in her bed. It was now three weeks since the endless flow had begun. Those we could not house slept in ditches or under trees by the roadside. They had learned to appreciate the immunity trees gave them from the searching eyes of bombers. As time went on and the zone from which they hailed grew closer, I felt the tension growing. Old men shook their heads and women looked at me anxiously as I passed. It was hard to keep cheerful with one's heart bursting with grief and indignation.

Aften ten years spent in a land at peace, I find it difficult to describe my reactions to the stress and turmoil of that spring. I remember a feeling of growing horror as the Huns approached. It was as if everything beautiful and fine and worth while was going to be destroyed. I had worked hard—I had simulated a courage I did not feel—I knew we were beaten. It seemed to me that the only thing that now mattered was to get our sanatorium children safely away. But before leaving I went to see the Comtesse Pierre de Viel Castel, who lived in the village. Anna Ripley was an American and I wanted to consult her about an appeal we planned to send to our countrywomen. She met me on her doorstep, shocked at news she had just heard. It seemed that her daughter's mother-in-law had been killed by the Nazis!

"My daughter is upstairs," she whispered, "but has not yet been told. She adores her mother-in-law, and she is shortly expecting a child—how am I going to tell her?"

"How did it happen?" I asked.

Madame de M. had, she told me, been shot dead sitting at her husband's side in the car they were driving in. He, as *Maire* of his village, was the last to leave after evacuation had been ordered, and had run into the German Bicyclist Corps. Luckily he himself had only been wounded and was therefore able to escape.

With the enemy so close, it seemed hardly the time for an appeal to Americans. Our friends across the sea were so far away. No words of sympathy had reached us. It struck us as strange that they should be so insensible to our woes. Indeed, at that moment everything seemed unreal, and we were dazed by a disaster we felt very near, for the wind blowing from the north was bringing the sound of guns ever more clearly to our ears.

The next day, June 6, in obedience to the Health Department's instructions, we set out for Pau in search of quarters for the children. Jacques had orders to go south and was able to take me in his small Citroen—our chauffeur had been mobilised. We left with a valise apiece, since we planned to be away for a few days only—just time to find a house, and then return to evacuate the children.

I shall never forget the sadness and the beauty of that last day at Motel. The fountains I so loved were throwing their sun-tipped jets into the still air; the children's laughter rang happily as they played near-by. I looked back as we drove away. The pink house with its blue roof was reflected in the waters of the moat. I prayed it would be spared.

Then we were on the road, caught in the traffic that flowed south. A few miles beyond Dreux, tank traps were being dug and a "75" enfiladed the road. At Blois we crossed the Loire, its slow grey waters and its golden sands. The town was crowded with troops and refugees. The latest news was bad. People were talking of treachery and of how the bridges of the Meuse had fallen to criminal carelessness or worse. Rivers no longer meant defence against so mechanised an army, they said. They grumbled that the refugees, of whom there were several millions, were like hordes of locusts. They wondered how long there would be enough food to feed them and their horses—or petrol for their cars. In a few days they anticipated that they, too, would be evacuating their homes, leaving all they possessed. It was heartbreaking to witness the gnawing anguish—the horrible disillusionment that had descended upon the proud people of France.

We reached Châteauroux for dinner and spent that night with Jacques' brother in his family home. During the night

German planes dropped bombs close to our cloth factories and we were awakened at dawn by anti-aircraft fire. When we left at eight o'clock my sister-in-law, who had already been to Mass, serenely bade us good-bye.

The impersonal manner in which my French relatives discussed the progress of events always surprised me. There was no wishful thinking, no casual assumption of France's eventual victory as in England there would have been. Listening to them I wondered whether my lively imagination was at fault, for even then I anticipated the horrors of a Nazi occupation. 'Perhaps', I reflected, 'their tolerant civilisation scorns to apprehend the inhuman methods of a ruthless tyrant.' Whatever their thoughts may have been, their fortitude was admirable.

Leaving Châteauroux we pursued our way to Périgueux. The road runs over hills in a long straight line. Below are rich pastures on which graze the white Limousin cattle. The country spread before me like a landscape painted by the Primitives. Gothic tapestries came to life, and I visualised ladies riding caparisoned steeds, a hooded falcon on an extended wrist. But I lived in the twentieth century. Tanks, I reflected, would crush this rich earth, those beautiful trees would be felled, homes that had withstood the wear and tear of centuries would be shattered by these modern demons of destruction.

We found Pau overcrowded. Proximity to the Spanish frontier had attracted many whose activities were considered suspect. Distrust was rampant; arrests were numerous. I felt stifled in a malodorous atmosphere of disloyalties. We rushed our search for a house capable of accommodating some hundred children, and finally found a large villa which, although quite unsuitable for permanent use, could serve as a temporary home. The Government commandeered the hotel where we spent the first night. Jacques' youngest brother, who lived in Pau, kindly asked us to share his apartment for the remainder of our stay.

Accustomed to rising with the lark, we left Pau at 4 a.m. on the third day, glad to be homeward bound. It seemed strange to see our way so clear; no one was going north and yet the south-bound traffic never infringed the regulations and our half of the road lay free before us, stretching through an endless row of caravans. I thought of Epsom Downs on Derby Day, but here the gamble was one of life or death and in the stark disillusionment of the faces I saw I realised the stakes were heavily loaded. I wished Degas could have painted some of those scenes —a woman half nude bending over a basin in an unforgettable pose—another combing her golden hair against the rising sun.

At Périgueux we drew up at a café for much-needed refreshment, and were greeted by two friends.

"Where are you going?" they asked us.

"To Saint Georges-Motel," we answered.

"You are crazy," they said, "the Germans are already there; the Government has moved to Bordeaux."

"Nonsense," said my husband, "they exaggerate," and we resumed our way. Visions of the Nazi Bicycling Corps swam before my tired eyes. I would so much rather be shot than taken prisoner, I reflected. Searching the traffic that now appeared to be flying south, I looked for our cars which, if the news were true, must be conveying our household to Pau. Suddenly I recognised one of them and our butler sitting next to the driver. He too had seen us and that evening telephoned to Henri Balsan's house, where he rightly concluded we would spend the night. Telephonic communication between the French departments having been stopped, it was fortunate that he was still near enough to reach us. We were then told that the Germans were indeed in our village, which had been evacuated. Saint Georges had been bombed, but neither the château nor the sanatorium had been hit. The hospital at Dreux, on the contrary, had received a direct hit, and we heard that our agent's wife, who had that day gone to be delivered of her child, had been killed, together with her newly-born child. One more tragedy among so many when nerves are taut and sensibilities flexed is best ignored, and we chose rather to rejoice in the news that the sanatorium children had safely escaped. Albert, our butler, further told us that at the last moment Basil Davidoff and Louis, my husband's valet, who both spoke German, had decided to remain in the château for its protection. Louis, being a Luxembourgeois, would, we hoped, be spared by the Germans, and Davidoff, a White Russian officer, could surely be considered safe. Nevertheless, we heard later that Louis had been nearly shot as a spy when the Germans moved in.

We had arrived at the Henri Balsans' in the afternoon and our hosts still had a room to give us. Later, as the evening wore on, other members of the family kept driving up. Like ours, their homes were in the north. When every available bed had been allotted, mattresses were laid on the floors—even armchairs had their occupants. Never was hospitality more generously extended. I wondered how our host would be able to provide dinner for twenty unexpected guests, for Le Plessis is far from any town and French villages have little food to offer. I was therefore surprised by the excellence of our meal, which, although limited to soup, macaroni, vegetables and a sweet, was served with the precise ritual of a banquet. How helpful such conventions are, I thought, as I listened to the pleasant flow of general conversation; we might be invited guests, not evacuees fleeing an invading enemy. This illusion was still further maintained by a lovely old lady who sat at Henri Balsan's right. With an aristocratic disdain for trouble and fear, she completely ignored the war and in the tradition in which the captain of a sinking ship gives orders to his crew she was compelling us to go down with flying colours! How gallantly she took that evening in hand—how humorously and wittily she steered the conversation away from the rocks and depths of the present to smooth waters of the past. Her sons and grandsons were with the armies —their womenfolk dispersed—her home in enemy hands—but not one word of all this escaped her. It was as if she wished to inspire the young women and girls around her, for whom she anticipated the humiliation and the sorrow of defeat, with the tradition of courage and endurance Frenchwomen have ever shown.

Emotionally harrowed by the news the radio brought of captured towns, defeated armies and the incredible advance of the enemy, we wondered where their forces could be checked. With the Belgians no longer at war, the Italians our proclaimed enemy, and the English from their shores appealing to our distraught Government to make a stand, what would happen next? For us there was but the simple decision to proceed south and there make preparations for the children who would soon join us at Pau. But even here a worry beset us, for Jacques had mislaid his petrol coupons and without them we could not go on. We had just enough left to take us to the filling station we had last stopped at on our way north, and we hoped the little woman in charge might have found our coupons and kept them for us. All the way we worried over those coupons—it was perhaps as well to have a personal need at such a time—and when we found them our joy was great, and we blessed the honest woman who had kept them for us.

In Pau we again heard rumours of an impending armistice. With France under enemy occupation, my income as a French citizen would be frozen in America, and we would no longer be able to maintain the sanatorium. The children somehow had been fitted into the villa we had found for them, but we now had to plan to return those who were cured to their parents and to send those who still required care to other institutions. It was difficult to obtain reliable information, so we decided to motor to Bordeaux, the rumoured seat of government. Bordeaux is a beautiful city. Upset as I was, the lovely old houses awakened my admiration. Reaching the American Consulate, we saw a long line of cars and crowds of excited people running in and out of its doors. The Stars and Stripes over the entrance held for us a false promise of peace. Inside, queues of frenzied people surrounded every official. It was impossible to reach one. Hemmed in the crowd, we were greeted by two American friends. One of them, an important official in the Red Cross, looked harassed and insistently begged me to leave the country. He told us that I figured on the Nazi hostage list. Only a few months back, Baron Louis de Rothschild had been imprisoned in Vienna and millions had been extorted from his family before he was returned. We were advised to cross the frontier at once— for it would soon be closed.

Impressed by this evident anxiety for my safety, we decided to approach Jacques' chief, the Ministre de l'Air, for permission to leave the country. He was difficult to find, because the Government was only then moving into its new quarters. But when at last we found him, the fact that an armistice had been granted made Jacques' demobilisation easy and he was not only given permission, but also advised to take me to America immediately. It remained only to obtain our visas. Urgent though the matter appeared to be, we nevertheless lunched in one of Bordeaux' famous restaurants, and my husband and the woman who shared our table—the owner of extensive vineyards—were soon engrossed in a discussion on vinticulture, stimulated by an excellent bottle of claret; the war was not mentioned. As people were clamouring for seats, we decided to have coffee elsewhere and drove through a deluge of rain to the principal café, where with difficulty we found an unoccupied table. The room was packed with a silent crowd. Suddenly the radio broke into the familiar bars of the 'Marseillaise', which by now I had learned to associate with disaster. We all rose to our feet as if impelled. Then came the short and shattering announcement: "The French Government has asked for an armistice, which has been granted." In the ensuing stillness, as men squared their jaws and women wept, we were terrorised by three terrific claps of thunder which rent the air in rhythmic sequence, as if the heavens themselves were moved. "It's France that is being crucified," I said, and as if in a nightmare we found our car. At the American Consulate the same frenzied masses were besieging the staff. The news of an armistice had but spurred their fears; to cross the frontier had become their only preoccupation.

I felt sorry for the officials. Unable to cope with so many distraught people, understaffed and overworked, they were, moreover, struggling to decipher new and urgent passport regulations which the State Department was sending out. I finally captured a secretary, who with evident reluctance listened to my application for a visa. Handing him our passports, I requested a visa to permit us to go to our home in Florida, a permission always granted in the past. But he answered:

"You can no longer claim a visiting visa—you will have to go over as an emigrant."

"Very well, we will go as emigrants."

Nevertheless he handed back our passports. "You will first produce your birth certificate, your marriage certificate and your divorce certificate," he grimly told us.

"Our papers are in Paris with our lawyer, who has most certainly been evacuated. How do you expect me to produce them?"

I saw a gleam of satisfaction in his eyes at the thought that he had got rid of us; for during our somewhat heated conversation he had been darting about looking up new regulations, dictating to his secretary, arguing with a Frenchman who wished to return to his business in New York and rushing out to see the Consul, all the while keeping up a running commentary on the impossibility of working under such hectic conditions, and furthermore viewing with disfavour the idea of remaining in Bordeaux under German occupation. Then looking at his watch and throwing me a glance he said:

"It's six o'clock, you had better come back tomorrow."

"Don't waste any more time," said our kind counsellor of the morning. "You will never get anything done here. Have your passports visa-ed for Spain and Portugal at Bayonne, where they have consulates, and trust to getting your American entry in Lisbon. And hurry," he added ominously, "for the frontier may be closed at any moment, and then you will no longer get out."

No room being obtainable in Bordeaux, we took the road to Bayonne. The surrounding country appeared to be alive with cars and we looked in vain for lodgings. It was now getting dark. Passing through a village we inquired of a man who was directing the traffic if he knew of a vacant room. With a quick look at Jacques' uniform, he smilingly said:

"*Mais, mon Colonel,* my wife and I will be proud to have you and *Madame la Colonelle* share our home. We have only one small guest-room, but it is at your disposal."

How gratefully we accepted, and when we saw his kindly wife, the clean and comfortable room they gave us, the generous hospitality it pleased them to extend to us, we felt we had indeed been lucky. We sat in the small living-room that looked over their garden talking to our hostess and wondering what had happened to our host. He was, his wife told us, a retired captain of the Merchant Marine. Suddenly, looking very pleased, he returned with a large bottle of Moet et Chandon 1928 under his arm. He had cooled it, he informed us, in the bath filled with cold water. I have never drunk better champagne nor enjoyed any more. From sad and weary, we became hopeful and refreshed.

Madame had laid the table and asked us to share their meal. After a good soup she gave us an excellent omelette, a salad such as I had never tasted—the vinegar was made from Bordeaux wine, its flavour warm, delicate and perfumed—and we finished with juicy apricots, while two bottles of Bordeaux, one light and one with more body, seemed to disappear with astonishing rapidity. During our meal our hostess's father looked in. He was the gamekeeper of an important local magnate, and from his remarks we gathered that had he only had notice of our arrival a rabbit or two would have graced the board. Our host, having absorbed a good share of the champagne and of the two bottles of red wine, had become very loquacious. He was by now more impressed by my appearance than by my husband's uniform, and if it had not been for the constant reminders from the radio that we were at a very critical moment of a very disastrous war, he would have become quite gay.

We left at four the next morning, warmed by their kindliness. They even insisted upon giving us coffee before seeing us off. At Bayonne it was impossible to get accommodation, but at the hotel where we lunched the *mécanicien* offered us a room in his house near-by. It was, we found, in a quiet little street and the room looked out on a garden. There were two sofas on which we slept.

We found the Portuguese and Spanish Consulates in a state of siege. Crowds of excited people were trying to force an entry through doors that were guarded by consular officials assisted by police. Any newcomers, we realised, would have little chance of reaching those portals. Fortunately it occurred to Jacques that a former Spanish Ambassador to France who was a friend of ours now lived at Biarritz, and we decided to motor the few miles to obtain a letter of recommendation which would gain our admittance to the Spanish Consul. Unfortunately the Ambassador was away, but was expected back the following day. Such delays, we knew, might be fatal, and were hard to bear, for the possibility that the frontier might at any moment be closed was ever in our minds.

Torrential rains increased the difficulties of circulation, so we bought mackintoshes and umbrellas. We had our meals at the hotel, where an overworked staff efficiently served hundreds of travellers. I marvelled at the patience the waiters showed. No doubt they realised how harassed and worn their customers were. Many had lost their relatives, and we witnessed touching scenes of reunion when, in the flood of evacuees, a man would unexpectedly come upon his wife and children. With all means of communication severed one felt strangely dependent on a fortunate chance. So we deemed ourselves lucky when we met Baron Almeida in Biarritz, for he kindly offered to help us reach the Portuguese Consul. In motoring from Biarritz to Bayonne we picked up a man and his wife who were on foot. The man we were to see again.

We had been told that the Spanish authorities required a visa for Portugal as a guarantee that refugees would not be stranded in Spain, where food was none too plentiful. Our first visit was therefore to the Portuguese Consul. So anxious were we to reach him that we arrived at 6 a.m., although the doors would not open before 8. It was a gloomy dawn, and the rain was coming down harder than ever. Long lines of angry and disconsolate people stretched like black and dripping beetles far into the street. From this street a narrow passage between overhanging houses was the only entrance to a small court from which a flight of wooden stairs led up an outer wall to the consular offices on the fourth floor. Slowly we managed to squeeze our way, but when we reached the court it was equally crowded. Newcomers were viewed with hostility and protesting murmurs arose at our appearance. Even at that early hour I could see no possibility of reaching the Consul, for the crowd was rough; among it were a number of Portuguese loudly proclaiming their right to return to their own country. On a raised step in the court I recognised a few acquaintances who, like us, were waiting. The Consulate was not yet due to open, but suddenly in response to the clamour a window opened above and the Consul's head appeared. "We want our passports"—"We have a right to our passports," shouted the Portuguese. The Consul, with a wave of desperate hands, shouted back, "How can I help you all when I cannot even save my wife?" At this the crowd grew menacing; we were being hemmed in ever tighter. I wondered what would happen next. Then the window above closed. The Consul must have taken counsel, for in a few minutes he shouted down to us, "You will all have your visas, but you must be patient." Then the tension eased—there were even spasmodic cheers. We waited two hours, standing in the crowd in the rain, before the door at the top of the wooden stairs opened and to our surprise we saw the man to whom we had given a ride the previous day, streaking through the crowd down the stairs towards us, while from above Baron Almeida signed to us to come up. It seemed that our fellow traveller had acted on a chance remark of ours—that the Portuguese Consul needed additional help.

There were a lot of people between me and the stairs, and I felt desperate as I began to push through them, but with Jacques behind me and our rescuer stretching down to me from above I managed to get through and up those flights to the safety of the Consulate. I had just time to regain breath before the door opened and, clutching my visa, I faced those stairs and a mob now furious at having been cheated. 'They will never let us down,' I thought, and so evidently did our rescuer; for with a quick look at the low hand railing and the frail wooden stairs he suddenly shouted, "Look out—look out—the stairs are giving way—they were never meant to bear so great a weight." In the ensuing rush down we reached the safety of the street before the mob turned, and with cries of rage once again charged up the stairs. It is rare that one good turn is so quickly rewarded, and in so great a measure. Passports were now more precious than jewels; and it almost became a nervous habit with me to explore my handbag for the reassurance mine brought me.

But there was still the Spanish visa to be obtained before we could cross the frontier. The Spanish Consulate was on the second floor of a patrician house in one of Bayonne's principal streets. The imposing staircase swept upward in wide steps and on each a recumbent figure lay half asleep. As we picked our way through they looked up and pointed to a sign prominently displayed on the Consulate door. It announced that no more visas would be issued that day. Since the day was still young, I felt that the staff was probably indulging a midday siesta. We rang the bell repeatedly until the door was carefully opened and a head appeared. Waving the Ambassador's seal in the startled man's face, we succeeded in pushing our way in. When a few minutes later we emerged with our visas I was shamed at the sight of those tired unhappy people facing the discomforts of another night on the stairs. Reflecting on what prerogative had accomplished, I almost felt a transgressor.

We returned to Biarritz on our way to the frontier. I hoped there would be no more miserable and disconsolate crowds, for I hated pushing my way through, but Jacques in a French officer's uniform could hardly resort to such methods; neither, I shrewdly calculated, could he refuse to follow me, since alone I might easily have been manhandled.

Of the Hôtel du Palais at Biarritz I have two memories and they are very clear. As we entered the hall where deserted cock-tail-tables still stood I saw a young man bent over one in a gesture of such complete despair I thought he was dying, until at my approach he raised his head. 'Will it be the ocean so close or a pistol shot so much quicker,' I thought, as his eyes met mine and revealed his plight in the curse that lay upon his race. Then I went upstairs to collect some things we had left. In the hall I saw a row of at least twenty trunks, beautifully polished and labelled "Mrs. Tailer-Smith". I met their owner, an American and a friend of my mother's.

"Are you staying here?" I asked her. "The frontier may soon be closed."

"But I could not leave without these," she answered, pointing to the twenty trunks. Looking at her placid countenance and her twenty trunks, I said, "You will be all right. Good-bye and good luck."

And now we were actually on our way to the frontier, but when we reached it the barriers were down, the Customs closed. Would they open tomorrow? We were assured they would. With my husband's habit of everywhere finding a friend we turned to the director of the Bidassoa, a furniture factory that lay near-by, and he kindly offered to put us up. The next morning at six we brought our car to the bridge over the river which divides Spain from France, and while my husband went to the Customs I strolled out to where the sentries were on guard.

A great sadness filled me at leaving France, where I had found such happiness. I knew my husband would return to his country and I hated being the cause of his going. While I was standing on the bridge, the frontier opened, and I saw Sir Charles and Lady Mendl in a beautiful Rolls-Royce driven by a chauffeur pass by. They had a diplomatic passport, and were followed by a station wagon, driven by a Mr. McMullen, a friend of theirs. It was filled with Vuiton trunks.

Once in Spain, life assumed a more normal aspect. It was easy to obtain good rooms a San Sebastian, but our passports were limited to a few days. I noticed that we had neither butter nor sugar and realised that food was not plentiful, and that strangers were unwelcome. Nevertheless we experienced great difficulty in getting places on the train to Lisbon, for which the Travel Bureau was asking extortionate prices. The French Government allowed each of its nationals to take thirty thousand francs out of the country, but with the fall of France her currency was no longer honoured. My husband had a limited number of English pounds and American dollars, but these were not sufficient to pay the prices for our tickets to Lisbon. We decided to sell our Citroen, which was worth more in Spain than in France, since few cars were on the market. But then we were informed that it was illegal to buy French cars from refugees. We were learning the hard way, and I felt outraged by the incredible bargain the haggling dealer secured our car for. He and the travelling agency then arranged to give us the places on the train they had before told us they were unable to procure.

I shook the dust of Spain from willing feet as I climbed into the train, but at the Portuguese frontier the worst of all trials awaited us. They actually took our passports from us, giving us slips of paper in exchange for which, they said, our passports would be returned to us in Lisbon. This procedure struck me as a refined and needless torture. In the state of nervous tension to which all refugees had been reduced it was like removing a life-belt in midstream from a worn-out swimmer. In fact I clung to my passport with the same desperation with which a drowning person would have clung to his belt, but to no avail.

"It will be returned to you in Lisbon at the Passport Office," they said.

We had expected to reach Lisbon at 7 p.m. that evening, but arrived at 4 a.m. the following morning. There were no reservations at the hotel we had wired to; every room in the city, the concierge told us, was occupied. We might, if lucky, find one at Estoril, some twenty-five miles out of town. So we taxied there and at 6 a.m. finally found a bed and room. I was glad to lie down, but visions of my passport haunted my dreams and at 8 a.m. we were again on the road to claim it.

There was, of course, a long queue awaiting the opening of the Passport Office, which, with the lazy ease bred by the sun, opened late, closed early for lunch and siesta, and opened again as a deferential gesture before closing for the night. We arrived in time to join the end of the queue and reached the office just as it closed. So we went to the American Consulate, where we were informed that no visa could be granted without a passport. A welcome cable from my brothers, however, told us that we had reservations on a seaplane the following Friday. We had hardly three days to secure our passports and visas. It was forty-eight hours before we got them back. Driven to despair we threatened to remain in Portugal at the expense of the authorities; at this they made a thorough search of their files and produced our passports. Then the American Consul most kindly put pressure to bear and we obtained our American visas.

The evening before leaving Lisbon we dined with the Duke of Kent, who, having heard of our arrival, invited us to a lovely palace the Portuguese Government had put at his disposal during his official visit. Having no evening clothes, we at first declined, but he insisted that we should come as we were, and he promised to take news of us to my sons in England. I sat next to him at dinner—it was just a year since we had met at Blenheim for my granddaughter's coming-out ball. Two years later he was killed in an aeroplane accident. How odd it seemed to sit at a formal dinner again free of anxiety and care—how little these people knew of the storm and stress of a country overrun by a ruthless enemy. That we had no evening clothes seemed strange to them. What a world of difference now lay in our outlooks! I shall not, however, forget the Duke's considerate kindness to us that evening. He brought England and my children closer to me, and I felt warmed by his solicitude. He was a man of great charm and had a sympathetic understanding of all things beautiful, inherited from his mother, Queen Mary.

The next morning—thanks to the good offices of the American Consul and my brothers—we left Lisbon on the Clipper. I had an inhibition against flying, and this was my first voyage. As we moved through the waters and rose to our flight, I looked at the blue sky above and the slowly fading coast beneath and felt I had embarked on a celestial passage to a promised land.

INDEX

Gordon, Kate M., 172
Göring, Hermann, 209
Gorky, Maxim, 126
Gosfords, The, 92
Gounod, 10, 78
Gouthière, 9
Gramont, Duc de, 26, 188, 191
Grand Trianon, 19
Granada, 47, 48
Granard, Lady, 14
Green Park, 96, 97, 102
Gregory, Lady, 158
Grenfell, Lilian, 33, 35, 54 67-9, 92, 94, 98, 186
Grimaldi, 206, 210
Gross, Dr., 191
Grossmith, George, jun., 78
Grosvenor House, 77
Guest, Ivor, 42, 54, 114
Guitry, Sacha, 214
Guy Fawkes Day, 40
Guys, 39

HAAKON, King, 90, 92
Hackwood, 63, 138, 160, 211
Haig, Field-Marshal Earl, 185
Haldane, Viscount, 155, 186-7
Hamilton family, 44, 54, 57
Hamilton, Sir Ian, 103
Hammersley, Mrs. 33
Hampden House, 57, 99
Harcourt, Viscountess, 174
Harper, Miss, 22, 30, 38, 192
Harrow School, 103
Hartington, Lord, 87
Harvey, Colonel George, 151, 190
Hatfield, 132
Hatherly, 163-4
Havre, 19
Healy, Timothy, 135
Hegel, 18
Heine, 18
Helleu, Paul, 108-9
Henry Esmond, 17
Henty, G. A., 17
Herald, New York, 50
Herald, Paris, 50
Herculaneum, 52
Hermitage, The 127
Herriot, Edouard, 197-8
Hichens, R. S., 157
Higgins, Ethel, 164
Higgins, Harry, 78
Higgins, Mrs. Harry, 78
High Park, Blenheim, 34, 66, 94, 106
History of English Literature, 103
History of Greece, 25
History of Trade Unionism, 155
Hitler, 161, 208, 230, 236
Hofburg, 142
Hohenzollern family, 116

Holland, 2, 239-40
Holland House, 76
Home for Prisoner's Wives, 152, 176
Home for Swiss Girls, 12
Home Rule, 87, 135-7
Hooghly, 24
Horowitz, Vladimir, 219-20
'House of Vanderbilt, The,' 3
Howland, Meredith, 110
Howland, Mrs. Meredith, 110
Hudson, Thomas, 34
Hunt, Richard Morris, 8, 19
Huntington Collection, 77
Hurlingham, 79
Hyde Park, 58, 72, 74, 136, 176

IBSEN, 79, 104
Idlehour, 6, 11, 15, 21, 22, 46
Ilchester, Earl of, 76
Importance of Being Earnest, The, 79
India, 23-5, 139-41
Indian Mutiny, 24
Industrial Democracy, 155
Influence of King Edward, The, 91
Inge, Dean, 151
Inter-Ally Council on War Purchases and Finance, 183
International Woman Suffrage Alliance, 171
'Internationale,' 199
Irish Nationalist party, 135
Islip, N.Y., 18
Ivanhoe, 17

JAIPUR, 24, 140
James, Henry, 104, 217
James, William, 104
Jay, Julia, 30, 41
Jay, Mrs. William, 29, 30, 37, 38
Jennings, Sarah, *see* Marlborough, First Duchess of
Jersey, Earl of, 67
Jersey, Lady, 67
Jockey Club, French, 110, 145, 188
Johnson, Johnny, 221
Jones, Dean, 64-5

Kaiser Wilhelm der Grosse, 172
Kant, 18
Kapurthala, Maharajah of, 208
Karsavina, 220
Kedleston, 138, 211
Kelly, Mrs. Florence, 172
Kemal, Mustapha, 13
Kenilworth, 17
Kent, Duke of, 258-9
Keppel, George, 120
Keppel, Mrs. George, 120-1
Kerr, Philip, (Lord Lothian), 161
Kimbolton, Lord, 5
Kingsley, Charles, 17